The
Pricing
System

The
Pricing
System

ROBERT HANEY SCOTT
Professor of Business Economics
University of Washington

HOLDEN-DAY, INC.
San Francisco

Dusseldorf   Johannesburg   London
Singapore   Sydney   Toronto   Panama

THE PRICING SYSTEM

Library of Congress Catalog Card Number: 72-83239
ISBN: 0-8162-7665-X

Printed in the United States of America

1234567890 MP 8079876543

*For Joy, and for William, Ann, Sarah, and Elizabeth,
with all my love*

Preface

With many fine price theory texts already available, one must set forth a reason for attempting yet another. The reason is simply to emphasize more strongly the general equilibrium framework in contrast with the usual strong emphasis on partial equilibrium. In the initial chapters partial equilibrium tools are developed in the process of constructing the general equilibrium model. In most price theory books partial equilibrium analysis is developed step by step in separate unrelated parts. Then, in a late chapter a set of equations is provided to illustrate the manner in which the parts of the system can be put together.

Unfortunately, it is often the case that instructors never quite reach the last chapter of a text, and, if they do, they are so rushed for time that analysis of the interrelatedness of all the parts of the economic system fails to receive its due attention. This is unfortunate for a very important reason: The students of today will form the economic policies of tomorrow. If the economic policies of today reflect many years of past instruction in partial equilibrium, then it is easy to show that they are deficient on that account. For the typical approach of all levels of government is ad hoc rather than broad in perspective. To illustrate, take the case of a military procurement board during the Korean War. The subject of price controls arose, and the generals on the board were asked to submit their position on the question before a Congressional Committee. The position they suggested at first was simply to request price controls on all items in the military procurement program and leave all other prices to the market. A friend explained to them just why this program would probably fail in a short time since the prices of military goods are related to the prices of all other goods; but the way the generals thought about the problem is typical.

If the community wishes to support an industry, the usual first suggestion is to raise the price of the good produced by that industry as if this course of action would have little or no side effect. The sundry support programs in agriculture provide excellent examples. A rise in the price of raw cotton affects the textile industry and the synthetic fiber industry: it affects the price of land and land use; it affects the demand for farm machinery and employment; and through these channels eventually, however minutely, it affects *all other prices* and *all quantities* in the economy. These distortions in the allocation of resources in many segments of the economy are unanticipated evidently because of a lack of acknowledgment of the significance of the many interrelated forces always at work in the economic system. This may explain why many of our economic programs and policies turn against us after a time.

The simple proposal that all such governmental programs and policies be done away with is appealing, but it will not suffice for it is the politician and not the economist who determines whether programs do or do not exist. Hence, it is of paramount importance that the politicians and the public at large be given greater insight into the workings of the economic system *as a system* if ever there is to come about a significant improvement in the way such matters are handled. Thus, unlike many excellent price theory books that provide students with rigorous exercise in the techniques of economic analysis without raising issues of policy, this book is designed to point up the way in which economic analysis must be used to help us understand the effects of different policies so that we can cope with them more effectively and bring about better policies than we now have.

Any general equilibrium system which is intelligible to intermediate-level students must be oversimplified. Therefore, the presentation of a two-person, two-factor, two-good general equilibrium model begs many questions. But to assume an economy without capital, for example, is surely no worse an abstraction for expository purposes than to assume the existence of a demand curve for wheat, as is often done in partial equilibrium analysis. For wheat comes in many varieties—those suitable for soda crackers will never do for cake mixes—and the demand for "wheat" depends on many factors left unexplained. The point is that the world of economic theory is abstract, and, however, unsatisfactory this situation is, partial equilibrium analysis is no less abstract than general equilibrium analysis. It is only that in dealing with a larger number of parts of a system at one time there are more occasions to make abstractions explicit.

Many instructors, steeped in the many facets of economic theory, will feel that some of the abstractions are unnecessary, for economists do know more about the issues than the analysis might indicate at any one stage of the development of the system. Hopefully they will remember that the objective is to provide intermediate-level students with an intuitive understanding of the operation of a system, and that many detailed ramifications are omitted so as not to disrupt unduly the orderly progress toward that objective.

I wish to apologize, therefore, to instructors who prefer a more refined and exacting development of theoretical issues as one moves along to construct the general equilibrium paradigm. My only hope is that students will progress rapidly enough along these paths of abstract theory to gain insight into policy questions before they become burdened and dismayed by excessive detail. And then they may be interested enough in the issues to pursue the details further in more advanced courses. This book, therefore, is not intended as a reference work but rather as a theoretical "laboratory" in which a few basic analytical "experiments" are provided to expose the student to the world of economic theory.

My deepest indebtedness is to my mentor who introduced me to the world of economics, Richard S. Howey. I am one of thousands of students whom he has guided through the rigors of E. H. P. Brown's *Framework of the Pricing System*. This classic work has greatly influenced my thinking. Anyone familiar with it will recognize this as he turns these pages. I also wish to express my heartfelt gratitude to my parents and my brothers, whose steadfast confidence supported me in my studies when, as is wont to happen, the going got tough. And to my wife and children who, to me, provide the essence of purpose in life itself, I wish to express my humble thanks. I am also indebted to my many students who read the manuscript, catching errors and oversights here and there and helping to improve it in every way. For direct assistance and indirect encouragement I am indebted to Edward J. Chambers, William Pigott, Dudley Johnson, Barney Dowdle, Philip Bourque, Walter Oi, John McKean, Richard H. Swanson, and many editorial reviewers.

The School of Business Administration in the University of Washington provides an atmosphere of encouragement through stimulating colleagues, adequate time, secretarial services, library facilities, and other amenities that make life at work so pleasant. For this helpful environment I am very grateful.

Along with responsibility for the contents of these pages, which I gladly accept fully and without reservation whatsover, I hope that I may be informed of all criticisms so that exchanges of views may promote better economics just as exchanges in the marketplace lead to greater economic welfare.

ROBERT HANEY SCOTT

Contents

9 THEORY OF MONOPOLY AND ITS REGULATION   204

10 OTHER FORMS OF MARKET STRUCTURE   234

11 SELECTED TOPICS IN PRICE THEORY   255

The
Pricing
System

1

Introduction to General Equilibrium

1.1 THE ECONOMIC PROBLEM

Economics is the study of the allocation of scarce means (resources) to alternative ends (uses). The economic problem arises out of the inequality between human wants and the means available to satisfy those wants. This inequality defines the term *scarce*, for all goods that are available only in amounts that are insufficient to satiate all human desire for them are scarce, and some way must be found to ration them among users.[1] Air, sunlight, and bacteria are examples of free goods to nearly everyone everywhere. For people in some regions, water, coconuts, and land are also examples of free goods. Examples of scarce goods, on the other hand, are everywhere about us. These are the goods of concern to economists—food, clothing, shelter, transportation, and entertainment. Goods that once

---

[1] On rare occasions an economist may be concerned with the availability of free goods, as in the case of rainfall where a dearth or an excess may affect agricultural output. But his concern in this instance is with the combination of this free resource with other scarce resources used in the production process.

were free, such as land, timber, and fresh air, have become scarce with population growth and industrialization.

The nature of economic, or scarce, goods has led to the false accusation that economists are only concerned with materialistic human desires. The accusation is false because the economist, as economist, makes no attempt to fashion the desires of people, that is, he is basically unconcerned with the formation of human desires. For whether people desire aesthetic cathedrals, and time to watch sunsets, or whether they want transistor radios and chrome-plated sports cars, an important part of the economist's job is to assist people in finding *the most efficient means* of acquiring the goods and services they want. Thus, economics, as a science, like other sciences, exists in an atmosphere that is *to as large an extent as possible* independent of issues of morality. A physicist can tell you how to construct a hydrogen bomb, but he has no unique power as a physicist to say whether or not you "ought" to drop it. Of course, as human beings, physicists and economists, like other scientists, have both the right and the duty to voice their opinions on the great moral issues of the day. But, they do so as individuals and not as physicists or economists.

If there were only a single end to which a scarce resource could be put, this resource would be of no great concern to an economist. The solution to the allocation problem becomes trivial; one simply allocates all of the available resource to the end in question. For an *allocation problem* to exist, there must be alternatives to consider. Economic goods, therefore, are scarce goods, and the economic problem is to decide what use to make of them. Thus, issues of primary concern to economists are those involving resources that are scarce, and that have alternative uses.[1]

1.2 THE SOLUTION: AUTHORITY AND MARKET PRICES

In society, the solution to the economic problem—the problem of allocating scarce resources—is determined either by an authoritarian system or by the pricing system or by some combina-

---

[1] There is some question today about the meaning of "scarce." Does scarcity exist in a technological sense or is it primarily the result of the historical evolution of *property rights?* Economists have become more and more concerned about the essence of the relation between property rights and the functioning of the economy.

tion of the two. The term *authoritarian* is sufficiently broad to encompass aristocratic societies of the past as well as dictatorships of both right and left. It also includes socialistic systems in which planning boards gain their duly constituted authority by legislative action. Whatever the source of their power, be it from divine right, from military might, from the votes of constituents, or, in the case of bureaucracy, by legal appointment, the authorities who make economic decisions nearly always make use of, or must adjust to, the second system that exists for solving the economic problem—the pricing system.

This book is concerned with the pricing system. Pricing systems exist in every country and every society. Some societies rely somewhat more upon the pricing system than others, but even in those societies in which the economy is largely regulated by authoritarian controls the authorities exercising control cannot ignore the pricing system. Those in authority, as well as other citizens, need to have a clear understanding of how the pricing system operates if they are to be effective in their jobs.

In most societies, and especially in capitalistic societies, the pricing system is the principal system that people rely upon for solutions to their economic problems. Prices serve (1) to ration the flow of consumer goods among consumers, and (2) to ration the flow of factors of production, such as land, labor services, capital goods, and materials, among producers. Businessmen are the principal producers in a capitalist society inasmuch as they compete for scarce factors of production. In a socialist society, managers of government enterprises are the principal producers.

1.3 FLOW OF GOODS AND FLOW OF MONEY

Prices are determined in markets where people meet to make exchanges. Markets exist for both consumers' goods and producers' goods. There also exist financial markets, markets for money and financial capital. In pursuing a discussion of general economic equilibrium it is useful to distinguish between these three types of markets, and in particular, to recognize the interdependence of these markets. A cursory description of the flow of goods and services, and of money, among these markets can be presented in the form of a diagram.

The consumers' market is represented at the top of Fig. 1.1. In this market consumers meet with producers in order

CONSUMERS' MARKET

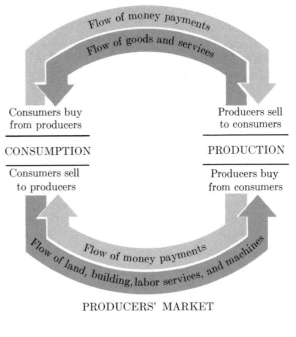

Consumers buy | Producers sell
from producers | to consumers

CONSUMPTION | PRODUCTION

Consumers sell | Producers buy
to producers | from consumers

PRODUCERS' MARKET

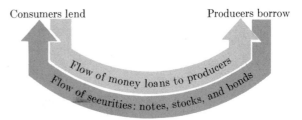

Consumers lend   Producers borrow

Figure 1.1   FINANCIAL MARKET

to exchange commodities that consumers use in everyday life. It is here also that producers receive the money revenues necessary to carry out production efforts. Consumer behavior is represented on the left-hand side of Fig. 1.1. To explain consumer behavior, the theory of consumers' choice, or as it is sometimes called, the theory of household behavior, must be introduced. Consumers face a constraint on their purchasing behavior. The prices they must pay for the goods they buy form part of the constraint. The other part is in the form of the amount of income they receive each period. Together, income and price form the consumer's budget and impinge upon the ability of consumers to satiate their desires for scarce goods. In Chap. 2, the theory of consumers' choice is described in greater detail.

Producers' behavior is represented on the right-hand side of Fig. 1.1. To explain producer behavior, the theory of production must be introduced. Producers also face a constraint. They face the prices that they must pay for the factors of production they buy and the demand for their product determines the amount of revenue that they receive each period from sales of their products. In Chap. 3 the theory of production is developed in greater detail. However, Chaps. 8 and 9 also concern production inasmuch as they contain discussions of the theory of the firm.

The producers' market is also represented in Fig. 1.1. In this market businessmen meet with laborers, landowners, owners of capital, and other businessmen who supply factors of production. It is also in the producers' market that money incomes are earned, for money purchases of factor resources by businessmen provide money income to those consumers who own resources and who sell these in the producers' market.

Toward the bottom of Fig. 1.1, the financial market is represented. In this market consumers meet with producers in order to lend and borrow. Consumers receive money incomes, part of which they use to purchase financial securities. Producers borrow by selling financial securities and use the proceeds to purchase machinery and other capital goods. Producers also pay interest to consumers who hold securities. Interest payments represent income to suppliers of capital, and expenses to users of capital. The financial market is discussed in more detail in Chap. 5.

This diagrammatic depiction of economic activity is greatly oversimplified. However, it serves to indicate the *interdependence* of the variety of economic *activities* that each citizen engages in every day of his life. The classification scheme employed in the diagram does not entail mutually exclusive classes of individuals, that is, a consumer may also be a producer, and a producer may also be a laborer so that no one individual fits into one class alone. However, conceptually the differentiation of the classificatory scheme applies to the various activities of individuals and it is assumed that these activities can be classified accordingly into mutually exclusive categories.

Payments to producers for goods determine the amounts of money revenues that producers have available for purchasing factors of production. Owners of factors of production earn incomes by selling these factors in the producers' market. With these incomes the owners become consumers and enter the consumers' market where their expenditures become revenues to producers—and the circular flow of economic activity is complete. Of course, incomes and revenues are determined by prices and quantities. The analysis of the interdependent determination of prices, quantities, incomes, and revenues is called *general equilibrium analysis*.

Since prices and quantities are observable and measurable, the term *equilibrium* in the phrase "general equilibrium analysis" refers to the numerical values assumed by prices and quantities of goods and services and prices and quantities of factors of production as they are determined in their respective markets. These prices and quantities are *dependent variables* in a general equilibrium system inasmuch as the values they assume depend upon the interaction of market forces, and these variables are in *equilibrium* if there is no tendency for them to change from the values that they assume. Equilibrium values may be *stable* or *unstable*. A plate balanced on the end of a pencil is an unstable equilibrium position because any movement of the pencil sets in motion certain forces that tend to pull the plate further and further away from its balanced position until it falls to the floor. A marble in a bowl, on the other hand, may illustrate the case of stable equilibrium—any movement of the bowl will set the marble in motion, but if the bowl remains upright other forces will gradually pull the marble back to its original position in the bottom of the bowl.

While it is usually assumed that the general equilibrium solution to the values of prices and quantities in a free pricing system will be a stable equilibrium solution, there is still concern among economists over the precise nature of the conditions that are necessary to ensure that the equilibrium solution will be stable.

The first six chapters of this book are devoted to the construction of a general equilibrium system of analysis for explaining the determination of prices and quantities. As such, the general equilibrium pricing system explains how resources are allocated by means of the free-market mechanism. Hence, it explains how the economic problem is solved in the absence of authoritarian intervention.

In the process of building the general equilibrium model there is great reliance upon *partial equilibrium analysis.* Partial equilibrium analysis differs from general equilibrium analysis in that only a part of the general equilibrium system is examined at one time. In partial equilibrium analysis it is assumed that certain forces are of negligible influence and can be ignored for the purpose of understanding the issues immediately at hand. It is in this sense that the analysis is "partial."

1.4 THEORY AND PREDICTION

Economists rely to a great extent upon theory. Because of the logical consistency of their theoretical description of the pricing system, and because of its elaborate content, economists can be formidable opponents in a debate. Some observers contend that the economist's theory of pricing is little more than a logical system, more akin to an abstract mathematical logic than to an explanation of the mundane economic affairs of man. While there is certainly merit in this criticism, it is also true that economists are capable of predicting a great number of everyday events by means of their analytical system. In the final analysis, the measure of success of a theory is its usefulness in predicting events in the real world.

When a scientist asserts that his theories, having been verified to some extent, enable him to predict events in the real world, he may fail to convey accurately just what he means. Scientific predictions are offered as conditional statements, that is, they are of the "if . . . then . . ." form. Usually there is a long list of "ifs," either explicit or implicit, setting forth conditions that must hold for the prediction to come true. Thus, scientists seldom if ever make unconditional forecasts or predictions. Furthermore, scientific predictions of actual events, besides being conditional, are usually offered as approximations and as probabilistic assertions. To predict that a falling body will reach the earth at a certain time always entails some allowance for a margin of error. Often an *interval* of time replaces a certain *given* time, and the statement that the falling body will reach the ground during a certain time interval is itself offered with a certain degree of confidence based on the probability of occurrence of the event. Therefore, in even the most exact sciences it is not at all unusual for exceptions to occur. The phrase "exceptions *prove* the rule" at one time meant "exceptions *test* the rule." Now, of course, it means that an exception or two simply are *exceptions,* and as such tend to support belief in the general soundness of the rule. When the exceptions *become* the rule, faith in the original rule is shaken. Alternatively, the original rule may be amended in a fashion so as to explain most of the exceptions as well.

As an example from economics, consider the possibility of an increase in the excise tax on cigarettes of, say, 6 cents a pack. An economist might predict that such a tax would lead to an increase in the price of a pack of cigarettes by 5 cents. He might expect the price to increase by nearly the same amount as the tax, but not quite the full amount. Implicit in his prediction are many conditions—that inflation does not affect all prices at the same time as the excise tax is imposed, that the cost conditions in cigarette production do not change, that smoking desires do not change, and so forth. Furthermore, the economist would predict that the increase in price would occur, say, within a 6-week period.

When an economist predicts that cigarette prices will increase in the wake of a tax increase, he predicts an approximate increase and an approximate time of occurrence of the increase. And with these qualifications in mind he is right a high percentage of the time; that is, out of 100 such predictions he will be right, say, 99 percent of the time. It is in this sense that the statement "Economic theory proves to be quite useful in predicting events in the real world" should be interpreted. Such an interpretation is consistent with that applied to other more exact sciences.

At lunch one day an anthropologist (A) and an economist (E) had a conversation that went something like this:

(A) "I read about the new tax on cigarettes and when I went into the smoke shop the next morning I placed 5 cents more than I usually paid on the counter. But, the shopkeeper returned the 5 cents saying that he had not paid the tax on the existing stock of cigarettes. Now, isn't it true that according to economic theory a profit-maximizing shopkeeper would have charged the extra amount?"

(E) "Not at all! To maximize his long-run profits he might feel that to keep his steady customers he would raise the price only when he too had to pay the tax."

(A) "Wait a minute! How can you have it both ways? If he does raise the price he's a profit maximizer, and if he doesn't he's also a profit maximizer."

The anthropologist wins the point, for the economist should have answered the query differently, as follows:

(E) "All that economic theory predicts is that a tax increase of this sort will lead to a price increase in the near future. It is not intended to predict *immediate* responses by any *single* individual. Your shopkeeper may have decided to retire and sell off his stock more rapidly by retaining a lower price. Or, he may have been motivated by any of hundreds of other factors. All that economic theory does predict is that out of thousands of shopkeepers, nearly all will, within a reasonable time period, adjust their prices upward in accordance with the prediction. And this did happen, didn't it?"

Thus the anthropologist's criticism of economic theory was unwarranted and it could have been countered had the economist replied in an appropriate fashion to the query.

Another example may be drawn from the insurance industry. Suppose that actuarial studies have shown that 15 houses out of 10,000 will be damaged by fire in the month of December. This prediction is very accurate; the longevity of insurance companies is itself adequate testimony of this. But, the student of actuarial science would never say that the chances are 15 in 10,000 that *your* particular house will burn this coming December. By examining your house and finding it neat, with no oily rags nor papers around, and with electrical wiring carefully installed, and so forth, the probability that your house will burn may be much lower than average.

Similarly, when an economist predicts that a subsidy on wheat will lead to an increase in wheat production, he would not wish to predict that any one certain farmer would plant more wheat this coming season, nor that hail or drought will or will not ruin this coming season's crop. When the predictive power of economic theory, or any science, is contested, this probabilistic frame of reference should be used.

For a theory to be useful in prediction it should be simple. To be simple a theory must be abstract. The dichotomy often drawn between "abstract" theory on the one hand, and "realistic" theory on the other is, in large measure, a false dichotomy, for an abstract theory widely useful in prediction is certainly "realistic" in the true sense of that term. An overly complex theory can be too realistic to be useful just as an overly simple theory can be too abstract to be useful. Thus, the final test of any theory is found in its application; if it works well, it is a good theory whatever arbitrary degree of abstraction or realism one assigns to it.

The general equilibrium model developed in succeeding chapters is an abstract model. It is intended as a paradigm of the pricing system in the economy in which we live. In order to keep the model simple, it contains two goods, two consumers, and two factors of production. The model is built in steps or sections, and then assembled, as a prefabricated building is constructed. While many graphs are used in the construction process, because of the complexity of the relations, great reliance is placed upon the use of equations. These are kept as simple as possible.

2

The Consumers' Market

A good has utility if it has the capacity to satisfy a human desire. Assume that a consumer, Mr. A, gains a certain amount of satisfaction each period from his rate of consumption of a good, good 1. Assume further that Mr. A's satisfaction can be measured in terms of a unit of measure called *utils*. The actual possibility of measuring satisfaction in this way is discussed briefly in Chap. 11. While this assumption of measurable utility can be dropped without damage to the analysis, heuristically it is a very convenient assumption to keep throughout the construction of the general equilibrium paradigm.

2.1 TOTAL UTILITY AND MARGINAL UTILITY

Let $Q_{A,1}$ represent the quantity of good 1 that Mr. A consumes each period. Let $U_{A,1}$ represent the number of utils of satisfaction Mr. A receives each period from consuming good 1. Under the assumption that the amounts of other goods consumed by Mr. A are held constant, the rate of flow of satisfaction to Mr. A from consuming good 1 can now be expressed as a function of his rate of consumption of good 1, as illustrated in Fig. 2.1.

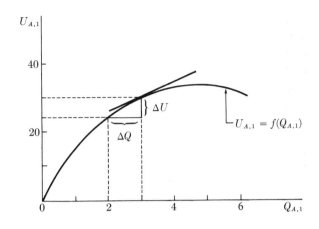

Figure 2.1

In general notation the equation for the curve may be written $U_{A,1} = f(Q_{A,1})$, indicating that the satisfaction received by Mr. A depends on the rate at which he consumes good 1. The highest point of the curve occurs at a rate of consumption of 5 units of good 1 each period. At this rate Mr. A receives approximately 33 utils of satisfaction each period. This satiates Mr. A's desire for good 1. Any rate of consumption greater or less than 5 units gives Mr. A less satisfaction than the maximum possible amount of 33 utils.

Marginal utility may be defined by the ratio $\Delta U / \Delta Q$. An illustration appears in Fig. 2.1. When Mr. A consumes 2 units each period, his satisfaction is 24 utils, and when he consumes 3 units his satisfaction increases to 30 utils per period. Hence, ΔU, the change in the amount of satisfaction Mr. A receives, is about 6. Also, ΔQ, the change in the rate at which good 1 is consumed, is 1. Therefore, marginal utility is 6 when the rate of consumption changes from 2 to 3 units per period.

Readers who have studied calculus will readily recognize the concept of marginal utility as a discrete approximation to the first derivative of the total utility function. Those who have not studied calculus need only imagine a line drawn tangent to the curve at some point on the curve, say the point where $Q = 3$. The slope of this tangent is then defined as $\Delta U / \Delta Q$, and in this way marginal utility is defined *at the point* on the curve where $Q = 3$, rather than being approximated by a discrete movement along a segment of the curve. In the figure the slope of the tangent would be something less than 6, so the discrete approximation overestimates marginal utility when Mr. A's rate of consumption is 3. A similar tangent to the curve drawn so as to touch the point where $Q = 2$ would clearly have a slope slightly greater than 6. Thus, between a rate of consumption of 3 units per period and a rate of 2 units per period the slope of the total utility curve is approximately 6.

The slope of a tangent to the total utility curve, or marginal utility, will differ at each different point on the curve. As the total utility curve emerges from the origin it has some positive slope. As the rate of consumption of good 1 increases, the slope of the total utility curve gradually declines until it is zero when Q reaches 5. When Q exceeds 5 the slope becomes negative; that is, an increase in Q results in a negative change in U ($\Delta U < 0$). Since a different slope exists for every Q, it is possible to draw a curve showing the slope of the total utility curve $\Delta U/\Delta Q$ as a function of the rate of consumption of good 1. Hence, in equation form, $\Delta U/\Delta Q = f'(Q)$. This is called the *marginal utility curve;* the function appears in Fig. 2.2.

By drawing the total utility curve in the particular shape chosen, the marginal utility curve falls, and it is an illustration of the *law of diminishing marginal utility.* This law, frequently a premise in economic theories, is that, given a constant rate of consumption of all other goods, when an individual increases his rate of consumption of any one good (i.e., when Q increases)

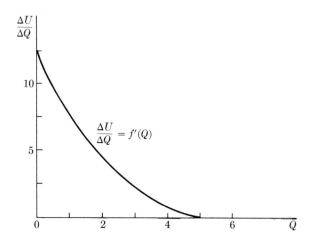

Figure 2.2

the additional satisfaction gained each period from a marginal increase in his rate of consumption (measured by $\Delta U / \Delta Q$) will diminish.

Another paragraph on the subject on marginal utility is necessary in order to dispel some slightly erroneous views of the concept that creep into economic literature from time to time. Marginal utility concerns the change in the rate of consumption of a good, *not* changes in the *stock* of a good available to the consumer. By avoiding the concept of a stock of goods the pitfall of assigning a utility value of a particular loaf of bread or glass of beer is also avoided. If you consume two loaves of bread each week, and then change your rate of consumption to three loaves of bread each week, there may occur some marginal increase in your total satisfaction each week from the consumption of bread. But, this change in satisfaction does not attach to any particular loaf, all loaves being identical in their ability to satisfy you.

Since *rate* of consumption is the basis of marginal utility, a unit of time over which consumption takes place should be specified or clearly implied. Furthermore, it is always assumed that no change occurs at the same time in the rate of consumption of any other good, for if it did it might affect the utility of the good in question.

2.2 INDIFFERENCE CURVES

Mr. A will, of course, receive satisfaction from his consumption of each of numerous goods besides good 1. In a general equilibrium framework the number of utils of satisfaction is expressed as a function of his rate of consumption of all the goods he consumes, $U_A = f(Q_{A,1}, Q_{A,2}, Q_{A,3}, \ldots Q_{A,N})$, for goods 1, 2, 3, $\ldots$ N. In order to retain simplicity in the abstract model it is assumed for now that Mr. A lives in a two-good world. That is, let $U_A = f(Q_{A,1}, Q_{A,2})$ represent Mr. A's utility function, which is illustrated in Fig. 2.3.

To gain perspective in the three-dimensional diagram, imagine the corner of a room from which an umbrella-shaped surface emerges. A point on this surface, such as point a, represents a set of three values. At a, $Q_{A,1} = 5$, $Q_{A,2} = 3$, and $U_A = 20$. Thus, if Mr. A consumes a package of 5 units of good 1 and 3 units of good 2 each period, he receives 20 utils of satisfaction

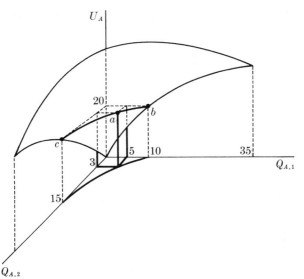

Figure 2.3

each period. If he consumes none of good 2 but 35 units of good 1 each period, his satisfaction is measured by the height of the appropriate dotted line on the far wall of the room. If one imagines a plane, parallel with the floor, at a height of 20 utils, such a plane will intersect, not only point a, but a set of other points including points b and c. The curve generated by the intersection of the plane with the utility surface can then be projected down to the floor as illustrated. By taking a number of such planes at different heights and representing different levels of satisfaction, a number of curves can be mapped onto the floor. If one then lifts up the floor and leans it against the far wall, it appears as in Fig. 2.4.

The curves appearing in Fig. 2.4 are called *indifference curves* and the graph is called an *indifference map* since the curves resemble contour lines on a geographical map. Points a and d both appear on the curve labeled $U = 20$. Since Mr. A receives 20 utils of satisfaction if he consumes the package of goods indicated at point a (5 of good 1, and 3 of good 2) and also 20 utils if he consumes the package indicated at point d (1 of good 1, and 10 of good 2), he has no reason to prefer position a over d nor d over a. Indeed, all of the packages of goods 1 and 2 represented on the curve are equally satisfactory from his point of view, and he is indifferent among them. If

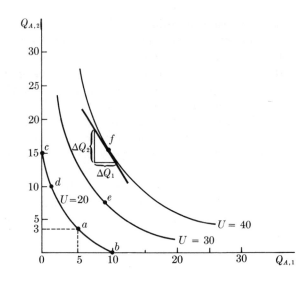

Figure 2.4

he were forced to choose a package from among them, he might resort to a game of chance to assist him in his decision.

Any point in a northeasterly direction from point a, say, point e, will be preferred to point a, for it represents a package containing more of each of the two goods. Point e would lie on a *higher* indifference curve. It is higher in the sense that it represents a higher level of total satisfaction for Mr. A. By the same reasoning, a southwesterly move will lower Mr. A's level of satisfaction. However, moves to either the northwest or southeast may result in a gain or a loss in utils of satisfaction each period for Mr. A, for they entail a higher rate of consumption of one good but a lower rate for the other. Whether or not Mr. A benefits from this change in his consumption pattern, depends on the extent to which the utils gained from the greater rate of consumption of one good offset the utils lost from the reduced rate of consumption of the other good. If, perchance, there is a net gain in utils, the new point is on a higher indifference curve; if a net loss, the new point is on a lower curve, and if the gains and losses of utils exactly match, then the new point is on the same indifference curve.

The slope of an indifference curve at any point, say, point f, is equal to the slope of the tangent to the curve at that point. It is called the *marginal rate of substitution* of 1 for 2 and is defined as the ratio $\Delta Q_2/\Delta Q_1$. In the evaluation of slopes, mathematical convention stipulates that the movement of a point be from left to right. Therefore, as Mr. A's consumption moves from one package to another down a single indifference curve, Mr. A substitutes more of good 1 in his package for some smaller amount of good 2. Mr. A's marginal rate of substitution of good 1 for good 2 will be denoted by $_A MRS_{1,2}$.

A discrete approximation to the marginal utility of good 1 can be also shown on an indifference map. To do so, specify the rate of consumption of good 2 by drawing a horizontal line through the appropriate amount on the vertical axis. A move rightward along this line is a move from one indifference curve to another. For a given horizontal distance, ΔQ_1, simply evaluate the attendant change in satisfaction, ΔU, by noting the values attached to the appropriate indifference curves. In this way observe $\Delta U/\Delta Q_1 = MU_1$. If the law of diminishing marginal utility holds, as you consider points further to the right (increasing rates of good 1), ΔU should diminish for each ΔQ_1 of a given amount. By drawing a vertical line rather than a horizontal one, the marginal utility of good 2 can be evaluated in similar fashion.

There exists a unique relationship between the marginal rate of substitution on the one hand and the two marginal utilities on the other:[1]

$$ MRS_{1,2} = -\frac{MU_1}{MU_2} $$

[1] In some texts the $MRS_{1,2}$ is defined as $-(\Delta Q_2/\Delta Q_1)$ in order to avoid the minus sign that remains. The reader who has studied calculus will recall the rule for the differential of a function of two variables:

$$ dZ = \frac{\partial Z}{\partial x}\, dx + \frac{\partial Z}{\partial y}\, dy $$

Upon applying this rule to Mr. A's utility function, $U_A = f(Q_{A,1}, Q_{A,2})$, observe that

$$ dU_A = \frac{\partial U_A}{\partial Q_{A,1}}\, dQ_{A,1} + \frac{\partial U_A}{\partial Q_{A,2}}\, dQ_{A,2} $$

Let $dU_A = 0$, consistent with remaining on a given indifference curve; then

$$ \frac{dQ_{A,2}}{dQ_{A,1}} = -\frac{\partial U_A/\partial Q_{A,1}}{\partial U_A/\partial Q_{A,2}} $$

On the left is Mr. A's marginal rate of substitution of good 1 for good 2 (the slope of an indifference curve at a point), and on the right is the ratio of the two marginal utilities. Thus, by differentiation we arrive at the solution found by discrete approximation in the text above.

For by definition

$$MRS_{1,2} = \frac{\Delta Q_2}{\Delta Q_1} \qquad MU_1 = \frac{\Delta U}{\Delta Q_1} \qquad MU_2 = \frac{\Delta U}{\Delta Q_2}$$

Hence $\qquad \dfrac{\Delta Q_2}{\Delta Q_1} = -\dfrac{\Delta U/\Delta Q_1}{\Delta U/\Delta Q_2} = -\dfrac{\Delta U}{\Delta Q_1}\dfrac{\Delta Q_2}{\Delta U}$

Since $MRS_{1,2}$ applies to a single indifference curve, the increase in utility, $+\Delta U$, from consuming more good 1 exactly offsets the decrease in utility $(-\Delta U)$ from consuming less of good 2. Thus, the ΔU's and the minus sign cancel out of the right-hand side of the equation, leaving the ratio of ΔQ_2 to ΔQ_1, which is the definition of $MRS_{1,2}$.

It is assumed that indifference curves have certain properties. First, they must never cross one another. If they did it could be shown that one package of goods would yield more satisfaction than another package, and at the same time yield less satisfaction than this other package—an inadmissable contradiction. Second, indifference curves must be negatively sloped in the range relevant to the analysis. If they were positively sloped it would mean that more of both goods would yield no greater satisfaction to Mr. A, a condition which could exist only if Mr. A's desire for some commodity were satiated.

A selection of indifference curves taken from a complete utility surface appears in Fig. 2.5. The point in the center of the ellipses has been called a "bliss point" inasmuch as any movement

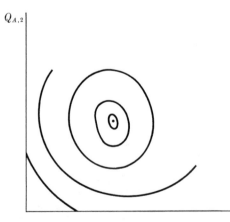

Figure 2.5

$Q_{A,1}$

away from it, even a movement to a higher rate of consumption of both goods, would leave Mr. A worse off. The ellipses, therefore, where positively sloped, indicate that Mr. A's desire for a good is satiated. But if consumption is not forced upon anyone, no one would freely consume commodities beyond satiation of his desires. Therefore, while indifference curves can be positively sloped for purposes of analysis, the relevant range of the indifference map is only that range where indifference curves are negatively sloped.

The third condition imposed upon the shape of indifference curves is that they appear convex as viewed from the origin. This condition means that the slope of each indifference curve $MRS_{1,2}$ must diminish in absolute value as more of good 1 is substituted for good 2 along a given indifference curve. An indifference curve might be negatively sloped throughout and yet have a lump in it forming a shape that is concave from the origin. The lower portion of the concave part of the lump would show $MRS_{1,2}$ as increasing, that is, as Mr. A's rate of consumption of good 1 increased, he would be willing to give up an even larger amount of good 2 than previously in order to obtain another unit of good 1. Thus, to Mr. A, good 1 becomes more valuable as his rate of consumption of it increases. The value of good 1 to Mr. A is measured by his willingness to give up good 2 in order to obtain more of good 1. A concave portion of an indifference curve might exist, for example, when one of the two goods in question has greater marginal utility for Mr. A, the greater his rate of consumption of it, that is, when one of the two goods does not adhere to the law of diminishing marginal utility.[1] One can certainly imagine that for certain individuals in certain circumstances exceptions to this law do occur. But exceptions are sufficiently rare to enable one to invoke, with few misgivings, the condition that indifference curves must be convex from the origin for most analytical pur-

---

[1] Even if concave portions of indifference curves did exist, however, it would be difficult to observe them. This is because maximizing consumers would not likely consume a package of goods represented by a point on the concave portion since there would doubtless be some other package that they could consume with their budget which would yield a higher level of satisfaction and which would be on a convex portion of an indifference curve. The analysis of the consumer's budget that follows should clarify this point.

poses. For the relevant range of concern, therefore, indifference curves are assumed to be downward sloping and to be convex from the origin, and it is assumed that they do not cross one another.

Economists make no serious attempt to describe the forces which create the particular indifference map that Mr. A happens to have. Wants, desires, and tastes of a consumer arise from personal, social, and psychological forces that are beyond the economist's capacity to explain. Any individual's environment contains innumerable forces of religious, ethical, cultural, political, and social origins, each of which contributes to the formation of some part of his tastes for economic goods. For purposes of economic analysis, therefore, tastes of consumers in the form of utility functions or indifference maps are assumed to be given. Furthermore, the model can handle a change in taste and predict the effect on prices and quantities of a change in taste. However, it is important for the model of the pricing system that these tastes are not in turn affected by the system itself. For if they were, tastes would be interdependent with the system, and without an explanation of tastes economists could not explain the determination of prices and quantities. For now, tastes of consumers are assumed to be given by utility functions and observable for each individual.

2.3 THE BUDGET: PRICES AND INCOME

Having established Mr. A's utility function, the next stage in building the consumers' part of the general equilibrium model is to specify the constraints that impinge upon Mr. A's consumption of economic goods. These were mentioned in Chap. 1. First, Mr. A's income acts as a constraint on his command over scarce economic goods, and second, it is assumed that the prices of goods 1 and 2 are given. The assumption of given prices is relaxed later on, for the purpose of this exercise is to show how prices and quantities are determined in a market pricing system. But it is essential to take prices as given at this stage of the development of the paradigm.

A budget emerges from given prices and a fixed income. Let P_1 represent the price of good 1, and let P_2 represent the price of good 2. Also, let I_A represent Mr. A's income. The ratio $1/P_1$ reveals the amount of good 1 that a dollar will purchase. If

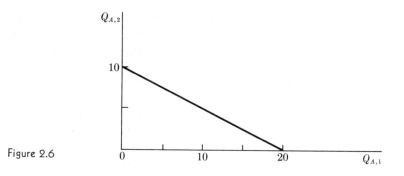

Figure 2.6

$P_1 = \$.50$, then \$1.00 will buy 2 units of good 1. Thus, the reciprocal of the price of a good is an expression of the value of a unit of money in terms of the amount of goods that a unit of money will purchase. The ratio I_A/P_1 reveals the amount of good 1 that Mr. A could purchase if he spent all of his income on good 1. Similarly, I_A/P_2 reveals the amount of good 2 that Mr. A could purchase if he purchased only good 2. In equation form the budget constraint appears as $I_A = P_1 Q_{A,1} + P_2 Q_{A,2}$ if Mr. A spends all of his income on goods 1 and 2 each period. If $P_1 = \$.50$, $P_2 = \$1.00$, and $I_A = 10$, the equation is satisfied by any of a theoretically infinite set of pairs of values of $Q_{A,1}$ and $Q_{A,2}$ which, when graphed, form the line appearing in Fig. 2.6. This line could be called Mr. A's *expenditure possibility line*, his *budget line*, or his *budget constraint*. This line delineates the set of all bundles available to Mr. A from those that are unavailable given his income and the prices he faces in the marketplace.

The slope of the budget line is the ratio $\Delta Q_{A,2}/\Delta Q_{A,1}$, but it may also be expressed as the ratio $-P_1/P_2$. If P_1 fell from \$.50 to \$.25, then Mr. A could buy twice as much of good 1 with his \$10.00 income. The budget line would intersect the horizontal axis at 40 rather than 20, but since P_2 remained unchanged, the line would still intersect the vertical axis at 10. Thus, the slope of the line in absolute value falls with a decline in P_1 while the line remains hinged onto the vertical axis.[1] In case of a change in the price of good 2, of course,

---

[1] Take the equation $I_A = P_1 Q_{A,1} + P_2 Q_{A,2}$ and rearrange terms to obtain $Q_{A,2} = I_A/P_2 - (P_1/P_2)Q_{A,1}$. With I_A, P_1, and P_2 each treated as a parameter, it follows from calculus that $dQ_{A,2}/dQ_{A,1} = -P_1/P_2$, which represents the slope of the budget constraint in Fig. 2.6.

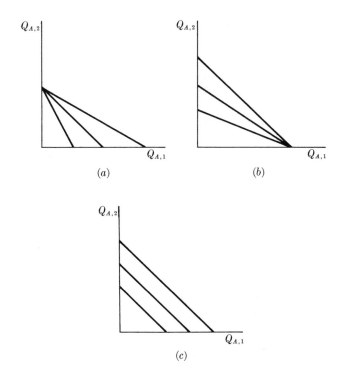

Figure 2.7   (c)

(a) Variation in P_1 with P_2 and I_A constant; (b) variation in P_2 with P_1 and I_A constant; (c) variation in I_A with P_1 and P_2 constant.

the line remains hinged to the horizontal axis, is lifted by a reduction in the price of good 2, and it drops toward the origin with an increase in the price of good 2. If Mr. A's income should increase from \$10 to \$20 per period, with no change in either of the two prices, the budget line would shift up and to the right while remaining parallel with the previous budget line. The new budget line would intersect the horizontal axis at 40. Figure 2.7a, b, and c illustrate the various movements of the budget constraint that result from fluctuations in P_1, P_2, and I_A, respectively.

2.4 EQUILIBRIUM FOR ONE CONSUMER

By superimposing the budget constraint on his indifference map it is possible to observe which package of goods 1 and 2 Mr. A will consume each period in order to maximize his satisfaction from his limited income. If the indifference map and the budget constraint appear as depicted in Fig. 2.8, Mr. A will freely choose to consume 10 units of good 1 and 5 units of good 2 each period if he is to maximize the utility available from his limited income. This package of commodities, represented by point a in the figure, rests on the highest indifference curve touched by his expenditure possibility curve. Any point on the budget constraint other than a, say, point b, will be on a lower indifference curve. At point a, the slope of the indifference curve just equals the slope of the budget line, that is, $_AMRS_{1,2} = -P_1/P_2$. For a consumer to maximize his satisfaction, this equality must hold.

If one assumes that rational consumers will behave in a fashion designed to maximize their satisfaction, or if this tendency is sufficiently pervasive to be acceptable as a general principle of behavior, then the above equality can be imposed along with the indifference map (utility function) and the budget constraint, and in combination these three equations provide a framework for a general theory of consumer choice. It must always be remembered, however, that this theory of choice is not a theory of *tastes*, for these are taken as given in the form of the utility function.

Since
$$MRS_{1,2} = -\frac{MU_1}{MU_2} = -\frac{P_1}{P_2}$$

then
$$\frac{MU_1}{P_1} = \frac{MU_2}{P_2}$$

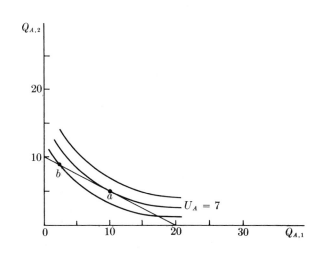

Figure 2.8

This equation represents another way in which the principle of the maximization of consumer satisfaction may be stated.[1] If a given consumer maximizes his satisfaction by his consumption pattern, then the marginal utility of good 1 is to the price of good 1 as the marginal utility of good 2 is to the price of good 2.

To clarify this statement of the principle, assume that this equality is not met. For example, assume

$$\frac{MU_1}{P_1} = 4 \qquad \frac{MU_2}{P_2} = 5 \qquad \text{and} \qquad P_1 = P_2 = 1$$

so that

$$\frac{MU_1}{P_1} < \frac{MU_2}{P_2}$$

If this consumer reduces his expenditure on good 1 by $1, he loses 4 units of satisfaction each period. If he then increases his expenditure on good 2 by this $1, he gains 5 units of satisfaction. Since the gain more than offsets the loss, he will engage in this transfer of the application of his funds. As he does so, however, he buys more of good 2, and, according to the law of diminishing marginal utility, MU_2 will decline. Similarly, with smaller purchases of good 1, MU_1 will increase. Both of

---

[1] The equality of the ratios of marginal utilities and prices may be found by using a factor in calculus known as the Lagrange multiplier. Let $I_A - P_1 Q_{A,1} - P_2 Q_{A,2} = 0$ by transformation of the budget equation. Add this function to the utility function in order to form a new function $V = f(Q_{A,1}, Q_{A,2}) + \lambda(I_A - P_1 Q_{A,1} - P_2 Q_{A,2})$, where $\lambda \neq 0$ is the Lagrange multiplier.

Set the partial derivatives of V with respect to $Q_{A,1}$, $Q_{A,2}$, and λ equal to zero, so that

$$\frac{\partial V}{\partial Q_{A,1}} = \frac{\partial U}{\partial Q_{A,1}} - \lambda P_1 = 0$$

$$\frac{\partial V}{\partial Q_{A,2}} = \frac{\partial U}{\partial Q_{A,2}} - \lambda P_2 = 0$$

$$\frac{\partial V}{\partial \lambda} = I_A - P_1 Q_{A,1} - P_2 Q_{A,2} = 0$$

In the first two equations move P to the right-hand side and then divide the first equation by the second to form

$$\frac{\partial U/\partial Q_{A,1}}{\partial U/\partial Q_{A,2}} = \frac{P_1}{P_2} \qquad \text{or} \qquad \frac{\partial U/\partial Q_{A,1}}{P_1} = \frac{\partial U/\partial Q_{A,2}}{P_2} \qquad \text{(and also} = \lambda)$$

which is the statement of the principle of maximization of consumer satisfaction, as noted in the text above; λ may be called the marginal utility of income (money) for it represents (loosely) the additional utility obtainable from spending another dollar on either of the two goods.

these forces will continue to operate until such time as the equality between the ratios of marginal utilities to prices holds. When this happens, there exists no further pressure for altering the components of the package of commodities that he buys each period; the consumer is then in a position of stable equilibrium, and the marginal utility derived from the last dollar spent will be the same in all uses. Thus, by examining the forces put into play when the equality is *not* met, an understanding of the principle of consumer maximization emerges.

2.5 THREE EQUATIONS, THREE UNKNOWNS, AND THREE INDEPENDENT VARIABLES

This completes the basic statement of the economic theory of consumers' choice. Upon review, the theory has the following components:

(a) $U_A = f(Q_{A,1}, Q_{A,2})$

A utility function derived empirically from Mr. A's own expression of his tastes for goods and presumed to have certain properties

(b) $I_A = P_1 Q_{A,1} + P_2 Q_{A,2}$

An equation expressing the principle that Mr. A will spend all his income

(c) $_A MRS_{1,2} = -\dfrac{_A MU_1}{_A MU_2} = -\dfrac{P_1}{P_2}$

An equation expressing the principle of the maximization of consumer satisfaction

(d) U_A, $Q_{A,1}$, and $Q_{A,2}$

Unknown dependent variables to be determined by the system

(e) I_A, P_1, and P_2

Independent variables given for the problem at hand

In many cases the system of equations can be solved simultaneously to determine a set of equilibrium values for the unknowns. This is illustrated in the following numerical example. For ease of computation, calculus is used, but the student who has not studied calculus should not be deterred, for he can simply substitute the solution values of the dependent variables into the several equations to convince himself that consistency obtains.

Let Mr. A's utility function take the specific form

(a') $\quad U_A = Q_{A,1}{}^{.5}Q_{A,2}{}^{.5}$

By taking partial derivatives of U_A with respect to $Q_{A,1}$ and $Q_{A,2}$, two equations for the respective marginal utilities are derived. They are

$$MU_1 = \frac{\partial U_A}{\partial Q_{A,1}} = .5 \frac{Q_{A,2}{}^{.5}}{Q_{A,1}{}^{.5}}$$

$$MU_2 = \frac{\partial U_A}{\partial Q_{A,2}} = .5 \frac{Q_{A,1}{}^{.5}}{Q_{A,2}{}^{.5}}$$

Therefore, $MU_1/MU_2 = Q_{A,2}/Q_{A,1}$ as the coefficients cancel one another and the exponents add to 1. Let $I_A = \$10$, $P_1 = \$.50$, and $P_2 = \$1$, then (c) becomes

(c') $\quad {}_A MRS_{1,2} = - \dfrac{Q_{A,2}}{Q_{A,1}} = -.5$

Therefore, $Q_{A,2} = .5Q_{A,1}$. Also (b) becomes

(b') $\quad 10 = .5Q_{A,1} + Q_{A,2}$

By substitution, $10 = .5Q_{A,1} + .5Q_{A,1} = Q_{A,1}$. If $Q_{A,1} = 10$, then $Q_{A,2} = 5$. Thus, Mr. A, if he maximizes his utility, will expend his limited income on goods 1 and 2 in this fashion. The solution is depicted graphically in Fig. 2.8 (page 23). U_A may be determined by substitution of these values of $Q_{A,1}$ and $Q_{A,2}$ into A's utility function. Hence

(a') $\quad U_A = Q_{A,1}{}^{.5}Q_{A,2}{}^{.5} = 10^{.5} \times 5^{.5} = 50^{.5} = \sqrt{50} = \pm 7.07$

This abstract numerical example is provided for the primary purpose of illustrating the logical consistency of the theory of consumers' choice. A casual observation of the way oneself and one's neighbor behave as consumers indicates that the theory describes reality quite well. First, consumers do spend most of their income each period. However, since savings play an important role, and should not be ignored, the analysis of savings will be integrated into the general model in Chap. 5. Second, individual patterns of consumption do change from month to month as consumers shop around to try different brands of goods, or different types of services; but if goods are defined into broad categories of food, transportation, shelter, entertainment, utility services, and so forth, when income and prices are given, the proportion of income spent on each of these tends to remain quite stable for quite long periods. This indicates that consumers' tastes, as described by their utility functions, are quite stable. Third, the bargain-seeking housewife, as a maximizing consumer, is testimony to the rational, assiduous, economically motivated behavior of by far the largest proportion of purchasers.

Another indication of the "reality" of the principle of maximization of consumer satisfaction can be gained through introspection. The principle is that marginal utilities are proportional to their respective prices. Hence, a very small, extra unit of income, when spent, will yield nearly the same addition to total utility regardless which good is bought with it. Assume that someone's income increased by $1 per month. Could anyone say which good he would buy with it? This is unlikely for the reason that if he is currently maximizing his utility from his income, he will be in a position such that an extra dollar's expenditure on any good that he already consumes a sizeable quantity of would yield very nearly the same additional satisfaction to him. He is indifferent as to the manner in which a very small addition to his income is spent.[1]

2.6 PRICE-CONSUMPTION, OR OFFER, CURVES

Before introducing a second consumer and thereby extending the size of the model, it is useful to examine some aspects of the model in its present form. What is called an *offer curve*, or *price-consumption curve*, is derived by connecting points of tangency of various budget lines (brought on by different prices of good 2 with P_1 fixed) with the various indifference curves on Mr. A's indifference maps. One is shown in Fig. 2.9. For

---

[1] This *may help* explain his susceptibility to lotteries, to tinkers who used to fix pots but nowadays beg for pennies, and to children who ask for mints and gum, if we think of him as spending his income for these "goods."

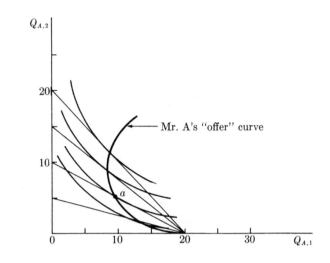

Figure 2.9

each lower price of good 2, the budget line rises and Mr. A will buy a new equilibrium package of goods each period as indicated by the appropriate point of tangency where $_AMRS_{1,2} = -P_1/P_2$. As P_2 falls, Mr. A will buy more of good 2. Thus, the price-consumption curve shows how Mr. A's purchases of good 2 vary with the price of good 2.

If Mr. A enters the market, not with income of $10, but rather with 20 units of good 1, then at point a he is willing to offer 10 units of his endowment of good 1 in exchange for 5 units of good 2. Thus, Mr. A's income may take the form of money, or of an endowment of good 1. In the former case the curve is called a price-consumption curve because Mr. A uses money to buy good 2 at the going dollar price. In the latter case the term *offer curve* is used because it is more descriptive of the barter exchange of goods. By letting P_1 vary instead of P_2, a price-consumption curve will originate on the vertical axis and will provide a description of the way Mr. A's purchases of good 1 will vary with changes in the price of good 1.

2.7 INCOME-CONSUMPTION CURVES

By keeping both prices constant and letting I_A vary, a different kind of curve is generated by points of tangency of the various budget lines with indifference curves. It is called an *income-consumption curve*. In Fig. 2.7c there is an illustration of the way the budget line varies with changes in I_A. In Fig. 2.10

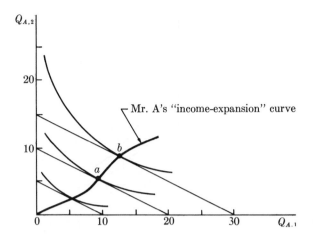

Figure 2.10

the expansion line itself is shown. If Mr. A's income increases from $10 to $15, his equilibrium position will shift from point a to point b, assuming that $P_1 = \$.50$ and $P_2 = \$1.00$ as in the original example.

The indifference curves have been drawn so that the income-consumption curve appears irregular in shape. In the numerical example above, the function chosen to represent Mr. A's utility was of a simple form. If this form were retained here, the expansion curve would be a straight line out of the origin. However, it is customary to assume that individual indifference maps have shapes to generate a wide variety of income-consumption curves.

2.8   INFERIOR GOODS

If an income-consumption curve bends back to negative slope over part of its range, one of the goods in question is called an *inferior good*. Good 2 is an inferior good if, as Mr. A's income expands beyond a certain point, he consumes a smaller amount of it each period than he did when his income was lower. Thus, a good is inferior if the quantity purchased each period varies inversely with income. In Fig. 2.11, as the point of equilibrium for Mr. A moves along the income-consumption curve from the origin to point a his rate of consumption of good 2 increases. Over this range of consumption good 2 is a superior good because quantity varies directly with income. But to the

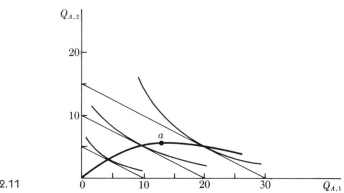

Figure 2.11

right of point a, as Mr. A's income expands his consumption package each period contains less good 2 than before. Hence, good 2 is an inferior good over this range of Mr. A's income-consumption curve.

2.9 GIFFEN GOODS

It is also possible to draw an indifference map such that the price-consumption curve bends back on itself. That is, as P_2 falls, after a time less of good 2 is bought each period. When this occurs the good is called a *Giffen good*, named after the man who first described this possibility. The example often used is that of a low-income receiver whose diet consists mostly of bread and who spends most of his income on bread. But when bread prices fall, he can buy the same amount of bread and have some income left over. He may then decide to substitute some meat for some bread. Hence, he ends up consuming less bread even if the price of bread has fallen. In the example, good 2 is bread and good 1 is meat. Figure 2.12 illustrates this. In the range from point a to point b, Mr. A consumes less of good 2 even though the price of good 2 is lower than before. Thus, a good is a Giffen good if quantity varies directly with price. A Giffen good is always an inferior good, a *very* inferior good; but an inferior good need not be so inferior as to be a Giffen good.

According to the *law of demand*, the lower the price of a good, the larger the quantity that will be bought each period. The case of the Giffen good is an exception to this law. In

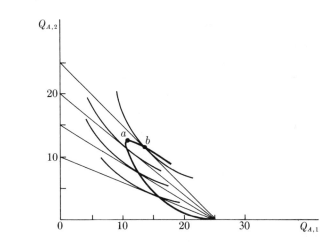

Figure 2.12

developing the general equilibrium model the possibility of Giffen goods is ruled out on the presumption that their existence is sufficiently rare that they can be ignored with negligible loss of generality and predictive content for the model.

2.10 COMPENSATING CHANGES IN PRICE AND INCOME

Assume that Mr. A maximizes his satisfaction by his expenditure on goods 1 and 2 each period as in the original example where $P_1 = \$.50$, $P_2 = \$1$, $I_A = \$10$, $Q_{A,1} = 10$ units, and $Q_{A,2} = 5$ units. This is shown as point a in Fig. 2.13. Now assume that

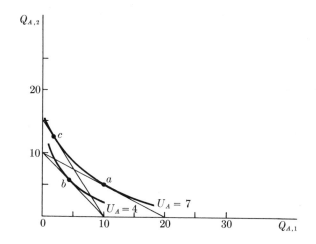

Figure 2.13

there is a change in the price of good 1, that it increases from $.50 to $1. Mr. A is now unable to reach the level of utility as represented by the indifference curve that passes through point a, but must be satisfied with some lower level of utility, say, $U_A = 4$, associated with the package of goods represented by point b. Now one can ask the question "What reduction in P_2 would just compensate Mr. A for the loss he incurred from the increase in P_1?" A *compensating* reduction in P_2 would be that reduction which is just sufficient to enable Mr. A to consume a package of goods that would give him as many utils of satisfaction as he had before P_1 increased. Point c in the figure represents such a package of goods. Initially, the budget line was that drawn through point b, but with the further compensating reduction in P_2 the relevant budget line became that drawn through point c.

It is also possible to compensate Mr. A by changing his income instead of changing P_2, or by combining some changes in income along with some change in P_2. Indeed, since there are three variables forming the budget constraint, there are six ways that changes can occur; and for each of these there are two ways of compensating Mr. A by using a single variable at a time and an infinite number of ways of compensating Mr. A if two variables are used in combination.

The concept of compensation is important in the subject of political economy, for every government is wont to interfere to some extent with the free flow of economic activity, and whenever it does the question of fair compensation arises. The nationalization of an industry is a clear case in point, but in more subtle ways the question arises in analysis of subsidies and taxes as well.

2.11 SUBSTITUTION EFFECT AND INCOME EFFECT

Here the concept of compensation is helpful in sorting out two types of forces brought into play when the price of a good changes. These forces lead Mr. A to change the quantity of the good that he buys each period. If, for example, P_2 falls, then Mr. A willingly substitutes some of good 2 for good 1. Furthermore, Mr. A's money income is effectively higher than it was before P_2 fell, because his $10 will purchase a larger quantity of goods than before. That is, the purchasing power of his $10 income has increased. With higher *real* income Mr.

A might choose to buy more of good 2 as well as more good 1. Thus, there is a *substitution effect* and also an *income effect* from a change in the price of a good that leads to changes in the quantity of the good bought each period. With the help of Fig. 2.14, the two effects can be shown to have independent existence.

Assume the initial budget curve is that drawn through point a, with $P_1 = \$.50$, $P_2 = \$1.00$, and $I_A = \$10.00$. Let P_2 fall to $\$.50$ so that the budget line is now the line through point b, and to maximize his satisfaction Mr. A buys more of both goods. He increases his purchases of good 2 by 4 units each period. How much of this increase results from his willingness to substitute good 2 for good 1, and how much is the result of his increased real income? To answer this question, the first step is to compensate Mr. A by reducing his income by that amount that just makes the previous indifference curve attainable. This reduction in income is illustrated by the parallel shift down and to the left of the budget line until it is just tangent to the indifference curve at point c, the same indifference curve that point a is on. If the substitution effect alone were responsible for Mr. A's increased purchase of good 2, he would buy package c instead of package a, and his rate of consumption of good 2 would increase by 3 units each period. In addition to this substitution effect there is the income effect that gives Mr. A a higher *real* income. It is represented by the budget line and the indifference curve on which point b lies. In shifting from point c to point b, Mr. A buys another unit of good 2 each period. Thus, the total increase of 4 units of good 2 pur-

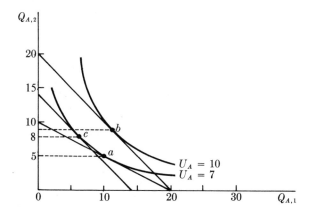

Figure 2.14

chased each period as a result of the decline in P_2 is divided into (1) 3 units that result from the substitution effect, and (2) 1 unit that results from the income effect.

In this example, the change in price was observed initially and the corresponding change in income was noted secondarily. Unfortunately, when dealing with discrete and sizeable shifts, if the income change were observed first, and the price change second, there would be a slightly different result. That is, if the income change were noted by drawing a budget line parallel to the initial budget line rather than parallel to the subsequent budget line, the amount attributable to the income effect (as well as that attributable to the substitution effect as measured by the movement along the outer indifference curve instead of the inner one) might differ slightly from the results just noted. Thus, to evaluate the effects more accurately, it is necessary to avoid discrete changes in price of sizeable amounts and evaluate instead the total effect of a large sum of very small changes in price, as could be done if calculus were used.[1] But this qualification should not be allowed to impair one's insight into the nature of the two distinct types of forces that exert pressure on the quantity of a good bought as a result of a change in its price. The case of a Giffen good, described earlier, is one in which the income effect of a decline in price (arising in the case of an inferior good) leads to a reduction in purchases that is large enough to outweigh the substitution effect that leads to an expansion of purchases when the price falls. Hence, the net effect is a decline in purchases when the price falls. A discussion of cases in which goods are complements rather than substitutes is reserved for Chap. 3.

It might be noted that if Mr. A's income is increased the quantity of good 1 purchased may either increase or decrease, so that the income effect may be either positive or negative. On the other hand, the substitution effect is always negative, for a reduction in the price of good 1 will reduce the steepness of the slope of the budget constraint; and as long as Mr. A remains on the same indifference curve, which is convex as viewed from the origin, the quantity of good 1 purchased will increase. Thus, the substitution effect is always negative, for as the price falls the quantity purchased will rise, and vice versa.

[1] The interested reader may wish to examine the clear discussion of these issues provided in R. G. D. Allen, "Mathematical Economics," pp. 665–669, Macmillan and Co., Ltd., London, 1957.

2.12 EQUILIBRIUM FOR TWO CONSUMERS

The next step in the construction of the general equilibrium model of the pricing system is to introduce Mr. B, the second consumer. It is assumed that Mr. B has also a utility function and that he receives a certain income each period. However, at this point the assumption of given prices is relaxed. In its place is the assumption that fixed quantities of good 1 and good 2 flow into the marketplace each period. The abstract model will then be used to show how the prices of the two goods are determined, and how the amounts of these scarce goods are allocated among the two consumers. In this way the model draws us closer to a complete description of the determination of all the prices and quantities under a free-market pricing system.

With two consumers, the model has the following components:

(a) $U_A = f(Q_{A,1}, Q_{A,2})$ Mr. A's utility function

      $U_B = g(Q_{B,1}, Q_{B,2})$ Mr. B's utility function

(b) $I_A = P_1 Q_{A,1} + P_2 Q_{A,2}$ Mr. A's budget

      $I_B = P_1 Q_{B,1} + P_2 Q_{B,2}$ Mr. B's budget

(c) $_A MRS_{1,2} = -\dfrac{_A MU_1}{_A MU_2} = -\dfrac{P_1}{P_2}$ Equations expressing the principle of the maximization of consumer satisfaction

      $_B MRS_{1,2} = -\dfrac{_B MU_1}{_B MU_2} = -\dfrac{P_1}{P_2}$

(d) $Q_{A,1} + Q_{B,1} = Q_1$ Equations showing that all of goods 1 and 2 flowing into the marketplace are sold either to Mr. A or to Mr. B

      $Q_{A,2} + Q_{B,2} = Q_2$

(e) $U_A, Q_{A,1}, Q_{A,2}$ Dependent variables to be determined by the system

      $U_B, Q_{B,1}, Q_{B,2}$

      P_1, P_2

(f) I_A, I_B, Q_1, Q_2 Independent variables given for the problem at hand

Of the eight equations, two stem from utility functions, two from budget constraints, two from the principle that consumers will maximize their satisfaction, and two from imposing the condition that the market be cleared. Of the total of twelve variables, four are assumed to be given, leaving eight dependent upon the solution of the system of eight equations. The model is determinate in the sense that it has defined limits.

Two points should be made about the equation system. First, in a system of equations that are linear and independent there must be as many equations as there are dependent variables. But this equality of the number of equations and the number of unknowns does not ensure that a solution exists, nor that it is unique if it does exist.[1] Second, the set of equations may be partitioned, that is, one block of dependent variables may be found separately. This block consists of the prices and quantities $(P_1,P_2,Q_{A,1},Q_{A,2},Q_{B,1},Q_{B,2})$ but excludes the utilities of Mr. A and Mr. B, U_A and U_B. If one omits the two utility functions of part (a), and the two dependent variables U_A and U_B, the remaining six equations and six unknowns provide a complete system. This is important because it illustrates that one need not be able to measure utils of satisfaction in cardinal terms in order to solve for prices and quantities, so long as one can find the consumers' marginal rates of substitution. And marginal rates of substitution can be found if consumers can *order*,

---

[1] Solutions that do exist are also assumed to meet certain acceptable restrictions that are meaningful in economics. Thus, in the numerical example provided for single consumer equilibrium above it was found that the number of utils of satisfaction he realized was over 7. However, this number was arrived at by taking the square root of 50. In this case both $+7$ and -7 will satisfy the equation system. The solution is not unique. The -7 solution, however, is arbitrarily ignored because it is not an economically meaningful solution.

Professor Robert E. Kuenne discusses the importance of existence proofs for systems of nonlinear simultaneous equations in his book, "The Theory of General Economic Equilibrium," pp. 19–20, Princeton University Press, Princeton, New Jersey, 1963. He also devotes the entire ninth chapter of his book to an examination of the various attempts to establish appropriate criteria for existence and uniqueness of solutions.

The mathematically inclined student who is interested in pursuing the issue of the uniqueness of solutions might wish to examine discussions of implicit functions to be found in many calculus books and also books on matrix algebra: for example, R. A. Frazer, W. J. Duncan, and A. R. Collar, "Elementary Matrices," Cambridge University Press, London, 1960; Ivan S. Sokolnikoff, "Advanced Calculus," McGraw-Hill Book Company, New York, 1939; and for the relevance of the issue to economic policy see K. A. Fox, J. K. Sengupta, and E. Thorbecke, "The Theory of Quantitative Economic Policy," North-Holland Publishing Company, Amsterdam, 1966, especially Chap. 2.

or *rank*, their preferences. Thus, the solution set of prices and quantities depends on *ordinal* measures of satisfaction but does not depend on cardinal measures in terms of utils. Utils have been used all along principally for their heuristic value. (See Chap. 11 for further discussion of the measurability of utility.)

2.13 ADDING CONSUMERS AND COMMODITIES

Although the model will only concern two consumers, one can easily infer how the model would change if a third consumer, Mr. C, were introduced. Three additional dependent variables $Q_{C,1}$, $Q_{C,2}$, and U_C, along with three additional equations under points (a), (b), and (c) above and one additional given I_C, would all be added to an expanded model. Furthermore, the equations under (d) would have to be amended. In theory, if a finite number of consumers were added, the model would still yield a solution. Also, if another good (instead of another consumer) were introduced, good 3, the model would contain an additional given Q_3, three additional dependent variables $Q_{A,3}$, $Q_{B,3}$, and P_3, and three additional equations, two of which could be found under part (c) and one under part (d). The component parts of equations in parts (a) and (b) would also have to be altered appropriately. In this fashion the model would expand as the number of goods to be considered increased. In theory, then, the model is determinate for any number of goods and consumers.

2.14 THE EDGEWORTH-BOX DIAGRAMS

The model of the consumers' market provides the analyst with a theoretical explanation of the determination of prices of economic goods, and the allocation of quantities of these goods among the individual consumers. A graphical description of this two-good, two-consumer model is provided in Fig. 2.15. The diagram is called an *Edgeworth-box diagram* after Francis Ysidro Edgeworth who first suggested one similar to it.[1]

Having two consumers instead of only one, there are now two utility functions to deal with. Thus, Mr. B's utility function, similar in general shape to Mr. A's, is rotated by 180° and then superimposed on Mr. A's so that the two indifference maps lie one on top of the other. Quantities of good 1 are

[1] V. J. Tarascio argues it should be named after Pareto. See: A Correction: On the Genealogy of the So-called Edgeworth-Bowley Diagram, *Western Econ. J.*, vol. x, pp. 193–197, June 1972.

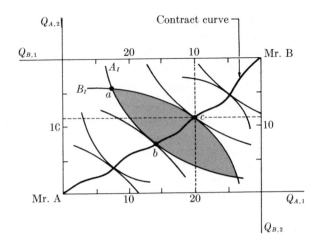

Figure 2.15

measured from left to right along the bottom horizontal axis
for Mr. A and along the top horizontal axis from right to left
for Mr. B. Similarly, the two vertical axes measure quantities
of good 2. The size of the rectangular box is determined by
the volume of goods 1 and 2 that flow into the consumers' market
each period.

If indifference curves are convex as viewed from the origin,
then there will exist a set of points each of which will represent
a point of tangency of one of Mr. A's indifference curves with
one of Mr. B's. A line connecting these points of tangency
is called a *contract curve*. Each point on the contract curve
is a point at which Mr. A's marginal rate of substitution of
good 1 for good 2 equals Mr. B's marginal rate of substitution
of good 1 for good 2; that is,

$$_A MRS_{1,2} = {_B}MRS_{1,2}$$

Since both of these marginal rates of substitution must also
equal the ratio $-P_1/P_2$, if the two consumers are to maximize
their satisfaction from the consumption of goods 1 and 2, the
equilibrium solution to the distribution of these goods among
the two consumers must be represented by one of the points
somewhere on the contract curve.

If the packages of goods received by Mr. A and Mr. B are
represented at point c, Mr. A receives 20 units of good 1 each
period and 12 units of good 2, while Mr. B receives 10 units
of good 1 and 8 of good 2. In this way the entire supply of
goods 1 and 2 is allocated among the consumers. Points b and

c and all other points on the contract curve are equilibrium points in the sense that if the solution rests on one of these points no forces exist that would press the consumers into altering the distribution of goods.

To see this more clearly, assume that point a represented the current allocation of goods. One of Mr. A's indifference curves A_I passes through this point and also one of Mr. B's indifference curves B_I. It is clear that any movement away from point a to some other point within the cigar-shaped shaded area of the diagram would represent a superior allocation of goods to the consumer than that represented by point a. Any such point would rest on higher indifference curves of one or both consumers, and they would both prefer and be happier with the alternative to a. Point b, resting on A_I, leaves Mr. A just as well off as before, for Mr. A is indifferent to the selection of point a or b. But at b Mr. B's position is greatly improved over what it would be at point a. Similarly, Mr. B is indifferent to the choice of point a or c, but A's position would be greatly improved by a shift from a to c.

Thus, if Mr. A and Mr. B enter a marketplace with packages as designated by point a, they will find that they can both improve their satisfaction by an exchange of goods. Mr. A would willingly give up some of his good 2 in exchange for some of Mr. B's good 1. At a, Mr. A's marginal rate of substitution of good 1 for good 2 is absolutely greater than Mr. B's; that is,

$$|_A M RS_{1,2}| > |_B M RS_{1,2}|$$

Hence, Mr. A is willing to substitute good 1 for a loss of good 2 in his own consumption package. And Mr. B is willing to substitute good 2 for good 1. The process of exchange will continue to benefit both Mr. A and Mr. B as long as their marginal rates of substitution differ. When some point on the contract curve in the range from b to c is reached, there will be no inducement to further exchange.

In Fig. 2.16, the indifference maps are omitted but the contract lines and offer curves are shown. Offer curves are generated by points of tangency of indifference curves and a rotated budget constraint. In order to draw them an origin must be designated. Rather than allotting Mr. A and Mr. B each a certain money income, let them enter the marketplace with an endowment of goods. Let Mr. A have 20 units of good 1, and let Mr. B enter with 20 units of good 2 *and* 10 units of good 1.

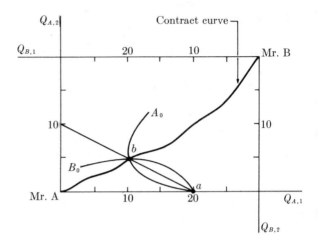

Figure 2.16

Thus, the origin of both offer curves is at point a in Fig. 2.16. If neither Mr. A nor Mr. B have bargaining power, that is, if the market is highly competitive, then point b will represent the equilibrium solution to the problem of allocating to Mr. A and Mr. B the scarce supplies of goods 1 and 2 that enter the market each period.[1] At point b, Mr. A and Mr. B have the same marginal rates of substitution for goods 1 and 2; therefore, both offer curves will intersect the contract curve at this point—the point at which "effective demand for each commodity equal[s] its effective offer" (Walras's law[2]).

[1] The assumption of a highly competitive market is "unrealistic" when two persons enter into a bargain over a single exchange as in the example. But one should remember that the graph is meant to depict the period by period flow of commodities and not a single exchange, and also that it is meant to be merely a model to portray the general tendencies and principal forces at operation in determining prices and quantities. Mr. A and Mr. B are meant to be *illustrative* of the large number of consumers that come to stores each day to compete for the available supplies of goods. The same diagram will be used, however, to cast light on the nature of multilateral bargaining arrangements in Chap. 9. Here, it is used as a paradigm to explain the determination of prices and quantities in the consumers' market.

[2] The full text of Walras's law is contained in the following quotation:

> We are now in a position to formulate the law of the establishment of equilibrium prices in the case of the exchange of several commodities for one another through the medium of a *numéraire:* Given several commodities, which are exchanged for one another through the medium of a *numéraire*, for the market to be in a stage of equilibrium or for the price of each and every commodity in terms of the *numéraire* to be stationary, it is necessary and sufficient that at these

The solution at point b gives the following values:

$$Q_{A,1} = 10 \quad Q_{A,2} = 5 \quad Q_{B,1} = 20 \quad Q_{B,2} = 15$$

$$_{A}MRS_{1,2} = {_{B}}MRS_{1,2} = -\frac{P_1}{P_2} = -\frac{0.50}{1.00} = -\frac{1}{2}$$

2.15 THE *NUMÉRAIRE* AND RELATIVE PRICES

It is important to point out that there has been an implicit assumption in the determination of P_1 and P_2 in all of the examples to this point. It is that there is a given nominal amount of money to be used to purchase the two goods and that this money changes hands once during each accounting period. In earlier examples, when it was assumed that Mr. A had an income of \$10 each period, to arrive at $P_1 = \$.50$ and $P_2 = \$1.00$ as he spent \$5 on each of the two goods, each of the dollars that he had changed hands once. In the above example, with two consumers, it is clearly important to point out that the theory determines only relative prices, that is, the *ratio* of P_1 to P_2. If good 1 is called the *numéraire;* that is, if a unit of good 1 is used as a standard for measuring the values of good 2 and all other goods, then relative prices are expressed in terms of the amount of good 1 that must be given up in order to acquire an amount of good 2 or 3, and so forth. In the example it is necessary to give up 2 units of good 1 to acquire 1 unit of good 2. Thus, specifying one good as a *numéraire* permits the determination of relative prices but not absolute prices. For absolute prices must be expressed in terms of some monetary unit of account, and to determine these prices the amounts of, say, dollars each consumer has and how often each dollar changes hands must be clearly specified.

In the earlier examples with budget constraints, the amount

---

prices the effective demand for each commodity equal its effective offer. When this equality is absent, the attainment of equilibrium prices requires a rise in the prices of those commodities the effective demand for which is greater than the effective offer, and a fall in the prices of those commodities the effective offer of which is greater than the effective demand.

[Leon Walras, "Elements of Pure Economics" (translated by William Jaffee), p. 172, Richard D. Irwin, Inc., Homewood, Illinois, 1954.]

of money income was specified and implicitly it was assumed that each dollar changes hands once. But, in the box diagram where it is assumed that each consumer enters the market with an initial endowment of goods rather than money income, only relative prices are determined; and in order to attach monetary values and prices in terms of a monetary unit of account to the goods in question, the further assumption of a money supply of some amount and its rate of turnover must be specified. If, for example, Mr. A has $5 and spends it all for 5 units of good 2, and a short time later Mr. B uses the same $5 to buy 10 units of good 1 from Mr. A, then a money supply of $5 changes hands twice during the market period and the monetary prices of $.50 and $1.00 are established for the respective goods. Therefore, whenever monetary values are used in examples it is important to remember that an *amount* of money and a *velocity* of money are implicitly assumed. The quantity of money and its rate of turnover are the two most important aspects of the study of money and banking as a special subject.

The box diagram and the algebraic model of the consumers' market can be used as an analytical tool to describe the likely results of many events: changes in incomes, changes in the supply of goods, excise taxes, quantity discounts, bilateral bargaining, and many others. A few of these special subjects will be given attention in Chaps. 7 to 10. But for now only one section of the model has been built, and it is time to set up the scaffolding for the construction of the second section, the producers' market. Fortunately, the very same scaffolding as that employed on the consumers' market can be used with only a few minor changes. Thus, construction of the producers' market will proceed more smoothly. Finally, of course, these markets must be joined before the paradigm is complete.

2.16 A DIGRESSION: THE THEORY OF CONSUMERS' CHOICE—DISCOUNT PRICING

This section is a digression from the principal goal of building a general equilibrium paradigm; it is included to illustrate how the theory of consumers' choice can be applied so as to assist our understanding of a market phenomenon called *discount pricing*. Other applications can be found among the problems at the end of the chapter.

Let Mr. A, living in a two-commodity world, have a preference function $U_A = f(Q_1,Q_2)$, where U represents Mr. A's satisfaction from consuming various packages of goods 1 and 2 each period of time. Let the usual assumptions for indifference curves prevail: that they do not cross, that they slope downward from left to right, and that they are convex as viewed from the origin. Call the slope of an indifference curve at any point the marginal rate of substitution of good 1 for good 2, $MRS_{1,2}$, and define the slope as $\Delta Q_2/\Delta Q_1$. Assume that Mr. A received a steady flow of 20 units of good 2 each period and that he then decides how much of good 2 he will offer in exchange for good 1 on the basis of the price of good 1. In this case good 2 is the *numéraire* and $P_2 = 1$ at all times. Figure 2.17 is prepared from this information and Mr. A's offer curve for good 1 is constructed by points of tangency of price lines (budget constraints) with indifference curves. Such points follow from imposing the principle that Mr. A will maximize his satisfaction. A necessary condition for this principle to hold is that $MRS_{1,2} = -P_1/P_2$.

Assume that the market structure permits the seller of good 1 to introduce discount pricing and that he decides to set $P_1 = 1$ for $0 < Q_1 \leq 10$ and $P_1 = .5$ for $Q_1 > 10$. The budget constraint is now the kinked line *abcd*, as depicted in Fig. 2.18. From casual observation it is easy to see that an indifference curve might, in some cases, be tangent to the kinked budget constraint not only at c but also at some point between a and b. Thus, discount pricing of this sort admits the possibility of a nonunique solution to the problem of determining the quan-

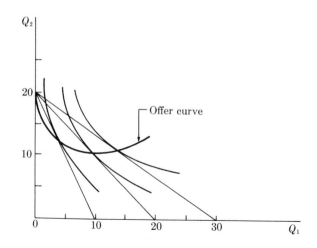

Figure 2.17

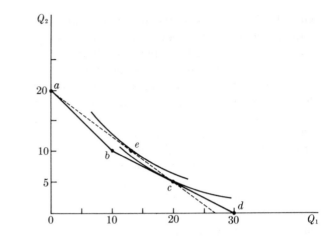

Figure 2.18

tity of good 1 that Mr. A will buy. To focus on effective discounts, however, assume that only one point exists such that $MRS_{1,2} = -.5/1$, namely, point c. Mr. A pays 15 of good 2 and purchases 20 of good 1; the effective rate of exchange becomes $^{15}\!/_{20}$ or .75, which is P_1. The slope of the straight dotted line drawn from a through point c is $-.75$. This line is tangent to a higher indifference curve at point e, a point which represents the quantity of good 1 that Mr. A would have bought if the price had been .75 for each unit purchased. This, then, illustrates a well-known phenomenon: more of a good will be sold each period if volume discounts are instituted.

Examples readily come to mind. Supplies of electricity and other utilities often have discount pricing. But, of course, all examples of discount pricing do not necessarily reflect what is shown here. A large quantity of a good may require less expensive packaging and handling. Insofar as commodities are really different commodities when they come in different quantities, different packages, and require different handling, a quantity discount may merely reflect these differences. In this discussion let us abstract from differences of this sort and concentrate on true discounts in which the item sold is entirely the same whether sold in large or small amounts.

In Fig. 2.19 the original discount budget constraint $abcd$ appears again. Now, however, the part of the constraint showing the lower price is extended leftward from point b to 15 on the ordinate by dots. Any of a large set of prices for the first few units of good 1 could have been imposed by the seller of good 1. The slopes of the few arbitrarily selected dotted lines indicate some such prices. Indeed, the seller of good 1 could have required that Mr. A pay an initial fee of 5 before he had permission to purchase even a single unit of good 1 at $P_1 = .5$.

It is easy to see that entrance fees, cover charges, and gate fees of all sorts are merely rather extreme forms of discount pricing. But the incidence of discount pricing is even more widespread than this. Telephone calls, packages of bridge-crossing tickets, and family fares on travel tickets are only a few examples which adequately show the great reliance placed on this type of pricing in our economy.

Typical telephone service pricing is indicated by the drawing in·Fig. 2.20. If Q_1 is the number of telephone calls made per month by Mr. A, he pays 5 units of the *numéraire* each month and buys at $P_1 = 0$ as many calls as he likes. Point c represents the point at which $MRS_{1,2} = 0$, and also the point at which the marginal utility of a phone call to Mr. A is zero. Thus, as long as any additional utility is to be gained by Mr. A from another call he will make the call, for the additional cost to him is zero. The equilibrium position becomes point c.

There is, however, a limit to the amount of monthly fee that the telephone suppliers can charge. For example, if the fee were 10, the horizontal line through 10 would represent the budget constraint. It is tangent to Mr. A's indifference curve at d. But note also that this same indifference curve intersects the ordinate at point a, the originating point of the budget con-

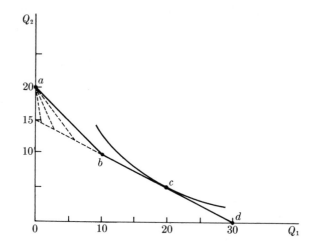

Figure 2.19

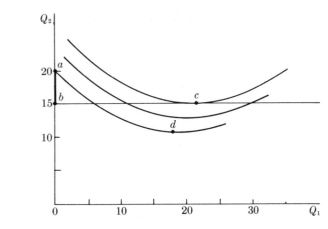

Figure 2.20

straint which represents Mr. A's periodic income. Thus, Mr. A is indifferent between points a and d because both points are on the same indifference curve. Thus, a fee of slightly less than 10, say, 9, would induce Mr. A to purchase the service, and he would be very close to d in equilibrium. (Incidentally, d could be under or to the right or left of c, depending upon the relation of the utility of good 1 to the utility of good 2. If goods 1 and 2 were substitutes, the utility of good 1 would increase as the amount of good 2 decreased, and hence point d would lie to the right of point c. If, however, the goods were complements, then smaller amounts of good 2 would mean lower marginal utility for good 1, and hence point d would lie to the left of point c.) A fee slightly more than 10, say, 11, would be rejected by Mr. A. He would simply remain at point a, a point on the highest indifference curve it is possible for him to obtain. If Mr. A can just be induced to move to point d, the supplier has been able to extract the largest possible flat fee from Mr. A. The situation is an example of an "all-or-nothing" offer; Mr. A is given his choice between the rate of purchase of good 1 indicated by point d or none at all.

In the first illustration of discount pricing above it was shown that by this means Mr. A could be induced to buy a larger quantity of good 1 than he otherwise would buy. To be meaningful this proposition must have a corollary, that by discount pricing Mr. A can be induced to spend a larger sum than he otherwise would for the *same* quantity of good 1. This is more astounding than simply to say he is induced to buy more, for if he buys more he receives more and the welfare implications are not easily made clear. But if he is induced to spend more for the same quantity, it is clear that his position is being exploited over what would be the case if a going price per unit rather than a discount price were imposed on him.

To illustrate the corollary, find in Fig. 2.21 an indifference map for Mr. A and assume he is in equilibrium at point c under the price of good 1 implied by the budget constraint. He consumes 20 units of good 1 each period. He pays a sum of 13.3 units of good 2 for these units of good 1 since $P_1 = \frac{2}{3}$, and $\frac{2}{3} \times 20 = 13.3$. Directly below point c there will be another indifference curve the slope of which will be absolutely less—the slope assumes a smaller negative value—than the slope at point c. (This will be so provided good 1 is not a Giffen good in the relevant range of prices.) Thus, Mr. A can be charged a flat fee of 12 plus the unit price indicated by the slope of the dotted budget constraint and he will then pay a total of 16 for 20 units of good 1. The average price he effectively pays for good 1 becomes .8, but he nevertheless purchases the same quantity at this higher effective price. The limit, of course, to the ability of the supplier to charge this price is again determined by point a and the indifference curve that intersects point a as discussed previously.

If Mr. A's offer curve has a minimal point, such as point a in Fig. 2.22, this represents the price and rate of output for which the total expenditure by Mr. A for good 1 is a maximum.

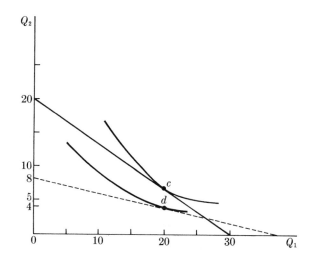

Figure 2.21

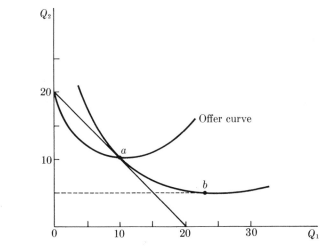

Figure 2.22

At any discretely higher price Mr. A's total expenditure on good 1 will fall, and at any lower price total expenditure will also fall. Thus, point a indicates the maximum revenues obtainable under straightforward pricing.[1] If good 1 were, for example, trips across a toll bridge, the total revenues that the bridge manager could collect are a maximum at the price indicated by the slope of the price line through point a. By charging a flat fee and permitting free trips over the bridge Mr. A can be induced to move to point b, and total expenditure on bridge service becomes larger than it is possible to collect under any unit pricing system. Annual parking permits also provide an example of this phenomenon.

In highly competitive markets it would not be possible for a firm to impose discount pricing to a significant degree. Mr. A could always go next door if he were aware that under discounts of this sort he spent more for the commodity. Or customers could group together and have a single person buy a large quantity and divide it among his friends afterwards at lower than average price until the supplier were forced to stop offering the discounts.[2]

---

[1] At point a it is said that the *elasticity of demand* for good 1 is -1. See the discussion of elasticity in Chap. 7 and subsequent chapters.

[2] For an excellent detailed discussion of this subject see: Walter Y. Oi, A Disneyland Dilemma: Two-Part Tariffs for a Mickey Mouse Monopoly, *Quart. J. Econ.*, vol. LXXXV, pp. 77–96, February 1971.

2.1   Examine the two-person, two-good model of the consumers' market carefully and list all the additions and changes in variables, givens, and equations that would be necessary if another consumer, Mr. C, were to enter the market.

2.2   Examine the two-person, two-good model of the consumers' market carefully and list all the additions and changes in variables, givens, and equations that would be necessary if another good, good 3, were to be introduced into the market.

2.3   Draw an indifference map for Mr. A with four indifference curves and label them with arbitrary amounts of utils of satisfaction. Assume a fixed rate of consumption of good 1 and show the marginal utility of good 2 for a given increment in the rate of consumption of good 2.

2.4   Assume that Mr. A has a budget of $40, that the price of good 1 is $5, and that the price of good 2 is $2. Draw Mr. A's budget constraint. Now let Mr. A's budget fall to $30 and draw another budget constraint. Draw indifference curves to show that good 2 is an inferior good.

2.5   Assume that Mr. A enters the market with a given amount of good 2 and illustrate how an offer curve for good 1 is generated by points of tangency of budget constraints with Mr. A's indifference curves.

2.6   Assume that the price of good 2 is $1 and the price of good 1 is also $1 if Mr. A purchases between 1 and 10 units of good 1 each month. But if Mr. A purchases more than 10 units of good 1 a month, the price for each unit beyond 10 is only $.50. This is illustrative of quantity discounts. Let Mr. A's income (budget) be $20.
  (a)   Draw Mr. A's budget constraint line.
  (b)   Draw an indifference curve that adheres to the rule of convexity as viewed from the origin, and that shows the possibility that either of two packages of goods 1 and 2 will maximize Mr. A's satisfaction.

2.7   Redraw the same budget constraint as outlined in Exercise 2.6(a). Draw an indifference curve showing that Mr. A maximizes his satisfaction by consuming 20 units of good 1.
  (a)   How many units of good 2 does he consume?
  (b)   How much does he spend on good 1?
  (c)   What is the average price of a unit of good 1 to Mr. A?
  (d)   Now draw the budget constraint as if the price of good 1 were set at that average price while the price of good 2 remains unchanged at $1 and show that under these conditions Mr. A would reduce his consumption of good 1.

(e) Do you believe that quantity discounts will lead to an increase in the amount of a good consumed?

2.8 (This exercise is an extension of Exercise 2.7.) First, draw a budget constraint for Mr. A. Next draw an indifference curve that is just tangent to the budget constraint roughly in the middle of the graph. Now draw another indifference curve that shows a lower level of utility than the first one that you drew. Finally, introduce a discount price mechanism so that the new budget constraint is steeper on the left-hand side of the graph and becomes flatter at some kink *and* such that the flatter portion of the budget constraint is just below the original point of tangency. Note that Mr. A is willing to pay *more* money (or give up more of good 2 if it, instead of money, is measured on the vertical axis) for the *same* amount of good 1 under discount pricing than he was willing to give up when a single price of good 1 prevailed. Mr. A is on the lower indifference curve, and the firm selling the product receives more money for the same volume of sales.

2.9 Some telephone companies charge a monthly fee and, in addition, 5 cents per call for each call made during the month. Assume that money income is measured on the vertical axis to represent "all other goods."

(a) Show that this method of setting telephone fares may lead to a larger dollar volume of sales of telephone service than would exist if the charge were simply 10 cents per call with no monthly charge.

(b) Assume a flat monthly charge for telephone service with a price of zero per call. Draw the budget constraint and show the indifference curve of Mr. A when he is at a higher level of satisfaction without a phone than he is with one. (*Hint:* It may help to let the indifference curves intersect the vertical axis.)

(c) Show how much Mr. A would just be willing to pay each month for phone service.

2.10 Products of high quality are typically exported when similar products of lower quality are not. Let Mr. A be American, and Mr. B be British. Assume that both A and B have identical indifference maps and the same budgets. Let good 1 represent superior quality pears and good 2 represent rather poorer quality pears, when selling in Oregon at prices of $.10 and $.05 each, respectively. After payment of transport costs, however, the same pears are sold in England at prices of $.12 and $.07, respectively, since it costs 2 cents per pear to ship them from Oregon to England. Show that if the negative income effect of the higher prices faced by the British is compensated for, the British tend to eat better pears than Oregonians. (This result need not always follow in a world of more than two goods.)

2.11 Draw a box diagram showing an offer curve for Mr. B and indifference curves for Mr. A. Assume that Mr. A is a monopolist and show how he will set the rate of exchange for goods 1 and 2 in order to maximize his own satisfaction given that he knows Mr. B's offer curve. (This is analyzed in Chap. 9 in the discussion of monopoly.)

2.12 (This exercise concerns what is known as the *index number problem*.) Label the horizontal axis Q_1 and the vertical axis Q_2, representing quantities of good 1 and good 2 purchased each period by Mr. A. Assume Mr. A's income is $6. If $P_{1,0}$ represents the price of good 1 in period 0 and $P_{2,0}$ represents the price of good 2 in period 0, plot Mr. A's budget line when $P_{1,0} = \$2$ and $P_{2,0} = \$1$. Label this budget line 0. Assume that under these prices Mr. A maximizes his satisfaction by consuming the package $Q_{1,0} = 1$, $Q_{2,0} = 4$. Label this package point a.

Assume now that in a subsequent period, period t, the prices of goods 1 and 2 are reversed so that $P_{1,t} = \$1$ and $P_{2,t} = \$2$. With Mr. A's income unchanged, plot his budget line in period t. Label this budget line t. Assume that under these prices Mr. A maximizes his satisfaction by consuming the package $Q_{1,t} = 4$, $Q_{2,t} = 1$. Label this package point b.

Draw in lightly an indifference curve tangent to the respective budget lines at both points, a and b, indicating that although Mr. A has changed his consumption package under the new set of prices, he is still as satisfied as he was before the prices changed. Note that

$$
\begin{array}{ll}
P_{1,0} = \$2, \; Q_{1,0} = 1 \\
P_{2,0} = \$1, \; Q_{2,0} = 4
\end{array} \quad \text{period 0}
$$

$$
\begin{array}{ll}
P_{1,t} = \$1, \; Q_{1,t} = 4 \\
P_{2,t} = \$2, \; Q_{2,t} = 1
\end{array} \quad \text{period } t
$$

A simple index of prices is the average of all prices. Since some commodities are of greater importance than others in a consumer's budget, it is desirable to weight each price according to its importance. The quantity of the good sold is often used as a weight for this purpose. The Lespeyres index (LE) uses base period quantities as weights; the Paasche index (PA) uses given period quantities as weights. For the two-good example, in percentages,

$$
\text{LE} = \frac{P_{1,t}Q_{1,0} + P_{2,t}Q_{2,0}}{P_{1,0}Q_{1,0} + P_{2,0}Q_{2,0}} 100
$$

$$
\text{PA} = \frac{P_{1,t}Q_{1,t} + P_{2,t}Q_{2,t}}{P_{1,0}Q_{1,t} + P_{2,0}Q_{2,t}} 100
$$

From the diagram one can see that Mr. A is on the same indifference curve after the prices have changed as he was before prices changed. Hence, his income, in terms of satisfaction, has not changed even though the package of goods that he now consumes differs from the original package. The simple average of prices is also unchanged, so that an index of the price level that is to indicate the consumer's *cost of living* should read 100.

Compute the LE index and the PA index and confirm that the former with base period quantities as weights (now used to estimate *cost of living* in the United States) overstates the true change in cost of living and that the latter with given period quantities as weights understates the true change in cost of living.

2.13 Assume Mr. A earns $20 per period. Because of his low income, he is eligible for the purchase of $10 worth of food stamps for $5. Draw an indifference map for Mr. A with income on the vertical axis and food on the horizontal axis. Show a budget line in the case in which the price of food is $1. Now show by dotted line the effective budget line that Mr. A faces when he takes advantage of the food stamp program. This line will have a kink in it, but the kink does not point toward the origin as it does in Fig. 2.18; rather it will point toward the northeast. Can you discuss why giving $5 in food stamps to Mr. A is effectively the same as giving him $5 in money?

3

The
Producers'
Market

Having built a paradigm of the consumers' market, the task is now to build one for the producers' market. In Chap. 4 the two markets will be joined. Fortunately, the two markets have many similarities, and tools of analysis that were developed to describe the consumers' market can also be applied to the producers' market. Thus, in many ways the exposition may now proceed more smoothly and more rapidly. However, although there are many similarities in the techniques of analysis, one should carefully note the important differences in the two markets as they arise.

When discussing the consumers' market, reference was made to Mr. A and Mr. B. By the end of the chapter the reader may have begun to personalize Mr. A and Mr. B as though they were his neighbors. But this would be a mistake for they are meant only to be abstractions. To explain why a *real* neighbor wears a new bright green tie every day, it is simpler and better to say it is because he is Irish than to compare the relative price of green ties with prices of other things. This is because often it is more appropriate to explain why a certain consumer has the particular tastes he does than to assume, as in Chap. 2, that his tastes were given. In the paradigm of the consumers' market, Mr. A and Mr. B were only meant to be *representative* of real consumers. When a physicist describes the orbit of an electron around the nucleus of an atom as if it were like the orbit of the moon around the earth, he engages in the same sort of abstraction. In general, planetary electrons seem to behave *as if* they were like the moon in orbit. Consumers, *in general*, seem to behave as if they were like Mr. A and Mr. B.

In this chapter, the same sorts of abstractions are used to describe the producers' market. Reference is made to producers α and β. These are producers of goods 1 and 2, respectively, and are meant to be representative of the behavior of *industries*. The difference, of course, between a firm and an industry is that an industry is comprised of all those firms that produce the same good. Thus, it is, roughly, the automobile "industry" and the Ford Motor Company, the wheat "industry" and farmer Jones' farm. But the reader should not personalize α and β; rather, he should think of firms and industries as abstractions. Their behavior, as described below, is meant to be representative of the way in which the production of goods 1 and 2 is carried out in a competitive economy guided by the pricing system.

In this chapter it is assumed that industries maximize output by spending all of their revenues on factors of production. This assumption enables the consistent use of the tools developed for the consumers' market. Of course, it is generally assumed that owners of real-world firms have as their objective the maximization of profits. To maximize profits owners must decide, among other things, what level of output to produce and then arrange production so as to minimize the cost of producing this level of output. Minimizing the cost of production of a given level of output can be shown to be equivalent to maximizing output for a given cost.[1] To proceed without clouding the issue, however, this unrealistic assumption that industries maximize output with the revenues available to them helps facilitate construction of the general equilibrium paradigm. The extended discussion of the motives of owners of real firms is reserved for Chaps. 8 to 10.

---

[1] The precise demonstration of this equivalence is to be found in the footnote on page 62. Also see Exercise 3.1.

Assume, then, that the producers' market contains two producers or industries α and β and that they employ two factors of production X and Y. In the consumers' market it was assumed that the rates of output of goods 1 and 2 were given, but now these rates Q_1 and Q_2 will be determined by interaction of forces operating in the producers' market and, in particular, by the rate at which each producer employs different amounts of X and Y under given technological conditions.

In later examples, X will stand for rates of use of labor services and Y will stand for rates of use of land or capital. Thus, factors of production are such things as labor, land, machinery, raw materials, and all the ingredients that producers buy when they undertake to provide goods for sale to consumers. It is not easy to come to complete agreement when defining factors of production in a specific sense. There are many kinds of labor, many qualities of land, many types of capital, and many types of raw materials. But, in principle, all problems of definition resolve into the general problem of agreement by the parties to a discussion of the terms to be used in the discussion. It is assumed here that agreement could be reached, given sufficient time to discuss the matter, regarding the meaning of the general terms *labor* and *land* in a practical real-world sense. For heuristic purposes, let the abstract terms prevail to facilitate construction of the model.

3.1   THE PRODUCTION FUNCTION AND MARGINAL PRODUCTIVITY

Let Q_1 represent the rate of output of industry α. Also, let the amount of factor Y be fixed. The more of factor X that α employs each period, the larger will be the rate of output. Therefore, Q_1 can be expressed as a function of the rate of employment of X in the production of good 1; that is, $Q_1 = f(X_1)$. This is called a production function, and it takes a shape similar to that depicted in Fig. 3.1 in most real-world situations.

The marginal productivity of X_1 is defined to be the slope of the total product function; that is, $_\alpha MP_X = \Delta Q_1/\Delta X_1$. As the amount of X employed increases from 0 to a, the slope of the total product curve increases; hence, the marginal productivity of X increases. To the right of a the marginal productivity of X decreases. Above point a the *slope* of the function is a maximum. This point on the function is called the point

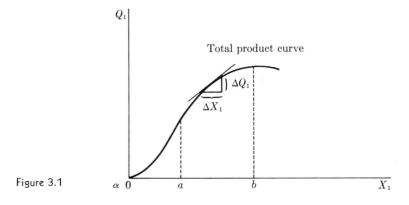

Figure 3.1

of inflection. If X were hours of labor per week, then an increase in the amount of labor service hired each week would, in the initial stages, lead to a greater than proportional increase in the output of good 1 because there are technical efficiencies that result from the specialized division and/or combination of labor in nearly every production process. Two men working together can move more furniture than two men working separately. However, as more and more labor service is employed, eventually the additional output obtained from an additional unit of labor service diminishes; this is the *law of diminishing returns*. In Fig. 3.1, diminishing returns obtain to the right of point a, for at point a the marginal productivity of X begins to decline.

3.2 THE LAW OF DIMINISHING RETURNS

The law of diminishing returns can be stated succinctly. As more of a given factor is employed each period, along with fixed amounts of other factors, eventually its marginal productivity will diminish. "Law of diminishing returns" is a phrase that is widely used in casual conversation by the public at large to refer to diminishing profitability. Although this interpretation of the law may have its uses, the rigorous meaning of the economist must not be confused with the public's meaning. In describing the employment of a factor of production, a time period should always be specified or clearly implied. Furthermore, when discussing the productivity of another unit of labor service, one should avoid thinking of the productivity of a certain man. The marginal unit of labor is not a marginal individual, but simply the difference between employing, say, 100 hours of labor service a week and 101 hours of labor service, each hour of labor service being technically identical. Also, the profitability of a firm may increase even though the marginal productivity of labor is decreasing, that is, even though there are diminishing returns from the employment of labor. This is because profitability depends upon the price brought by the good being produced. Thus, diminishing returns does *not* mean diminishing profitability. Also, the productivity of labor depends upon the amounts of other factors with which labor service has the opportunity to work. The more tools a laborer has at his disposal, in general, the more productive his own service will be. Thus, it is not quite correct to assert that, say, the construction of another factory in a certain location would lead to diminishing returns for "another factory" implies, not only the employment of more labor service, but also the employment of more land, machinery, and all other factors. The law of diminishing returns, when referred to by an economist, applies only in the case of variable rates of employment of one factor while the other factors are fixed in their rate of employment. Therefore, in a strictly technical sense, the law should be invoked only with considerable care.

The law of diminishing returns is a special case of the *law of variable proportions*, in which either factor may rise relative to the other. If more X is used with a fixed amount of factor Y, the ratio of X to Y increases. Thus, the law of variable proportions reads: As the proportion of X to Y increases, eventually the marginal productivity of X will diminish. Here, the relationship of the two factors taken together is emphasized.

3.3 ISOPRODUCT CURVES

In nearly all processes of production, the producing entity employs more than one factor of production. It is, therefore, appropriate to introduce factor Y into the production function along with factor X. Now the rate of output of good 1 is a function of the rates of employment of both X and Y; that is, $Q_1 = f(X_1,Y_1)$. This three-variable function could be shown in a graph in the same way that Mr. A's total utility function was shown in Chap. 2. The reader may recall that after graphing the total utility function, the indifference map was constructed by projecting indifference curves onto the horizontal plane. It is unnecessary to repeat that step here; rather one can move directly to the two-dimensional picture of a production function as shown in Fig. 3.2.

If 8 units of X are employed each period in conjunction with 5 units of Y, total output is 10 units of good 1 each period. This is represented by point a. The same rate of output can be produced with 15 units of X and 2.5 units of Y, as represented by point b. Thus, any of the variety of combinations of factors X and Y on the isoproduct curve (isoquant) labeled $Q_1 = 10$ is capable of producing 10 units of output each period. Each of these isoproduct curves represents a *frontier* in the sense that the designated rate of output is the maximum obtainable from the various packages of factors. (The isoproduct curves are drawn on the assumption that there exists a given state of technology.) It is possible to produce the rate of output with somewhat more of factor X along with somewhat less of factor Y. In this sense, factors X and Y are substitutes for one another. If more of both factors are employed, the rate of output increases.

At any point on an isoproduct curve the *marginal rate of substitution* of X for Y can be defined as the slope of the isoproduct curve. (Some authors prefer to call this the *marginal rate of technical substitution*.) Thus, $MRS_{X,Y} = \Delta Y_1 / \Delta X_1$.

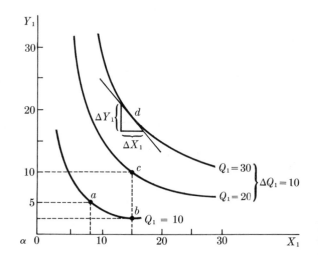

Figure 3.2

Since the curves are convex as viewed from the origin, the marginal rate of substitution declines in absolute value (that is, becomes less steep) with a rightward movement along a given isoquant. Therefore, as more X is used to replace Y in the production of good 1, the increments of X required for a given loss of Y must increase in order to keep output at the same level each period.

In order to observe the law of diminishing returns operating in Fig. 3.2, the reader need only imagine a horizontal line drawn through a point on the vertical axis, say, $Y = 20$, which indicates a given rate of flow of factor Y to this industry. Along this line consider a given increment of X and observe the increment in Q_1 that is forthcoming by comparing the labels on the two relevant isoquants. In this way the marginal productivity of X in the production of good 1 by industry α is measured for $MP_{X,1} = \Delta Q_1/\Delta X_1$. In similar fashion, one can compute the marginal productivity of Y.

3.4 EQUILIBRIUM FOR ONE PRODUCER

At this juncture in the development of the paradigm of the producers' market assume that producers of good 1 face a budget constraint in purchasing factors X and Y and that they engage in the employment of factors so as to maximize the output of good 1. If the prices of factors are given, along with the budget of α, the system will determine the equilibrium amounts of X and Y that will be purchased by α and the rate of production of good 1. The system may be presented as follows:

(a) $\quad Q_1 = f(X_1, Y_1)$ $\qquad$ The production function determined by the existing state of technology

(b) $\quad I_\alpha = P_X X_1 + P_Y Y_1$ $\qquad$ The budget constraint that indicates that all of α's revenues are spent on the factors of production

(c) $_a MRS_{X,Y} = -\dfrac{MP_{X,1}}{MP_{Y,1}} = -\dfrac{P_X}{P_Y}$ Equations expressing the principle of
the maximization
of output

(d) Q_1, X_1, and Y_1 Unknown dependent variables to
be determined by
the system

(e) I_a, P_X, and P_Y Independent variables given for the
problem at hand

The analogy of this set of parts to a system of equations to the
set used to describe the consumers' market is quite direct. For
the consumers' market a numerical example was provided, and
the steps taken to solve the system were shown. It is unnecessary to repeat this exercise. The interested reader can simply
substitute the values given for P_1 and P_2 in the consumers' market for P_X and P_Y and substitute the value of I_A for I_a. The
unknowns in the consumers' market were U_A, $Q_{A,1}$, and $Q_{A,2}$.
Here they are Q_1, X_1, and Y_1, respectively. Equations (a) to
(c) could also be amended appropriately, and then the same
numerical example could describe the solution of the system for
equilibrium values of the dependent variables.

At the outset of this chapter the reader was admonished to
note carefully the important differences in the model of the producers' market and the model of the consumers' market. The
equation system above is analogous in all respects with that
of the consumers' market. However, although it is quite realistic to refer to a budget constraint imposed on the consumers
in a household in the form of the paycheck received at the end
of each month, it is less realistic to do so in describing the
behavior of a firm or an industry. This is because managers
of firms can plan and decide upon various output rates and
various budgets since they often have ready access to markets
for money capital and can, therefore, borrow additional funds.

Of course, consumers also borrow at times, and this permits
some flexibility in their budgets as well. But business decisions
regarding output are nearly always less restrained by a fixed
budget than are those of consumers in a typical household.
However, if we think not so much about managers of a single

firm but more about the composite of firms that comprise an industry and the receipts that sales of industry output bring forth, then these receipts represent what consumers generally are willing to pay for the goods produced. These receipts, or revenues, are then used by managers of the various firms to employ the factors of production necessary to bring forth the output demanded by the consumers. It is in this abstract sense that the paradigm of the producers' market is offered. Borrowing and lending activities permit the budget to vary, and therefore the budget constraint is not a rigorous constraint in the real world. In Chap. 5 there is a discussion of borrowing and lending activities and how these can be introduced into the general equilibrium paradigm. Until then, the abstraction from borrowing and lending enables one to observe the nature of pertinent economic forces by assuming that industry output is limited by the extent of the producers' budgets. It is with these reservations in mind that one should view the equation system above.

A graphic description of the solution of the equation system is flexible and useful for further analysis and may be found in Fig. 3.3. If I_a, the revenue available for expenditures on factors X and Y, is \$25.00, and if $P_X = \$1.25$ while $P_Y = \$1.00$, the budget constraint as depicted will obtain. Point a represents the point of tangency of the budget constraint with the *highest* possible

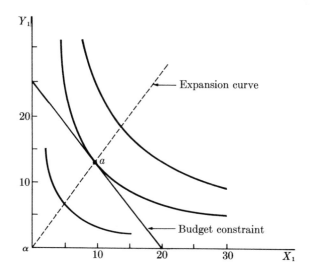

Figure 3.3

isoproduct curve. To maximize output, therefore, the managing authorities in charge of producing good 1 will purchase the indicated amounts of X and Y in each period.[1]

3.5 EXPANSION LINES

For given prices of X and Y, as I_a changes the budget constraint will shift while remaining parallel with the one shown. This shifting budget constraint will generate points of tangency with isoproduct curves which, when connected, yield an *expansion line* as shown. This line indicates the way that employment of factors will vary as the output of the industry expands.

[1] For a formal proof of the maximization of output under a given budget see the analogous situation for the consumers' market in the footnote on page 24 and compare this with the minimization of costs of a prescribed level of output as follows. From the production function for good 1, $Q_1 = f(X_1, Y_1)$, specify a given level of output $\bar{Q}_1$ and move $f(X_1, Y_1)$ to the left-hand side of the equation. Then, along with the budget equation, form the new function

$$W = P_X X_1 + P_Y Y_1 + \lambda[\bar{Q}_1 - f(X_1, Y_1)] \qquad \text{for } \lambda \neq 0$$

Here, λ is a Lagrange multiplier. Now take the partial derivative of W with respect to X_1, Y_1, and λ and set each equal to zero:

$$\frac{\partial W}{\partial X_1} = P_X - \lambda \frac{\partial Q_1}{\partial X_1} = 0$$

$$\frac{\partial W}{\partial Y_1} = P_Y - \lambda \frac{\partial Q_1}{\partial Y_1} = 0$$

$$\frac{\partial W}{\partial \lambda} = \bar{Q}_1 - f(X_1, Y_1) = 0$$

Moving the second terms in the first two equations to the right and dividing the first equation by the second gives

$$\frac{P_X}{P_Y} = \frac{\partial Q_1/\partial X_1}{\partial Q_1/\partial Y_1} \qquad \text{or} \qquad \frac{\partial Q_1/\partial X_1}{P_X} = \frac{\partial Q_1/\partial Y_1}{P_Y} = \frac{1}{\lambda}$$

which are different forms of the first-order conditions for the minimization of cost of a given rate of output as described in the text above. The third equation ensures that the constraint is satisfied.

Note also that $\lambda = P_X \, \partial X_1/\partial Q_1$, which is the *marginal cost* of output, or the total derivative of cost with respect to output. In increments, λ equals the price of factor X times the added amount of X that must be employed to produce, say, another unit of output each period, which is simply the cost of another unit of output each period. The condition must hold in the case of Y as well, so that the cost of another unit of output each period is the same whether produced by more of input X or input Y or some combination of X and Y.

As drawn in Figs. 3.2 and 3.3, the production functions show that doubling the use of both factors will double output. Indeed, any proportional increase in both factors will yield an equal proportional increase in the rate of output. This holds for any vector from the origin. Such production functions are called *homogeneous of degree one,* and they show *constant returns to scale* throughout.[1]

If *increasing returns to scale* exist, the rate of output increases more than proportionally with proportional increases in the use of both factors. And *decreasing returns to scale* exist if proportional increases in both factors lead to a smaller than proportional increase in the rate of output. Thus, the *law of diminishing returns,* in which the application of one factor alone is varied (or the *law of variable proportions*), should not be confused with the concept of *decreasing returns to scale,* in which all factors are varied proportionally.

In the literature one finds many analytical studies in which economists explicitly assume, for purposes of analysis, constant returns to scale. Whether or not this assumption is realistic is still a subject of concern. But most economists are willing to accept the proposition for purposes of discussion of particular issues because it is believed to be a sufficiently close approximation to reality. It is like assuming that the earth is flat for many practical computations in surveying, but with full recognition that if large distances are involved, the assumption may lead to considerable error. Thus, constant returns to scale may not hold throughout the entire range of a production function, but they may hold with only negligible error in the immediate domain.

As in the case of the consumers' market, the budget constraint may change its slope as a result of changes in the price of one or the other factor. If wage rates can be pushed up by, say, union power, there will be a tendency for employers to substitute capital for labor in the production process. Figure 3.3 can be used to describe this phenomenon. The assumptions of (1) a

---

[1] For any given set of prices of X and Y the expansion lines for these functions are always straight lines. However, expansion lines may be straight for other types of production functions as well. For example, they are straight for functions that are homogeneous of any degree. (See Sec. 3.10.)

given technology described by the production function, (2) a given budget, and (3) maximization of industry output, as three postulates in this argument, lead directly to the conclusion that if wage rates increase (say, P_X increases, causing the budget line to rotate leftward), then capital will be substituted for labor. [An analysis of a single firm's production function (as opposed to that of an industry) may be found in Sec. 3.10 and in Chap. 8.]

3.7 EQUILIBRIUM FOR TWO PRODUCERS

To continue with the construction of the model of the producers' market, the second producer is introduced. When only one producer faced the market, as in the example just above, it was assumed that he could buy all that he wanted of factors X and Y as long as he had the necessary income to pay for them at going prices. When introducing producer β, however, it is assumed that a *given* amount of X and a *given* amount of Y flow into the producers' market each period and are offered for sale to industries. The industries enter into competition for the scarce factor supplies and the prices of factors are then determined by the market forces. Also, these forces determine the share of each factor that each industry buys.

With two producers, the abstract model of the producers' market may be rigorously constructed as follows:

(a) $Q_1 = f(X_1, Y_1)$

$Q_2 = g(X_2, Y_2)$

Each industry's production function

(b) $I_\alpha = P_X X_1 + P_Y Y_1$

$I_\beta = P_X X_2 + P_Y Y_2$

Equations that express the principle that all of each industry's revenue is spent on factors of production

(c) $_\alpha MRS_{X,Y} = -\dfrac{MP_{X,1}}{MP_{Y,1}} = -\dfrac{P_X}{P_Y}$

$_\beta MRS_{X,Y} = -\dfrac{MP_{X,2}}{MP_{Y,2}} = -\dfrac{P_X}{P_Y}$

Equations that express the principle of the maximization of output by producers α and β

(d) $X = X_1 + X_2$
$Y = Y_1 + Y_2$

Market-clearing equations expressing the principle that all of the factors offered for sale are sold to the two industries

(e) $P_X, P_Y, X_1, X_2, Y_1, Y_2, Q_1$, and Q_2

Dependent variables, the prices and quantities of factors, equilibrium values of which are determined by the system

(f) I_α, I_β, X, and Y

Independent variables given for the problem; producers' revenues and available factor supplies; also given is an amount of money to be used in the exchanges $I_\alpha + I_\beta$

There are eight equations and eight unknowns. Hence, if certain properties of the equations are satisfied, a set of equilibrium values of the unknowns may be determined. The subset of six equations of parts (b), (c), and (d) can be solved first, leading to solution values for factor prices and quantities. Then, having determined the quantities of the factors that are bought each period by the two industries and inserting these values for X_1, Y_1, X_2, and Y_2 in the respective production functions, the rates of output of goods 1 and 2 are also determined.

The analogy with the consumers' market is straightforward in nearly all respects. One important difference is that, while it may be reasonable to assume certain uniformities in the shape of production functions, it is unlikely that preference functions have such uniform patterns. Individual tastes determine preference functions, and these are not as well understood as the technology of production.

3.8 ADDING GOODS AND FACTORS

The model of the producers' market can be expanded to allow for additional industries and to allow for additional factors of production. If, for example, another industry γ that produces good 3 were introduced, there would be three additional equations: a production function for γ, a budget equation, and an equation for γ's marginal rate of substitution of factors that expresses the principle of maximization of output. There would also be three additional unknowns to be determined by the system: X_3, Y_3, and Q_3. The market-clearing equations of part (d) would each have to be amended to include X_3 and Y_3 as well. I_γ, an additional independent variable, would also be given. With this set of additions and amendments, the system is solvable for three industries instead of two; and in theory the number of industries could be enlarged indefinitely.

If, instead of adding another industry, another factor of production Z is added, equations under (a) and (b) would need to be amended. Two additional equations for $_\alpha MRS_{X,Z}$ and $_\beta MRS_{X,Z}$ and one additional market-clearing equation for Z under (d) would be sufficient to solve for three additional unknowns P_Z, Z_1, and Z_2. The value of the independent variable Z would also have to be given. In this way the model can be amended to allow for the introduction of an indefinitely large number of factors of production. Thus, in theory at least, the system is solvable for any finite number of industries and factors.

3.9 THE EDGEWORTH-BOX DIAGRAM

The box diagram used to describe the equilibrium of the consumers' market is also useful in describing the equilibrium of the producers' market, and it appears in Fig. 3.4. The isoproduct curves representing rates of output of good 1 are convex as viewed from the α origin; those for good 2 are convex from the β origin. The size of the box is determined by the total amounts of X and Y flowing into the producers' market each period. The points of tangency of the two sets of isoproduct curves generate a *contract curve* which extends from one origin

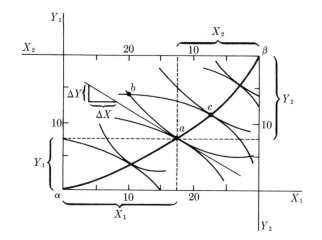

Figure 3.4

to the other. Point *a*, one point on the contract curve, may represent the solution to the problem of allocating the available supplies of factors X and Y to the two industries α and β. Managers of α buy X_1 and Y_1 each period as shown by the brackets outside of the graph. Similarly, β receives X_2 and Y_2 each period. In this way the quantities of X and Y are divided among the producers. At point *a*, there is one isoproduct curve for α that tells the output of good 1 that can be produced each period. There is also an isoproduct curve for good 2, indicating its rate of output. If production were represented by some other point on the contract curve, say, point *c*, then the factors would yield a larger rate of output for good 1 but a smaller rate of output for good 2.

Thus, in an important sense, *total* output cannot be increased if output is now represented by a point on the contract curve, for any movement along the contract curve to some other point on the curve will only result in a larger output of one of the two goods at the expense of a smaller rate of output of the other good. In this sense output is a maximum at point *a or at any other point on the contract curve*. However, if output at points *a* or *c* is compared with output at point *b*, then clearly more of *both* goods could be produced if the factors of production were reallocated among the two producers so that production took place at some point on the curve between points *a* and *c*. Thus, if production is not carried on at a point on the contract curve, output is clearly not maximized *even though all* of the resources of production are being utilized in the production process, that is, even though factors X and Y are fully employed.

A tangent line to both isoproduct curves at point a has been drawn and its slope noted. This slope represents the marginal rates of substitution of X for Y in the production of good 1 *and* of good 2, as well as the ratio of the price of X to the price of Y. In equation form, at point a, $_\alpha MRS_{X,Y} = _\beta MRS_{X,Y} = -P_X/P_Y$. This equation expresses the principle of the maximization of output, a condition that holds at any other point on the contract curve as well as at point a.

The final position of equilibrium, point a in this case, depends upon the purchasing power, or revenues, of the respective producers—how much they each have to spend on X and Y. If the public altered its purchasing pattern so that industry α received more revenues than before, and industry β received less, then the equilibrium point would shift rightward along the contract curve and vice versa.

To clarify how the equilibrium position on the contract curve is attained, it is helpful to examine some point off the contract curve. Assume that at this point $_\alpha MRS_{X,Y} = -2$ and also $_\beta MRS_{X,Y} = -1$. Thus, for good 1, another unit of factor X employed each period will be sufficient to replace the loss of two units of factor Y each period without change in the rate of output of good 1. At the same time, for good 2, the loss of one unit of factor X each period can be recovered by the additional employment of only *one* unit of factor Y, while the rate of output of good 2 is unchanged. Thus, a transfer of a unit of factor X from industry β to industry α and a simultaneous transfer of a unit of factor Y from α to β will leave β's output unchanged but will leave α with an extra unit of factor Y and a larger rate of output of good 1. The managers of α would hire more X and discharge some Y, while the managers of β would hire the additional Y and let go some X. The likely result would be a larger volume of both goods produced each period.

This is the argument that lies behind the suggestions often heard from economists that institutions to preserve *mobility* in the markets for factors of production should be encouraged. For when technological conditions change and as a result isoproduct curves shift their positions, total output of all goods can be increased if factors of production move from employment by one industry to other industries. Institutions that inhibit this free movement of factors will tend to prevent the maximization of output. Certain clauses in union contracts, selective taxes on securities, administrative regulations that prohibit "moonlighting," and compulsory retirement programs are but a few examples of forces that inhibit the mobility of factors and hence inhibit the attainment of maximum output. But these and other issues must not be allowed to divert attention from the principal problem at hand—that of continuing with the construction of the paradigm of a market economy at work. An extended discussion of the way in which production functions are related to cost functions and entrepreneurial decisions at the level of the firm is deferred until Chap. 8.

3.10 A DIGRESSION: HOMOGENEOUS PRODUCTION FUNCTIONS AND COMPLEMENTARITY

In this digression the first subject concerns the general form that is often presumed to exist for production functions. If one thinks of firms that consist of certain productive facilities utilizing certain amounts of labor, capital, land, and other resources and that turn out products with the utmost efficiency, then the industry output of the good presumably could be doubled simply by duplication of existing facilities, that is, by doubling all inputs used in production. For example, one might consider the production of services provided by drive-in restaurants, or filling stations. These facilities are rather easily duplicated. Each maintains roughly similar methods of production to those of each other facility in that each employs roughly the same amount of labor, capital, and land. A newly developing suburb, for example, providing for a 20 percent expansion in population of a metropolitan area will require roughly 20 percent more of each factor—labor, land, and capital—for the construction and operation of drive-ins, filling stations, and other facilities. For planning purposes in urban areas it may be that this assumption of proportionality between the rate of employment of inputs and the rate of output will serve quite adequately for predictive purposes.

As noted earlier in this chapter, a function for which proportional changes in the employment of each factor of production lead to proportional changes in the rate of output is called *homogeneous of degree one*. To understand the general meaning of *homogeneity* in this context one may construct the following definition: A function $f(X,Y)$ is homogeneous of degree n if

$$\lambda^n f(X,Y) = f(\lambda X, \lambda Y) \qquad \text{for } \lambda \neq 0$$

For example, assume $Q = 2xy$; then multiply x and y each by λ so that $2(\lambda x)(\lambda y) = \lambda^2 2xy = \lambda^2 Q$. Thus, the function is *homogeneous of degree two*. Consider the function $Q = 5x^{.3}y^{.7}$. In this function the exponents add to 1 so that $\lambda^1 Q = 5(\lambda x)^{.3}(\lambda y)^{.7}$. Thus, the function is homogeneous of degree one. The function $Q = 4x + 5y$ is also homogeneous of degree one, while the function $Q = 3x/y$ is homogeneous of degree zero. Functions of the general form $Q = aX^k Y^{1-k}$, where $0 < k < 1$, are all homogeneous of degree one and are sometimes called *Cobb–Douglas production functions* after the two men who attempted estimates of production functions of this sort for the United States.[1] The most immediately obvious characteristic of Cobb–Douglas production functions is that proportional changes in the rate of employment of all factor inputs will yield equiproportional changes in the rate of output. If one imagines a map of production isoquants such as that in Fig. 3.3, with prices of factors X and Y fixed over the relevant range of employment so that the ratio of P_X to P_Y is constant, the expansion curve generated from variations in the producer's budget will be a straight line out of the origin. Any expansion line so drawn, that is, drawn for any pair of prices for X and Y, will be a straight line if the production function is of the Cobb–Douglas type. This phenomenon of equiproportional changes in output that accompany proportional changes in employment of all factors is sometimes called the condition of *constant returns to scale*, for by *scale* of operations one has in mind the expansion curve representing different rates of output (returns) obtainable from different budget positions.[2]

---

[1] C. W. Cobb and P. H. Douglas, A Theory of Production, *Am. Econ. Rev.*, Supplement, March 1928. For bibliographic references and statistical estimates see George H. Hildebrand and Ta-Chung Liu, "Manufacturing Production Functions in the United States, 1957," New York State School of Industrial and Labor Relations, Cornell University Press, Ithaca, N.Y., 1965. Also see references cited in Chap. 8.

[2] Increasing returns to scale exist if output increases by more than an amount proportional with a given proportional increase in the rate of employment of all factors, that is, if the degree of homogeneity is greater

Marginal productivities in the Cobb–Douglas production function $Q = 5X^{.3}Y^{.7}$ can be computed with the aid of calculus by taking partial derivatives.[1] Consistent with the previous presentation of other marginal concepts, the marginal productivity of factor X may be defined and evaluated for this function as $MP_X = \Delta Q/\Delta X$. To find a particular value for this ratio one can assume given values for X and Y and solve to find Q; then let X increase by a unit, say, and again solve for Q. Now note the ratio of the ΔQ to the ΔX; this ratio is an approximation to the marginal productivity of a given amount of X when employed with a given amount of Y. One will obtain similar results, in general, from using calculus, so that $MP_X = 1.5Y^{.7}/X^{.7}$. By examination one can see that if the quantity of factor X employed each period increases, then MP_X decreases. The same would be true for factor Y where

$$MP_Y = 3.5 \frac{X^{.3}}{Y^{.3}}$$

Thus, it appears that the law of diminishing returns applies throughout the entire mapping of any Cobb–Douglas type of production function. The equations also show that MP_X will increase with an increase in the rate of employment of Y. For example, if laborers X have more tools Y with which to work, the marginal productivity of labor will increase.

Returning to the concept of constant returns to scale, it is appropriate to note that if prices of factors are assumed to be fixed, then constant returns to scale imply *constant costs of production*, that is, constant average costs. If prices of factors are given and if output rates change in equal proportion to budget changes, then the average cost per unit of output does not change. In similar fashion, increasing returns to scale imply

---

than one ($n > 1$); and decreasing returns to scale exist if output increases by less than the proportional amount ($n < 1$). For a discussion of the spacing of isoquants when illustrating returns to scale graphically see A. M. Levenson and Babette Solon, Returns to Scale and the Spacing of Isoquants, *Am. Econ. Rev.*, vol. LVI, pp. 501–504, June 1966, and a Comment by F. W. McElroy, *Am. Econ. Rev.*, vol. LVII, pp. 223–224, March 1967.

[1] If $Q = 5X^{.3}Y^{.7}$, by the exponential rule

$$\frac{\partial Q}{\partial X} = 1.5X^{-.7}Y^{.7} \quad \text{and} \quad \frac{\partial Q}{\partial Y} = 3.5X^{.3}Y^{-.3}$$

decreasing costs of production, and decreasing returns to scale imply increasing costs of production, when factor prices are fixed.

All of the above statements hold in cases in which the prices of factors are assumed to be fixed; but if this assumption is relaxed, then constant returns to scale no longer imply constant costs of production. For as output of a good expands the expansion may push up the supply price of the factor in a systematic way. In this case, the production function may not be homogeneous of degree one and may show increasing returns to scale, and yet the industry may face constant costs of production. Similarly, the production function may be homogeneous of degree one and yet costs of production may increase with output. The purpose of this paragraph is merely to stress that the concepts *constant returns to scale* and *constant costs of production* are *not* equivalent. The former implies the latter only if prices of factors are fixed.

At this point it may be appropriate to list some of the characteristics of a Cobb–Douglas production function so that the economic implications of assuming that the production function is of this form may be clearly evident:

1. It is homogeneous of degree one.
2. Constant returns to scale exist throughout, so that proportional changes in the employment of inputs lead to an equiproportional change in the rate of output.
3. The law of diminishing returns holds throughout (marginal productivities decline with increases in the utilization of a factor and no change in the employment of other factors).
4. Given fixed prices for factors of production all expansion lines will be radius vectors from the origin.
5. Given fixed factor prices movements along any expansion curve will yield constant average costs of production.
6. All production isoquants are asymptotic to both axes (hyperbolic functions) so that no output is possible unless some of each factor in the function is employed (and provided there is not an infinite amount of any one factor).
7. In proposition 6 it would appear that X and Y are complementary factors since some of each must be employed in order to achieve any output and since the marginal productivity of one factor always increases with increased amounts of the other factor; but exactly the opposite is

true. Factors used in production are substitutes for each other everywhere on the map.[1]

8. If factors of production are paid *in kind,* that is, paid with units of the good being produced, then all these payments together will equal total output when each factor price equals the marginal productivity of the factor. Thus, if the function $Q = f(X,Y)$ is homogeneous of degree one, it follows from Euler's theorem that

$$Q = X \frac{\Delta Q}{\Delta X} + Y \frac{\Delta Q}{\Delta Y}$$

Here, the amount of factor X employed times its marginal productivity (real wage or price), plus the amount of Y times its marginal productivity equals the total output.[2]

It may be appropriate in some cases to assume that production functions are of the Cobb–Douglas type, as, for example, when making statistical estimates of national industrial production functions. But these are broad and aggregative estimates. For if one chooses to narrow one's view and estimate the production function of a given firm, it will probably not contain the characteristics enumerated above. There will be complementary factors, fixed factors, perhaps variable factor prices, and very probably nonproportional changes in output with changes in budgets. In constructing the general equilibrium paradigm there is no reason to assume that production functions must conform to such a uniform shape; that is, the rationale of the pricing system in no way depends upon this uniformity. Thus, the assumption of such uniformity is only to be made when the analytical problem at hand dictates its usefulness.

An alternative view of production functions may be taken

---

[1] Complementarity, as opposed to substitutability, is the subject of discussion a few paragraphs hence (page 75); see this discussion for clarification of point 8.

[2] According to Euler's theorem if a function is homogeneous of degree n, and $n > 0$, then

$$nQ = nf(X,Y) \equiv X \frac{\partial Q}{\partial X} + Y \frac{\partial Q}{\partial Y}$$

so long as the partial derivatives exist. For a derivation of the theorem see Gerhard Tintner, "Mathematics and Statistics for Economists," p. 161, Holt, Rinehart and Winston, Inc., New York, 1960; or A. Kooros, "Elements of Mathematical Economics," p. 147, Houghton Mifflin Co., Boston, Mass., 1965.

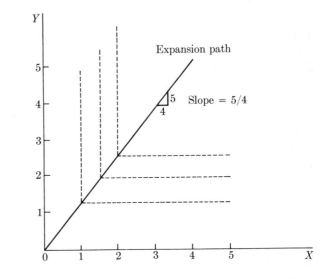

Figure 3.5

by assuming *fixed technical coefficients of production*. It illustrates the condition of perfect complementarity of factors of production because either managers of the firm choose to hire the two factors in strict proportions or the techniques of production are such that only by hiring them in this way is it possible to produce the commodity, that is, if factors X and Y must be hired in the ratio of, say, 4 to 5 and in no other way. If $X:Y$ as 4:5 it follows that $5X = 4Y$, also $X = \frac{4}{5}Y$, and $Y = \frac{5}{4}X$, which is the line drawn in Fig. 3.5 to represent the *expansion path* of output. The dashed lines indicate what production isoquants must look like when factors must be hired in fixed proportion. When production is carried on at a point on the expansion path, an increase in the quantity of any one factor employed each period unaccompanied by any increase in employment of the other factor will yield no change whatever in output; hence the isoquants representing given quantities of outputs are *kinked*. In addition, if it takes a unit of X each period to produce a unit of Q each period and also $1\frac{1}{4}$ units of Y to produce a unit of Q each period,[1] then $Q = 1X$ *and also* $Q = \frac{4}{5}Y$. For example, if one has 16 units of X and 20

---

[1] If $X = aQ$ and $Y = bQ$, then a and b are the *fixed coefficients of production*. In the numerical example above $a = 1$ and $b = 1\frac{1}{4}$. The amount of X needed equals the amount of Q, and the amount of Y needed is $1\frac{1}{4}$ times the value of Q if Q units of output are to be produced each period.

units of Y, then these amounts are sufficient to produce 16 units of Q. In general, one can state: Q = minimum of $5X$ and $4Y$. The expansion path of Fig. 3.5 has most of the characteristics of a function that is homogeneous of degree one. Constant returns to scale exist given fixed prices of factors and constant costs of production also exist. And yet, the fixed technical coefficients mean that the factors are perfect complements and that there exists no substitutability between X and Y. The use of factors in fixed proportion represents a single *technique* of production. Technical knowledge may provide more than one technique, however. Ditches can be dug with, say, ten laborers and $100 worth of spades. They can also be dug with one laborer and a $10,000 machine. For each technique the factor proportions are more or less fixed, but optimum output may be achieved by using only one or the other technique or by some combination of the two.

The problem of choosing among techniques of production is a problem in *linear programming*. Thus, the assumption of fixed technical coefficients of production is not as limiting as it might have appeared at first, for one can always specify a large number of techniques, and in doing so introduce substitutability and more closely approximate the analysis of the continuous production function. Linear programming, or *activity analysis*, as it is sometimes called, is now a widely used tool in business decisions and it grew from the economic theory of production functions.[1]

The subject of complementarity among factors of production (or among goods in the preference function of an individual) can best be understood when expanding the frame of reference to include three factors of production. Factors X and Y are complementary if, when the price of factor X falls, more X is purchased and also more Y is purchased after fully compensating for the *output* or *income* effects of the reduction in the price of X. In a two-factor production function, more of both X and Y could never be bought after adjusting for output changes, because more of both factors means more output. However, with a three-factor production function one can easily illustrate the existence of complementarity.

[1] There are many excellent descriptions of linear programming in textbooks. See, for example, R. G. D. Allen, "Mathematical Economics," pp. 332–342 and Chaps. 16 and 18, Macmillan and Company, London, 1957.

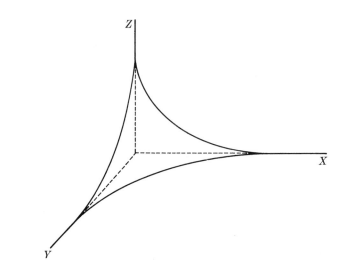

Figure 3.6

Assume a production surface such as that shown in Fig. 3.6. Any point on this surface indicates the amounts of factors X, Y, and Z that can be used to produce a given output each period. For a larger rate of output one could draw another production surface closer to the viewer and indicating some larger amounts of factors to be used in production. Thus, the production function would yield an entire set of such isoquant surfaces. These surfaces are concave as viewed from above or convex as viewed from the origin. The producer's budget constraint appears as a plane in this three-factor world. In Fig. 3.7 the budget plane

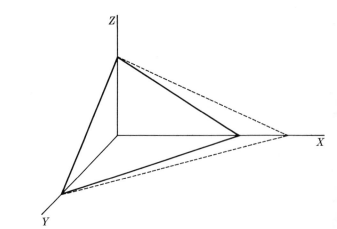

Figure 3.7

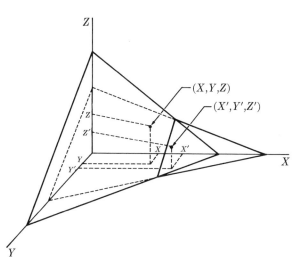

Figure 3.8

expresses the producer's income and the prices that he faces for each of the three factors of production, P_X, P_Y, and P_Z. He can purchase any package of factors represented by any single point on this plane with his revenues (income). If P_X falls while P_Y and P_Z remain unchanged, the new plane indicated by the dotted lines represents the new budget position of the producer.

Assume now that the isoquant surface just touches the producer's budget plane at point (X,Y,Z) (see Fig. 3.8), indicating maximum output obtainable from that budget for given factor prices or minimum cost of producing that rate of output. The isoquant surface is not drawn in the diagram to avoid clutter. Assume now that P_X falls *and* that revenues are lowered so that the new budget plane lies below the old one on the left side of the figure as the dotted lines indicate. Income was reduced by an amount just sufficient to leave a point of tangency of the new budget plane with the isoquant surface at point (X',Y',Z'). Thus, it is assumed that the isoquant surface (not shown) is shaped such that the new point is now the point of tangency.

Now notice that under the new lower price of factor X and having compensated for the effect on output of this change in price by changing the firm's revenues, the quantity of X purchased increases, the quantity of factor Y purchased also increases, and the quantity of factor Z purchased decreases:

$X' > X$, $Y' > Y$, and $Z' < Z$. Hence, factors X and Y are complements, while factors X and Z are substitutes. In production functions of the Cobb–Douglas type no complementarity among factors exists, for factors of production are everywhere substitutes for each other. (Complementarity in consumption can be described in analogous fashion if one assumes that utility is measurable cardinally.)

EXERCISES

3.1 Draw a map showing three isoproduct curves and label the middle curve $Q = 10$. Assume the price of factor X is $2.00 and the price of factor Y is $.50.

(a) What is the slope of the budget constraint?

(b) If 10 units of product are to be produced each period, from the diagram as drawn, roughly how many units of X and of Y will be employed each period? (Answers will vary according to how the isoproduct curves are drawn.) Draw the budget constraint in the appropriate place.

(c) Given the prices of X and Y above, how much will it cost to produce 10 units of output each period?

(d) Note that here it has been shown how to minimize the cost of a given rate of output while in the text the emphasis is on the maximization of output from a given budget. Show why these two approaches amount to the same thing.

3.2 If a producer wishes to produce a *certain* rate of output, and if factor X represents labor and factor Y represents equipment, show that an increase in P_X will lead to the substitution of capital for labor in the production process and explain briefly. (Recall the concept of *compensation* introduced in Chap. 2.)

3.3 For large rates of output the total product function appearing in Fig. 3.1 slopes downward indicating a range of output for which marginal productivity is negative. In drawing this function it is assumed that a fixed amount of one factor is employed with varying amounts of the other.

(a) Show this same negative marginal productivity on a map of isoproduct curves by drawing them elliptical (as shown in Chap. 8, Fig. 8.13) and by assuming a fixed amount of factor Y.

(b) If the price of X were zero, as it would be if X were free, show that increasing amounts of X would be employed up to the point where the marginal productivity of X is zero (the marginal rate of substitution of X for Y is zero) in order to maximize output for a given rate of expenditure (minimize cost of a given rate of output).

(c) By connecting all points where the marginal productivity of X is zero show the *ridge line* that separates those combinations of factors that are economically efficient from those that are not.

3.4 Carefully examine the model of the two-good, two-factor producers' market and list all necessary additions and givens, and equations that would be necessary if another good (good 3) were introduced.

3.5 Carefully examine the model of the two-good, two-factor producers' market and list all necessary additions and changes in variables, givens, and equations that would be necessary if another factor of production (factor Z) were introduced into the model.

3.6 Draw a box diagram for a two-good, two-factor producers' market. Show the contract line. Choose a point off the contract line and, by appropriately labeling isoproduct curves, show how it would be possible to increase the rate of output of both goods by reallocation of factors in employment on the production of the two goods.

3.7 Explicitly note the difference between decreasing returns to scale and the law of diminishing returns.

3.8 Give an example of a function that is homogeneous of degree three and show why it is so.

3.9 Show that only substitutability (no complementarity) exists among factors of production if the production function is of Cobb–Douglas form.

4

General
Equilibrium

In every economy there are two broad classes of things that are scarce and must be rationed: the goods and services that consumers use and the factors of production that producers use in the production of consumers' goods.[1] The fundamental scarcity, of course, is that of factors of production; for if each of these were freely available in unlimited amounts, then under existing technology it should be possible to produce any desired amount of consumers' goods and hence to satiate all human desire for economic goods. Thus, ultimately, output of consumers' goods is limited by scarcity of factors of production.

Conceptually, it is possible to distinguish the market in which consumers' goods are sold from that in which productive factors are sold. In Chap. 2, there is a description of the fundamental forces determining the prices of consumers' goods and quantities of these that each consumer receives. The model of the consumers' market illustrates how the pricing system solves the economic problem of the allocation of a given supply of scarce consumers' goods among individuals in the community. In Chap. 3, a description of fundamental forces in the producers' market illustrates how the pricing system determines the price of factors of production and the quantities of these that each producer may

---

[1] Of course, producers also use factors to produce capital goods, that is, to produce other factors. The subject of capital formation is raised in Chap. 5, Sec. 5.4.

purchase, and how the economic problem of the allocation of a given supply of scarce factors among producers is solved in a free-market economy. A *general equilibrium* system must show how all prices and quantities are determined, both those of factors and those of consumer goods, if the interrelations of the system are to be adequately portrayed and understood. By connecting the consumers' market and the producers' market, an abstract and analytical paradigm is provided for this purpose. It is to this connection that the present chapter is devoted.

4.1 CONNECTING THE CONSUMERS' MARKET AND THE PRODUCERS' MARKET

In developing the model of the consumers' market it was assumed that the quantities of goods flowing into the market each period Q_1 and Q_2 were independent variables given for the problem at hand. This assumption is now relaxed and Q_1 and Q_2 become dependent variables determined by the interactions of all of the elements of the system and particularly by the rate of production undertaken by firms α and β. This provides one connecting link between the consumers' and producers' markets.

A second link is provided by relaxing an assumption that was made in regard to the producers' market. It was that each producer's expenditure for factors of production—his budget— was given. Now it is assumed that the funds available to producers depend upon the prices of the goods each sells and the quantities that the consumers buy at those prices, that is, the firm's (industry's) revenues.

These two connecting links may be described by reference to the appropriate equation of the consumers' market and producers' market and by noting the changes that occur in the equations when the two models are joined:

	Equations from the consumers' market	*Equations after joining the markets*
(d)	$Q_1 = Q_{A,1} + Q_{B,1}$	$f(X_1,Y_1) = Q_{A,1} + Q_{B,1}$
	$Q_2 = Q_{A,2} + Q_{B,2}$	$g(X_2,Y_2) = Q_{A,2} + Q_{B,2}$

	Equations from the producers' market	
(b)	$I_\alpha = P_X X_1 + P_Y Y_1$	$P_1 Q_{A,1} + P_1 Q_{B,1} = P_X X_1 + P_Y Y_1$
	$I_\beta = P_X X_2 + P_Y Y_2$	$P_2 Q_{A,2} + P_2 Q_{B,2} = P_X X_2 + P_Y Y_2$

Thus, Q_1 and Q_2, treated as given in the consumers' market, are replaced by the production functions $f(X_1, Y_1)$ and $g(X_2, Y_2)$ in the new equations. And I_α and I_β, the firms' revenues that are given in the producers' market, are replaced by expenditure on goods 1 and 2 in the two new equations. The model now contains the following unknowns, the economically relevant variables about which the study of economics revolves:

P_1, P_2	Prices of consumers' goods
P_X, P_Y	Prices of factors of production
Q_1, Q_2	Total amount of each good produced each period
$Q_{A,1}, Q_{B,1}$	Quantities of each good that flow each
$Q_{A,2}, Q_{B,2}$	period to the consumers
X_1, X_2	Quantities of each factor that flow each
Y_1, Y_2	period to producers α and β
U_A, U_B	The total amount of utils of satisfaction flowing to each consumer each period

Altogether there are 16 unknowns in this two-good–two-factor–two-producer world. A noteworthy aspect of the model is that even after excluding U_A and U_B the remaining 14 unknowns may be calculated so long as the marginal rates of substitution of Mr. A and Mr. B are known. In other words, if utility is not measurable cardinally, there is nevertheless a solution for the remainder of the unknowns in the model provided that utility is measurable ordinally—provided that an indifference map can be constructed for each consumer showing marginal rates of substitution but not necessarily showing absolute values for levels of satisfaction in terms of an abstract unit of measurement called *utils*.

Values for the following four independent variables are given for the model in its present form: X, Y, I_A, I_B. In addition to the amounts of factors of production and the incomes of Mr. A and Mr. B, there is given implicitly an amount of money available to use for transactions purposes, and the average number of exchanges that each unit of money is engaged in each period. Thus, with 16 unknowns and 4 independent variables, the following set of 16 equations may be used to solve for equilibrium values of the unknowns.

(a)	$Q_1 = f(X_1, Y_1)$ $Q_2 = g(X_2, Y_2)$ $U_A = f(Q_{A,1}, Q_{A,2})$ $U_B = g(Q_{R,1}, Q_{B,2})$	Production and utility functions determined empirically by technological factors and the revelation of consumers' tastes
(b)	$P_1 Q_{A,1} + P_1 Q_{B,1}$ $\quad = P_X X_1 + P_Y Y_1$ $P_2 Q_{A,2} + P_2 Q_{B,2}$ $\quad = P_X X_2 + P_Y Y_2$ $I_A = P_1 Q_{A,1} + P_2 Q_{A,2}$ $I_B = P_1 Q_{B,1} + P_2 Q_{B,2}$	Budget equation for producers and consumers arrived at by invoking the principle that all incomes and revenues are spent on goods and factors, respectively
(c)	$_\alpha MRS_{X,Y} = -\dfrac{MP_{X,1}}{MP_{Y,1}} = -\dfrac{P_X}{P_Y}$ $_\beta MRS_{X,Y} = -\dfrac{MP_{X,2}}{MP_{Y,2}} = -\dfrac{P_X}{P_Y}$ $_A MRS_{1,2} = -\dfrac{P_1}{P_2}$ $_B MRS_{1,2} = -\dfrac{P_1}{P_2}$	Producers' marginal rates of substitution for factors and consumers' marginal rates of substitution for goods equated with relative prices in accordance with the principles of maximization of output and maximization of satisfaction
(d)	$X = X_1 + X_2$ $Y = Y_1 + Y_2$ $Q_1 = f(X_1, Y_1) = Q_{A,1} + Q_{B,1}$ $Q_2 = g(X_2, Y_2) = Q_{A,2} + Q_{B,2}$	Market-clearing equations derived by the assumption that all factors and all goods offered for sale are bought each period

By an examination of the above equations one can gain an understanding of many of the pertinent interdependent forces that operate throughout the pricing system to bring about a solution to the economic problem of allocating scarce goods and factors to alternative uses. First, it is noteworthy that factor resources are limited in supply. This is characteristic of most social communities. It is important, therefore, to understand the resource base of an economy in order to evaluate its economic potential. Second, these scarce resources of each community are guided into use in the production of different goods by the budgets and preferences of the consumers, for consumers' expenditures for goods give managers of the different firms the revenues with which to purchase factors of production. The more consumers spend on a good, the more revenues accrue to the firm that produces that good and the larger the quantity of factors that flow into its production. In the final analysis, therefore, what is produced is determined by the expression of consumers' desires in the marketplace.

Having connected the producers' market with the consumers' market, the model now resembles a duplex dwelling. Both dwelling units have many similarities, but also a few pertinent differences that reflect the tastes or technology of the respective occupants. In the fundamental structure of the duplex, the dwelling units are connected with one another. Now it is time to "finish" the structure by adding some finishing touches, one of which also serves as an important connecting link between the two units.

4.2 FACTOR OWNERSHIP AND INCOME

To construct another connecting link between the consumers' market and the producers' market it is necessary to relax the unrealistic assumption that Mr. A and Mr. B both have a certain income each period. Instead, each consumer is assumed to be endowed with ownership over certain amounts of each factor of production. Thus, formerly it might have been assumed that Mr. A had an income $I_A = \$20$ per period and Mr. B an income $I_B = \$30$ per period. Now let Mr. A be the owner of X_A units of factor X and Y_A units of factor Y. Similarly, let Mr. B be the owner of X_B units of factor X and Y_B units of factor Y. And let the consumers offer these quantities of X and Y for sale each period in the producers' market at the prevailing prices. It is clear that the incomes accruing to Mr. A and Mr. B will no longer be given as independent variables but will instead depend upon the prices that these factors will fetch in the producers' market and the quantities that each consumer owns and can offer for sale.

Under part (b) two of the equations are altered and will now read as follows:

(b) $P_X X_A + P_Y Y_A = P_1 Q_{A,1} + P_2 Q_{A,2}$

$P_X X_B + P_Y Y_B = P_1 Q_{B,1} + P_2 Q_{B,2}$

The left-hand sides of these equations represent substitutions for I_A and I_B. There are now two more independent variables than there were before (four expressing factor endowments have been added, and two expressing incomes have been removed). But there remain the same number of dependent variables and the same number of equations; hence the system is determinate, and there may be solution values for price and quantities. If one wishes also to determine revenues of the two firms and the incomes of consumers A and B, then I_α and I_β as well as I_A and I_B are additional dependent variables. There are also four additional equations:

(e) $I_\alpha = P_1 Q_{A,1} + P_1 Q_{B,1}$ Each firm's (industry's)

$I_\beta = P_2 Q_{A,2} + P_2 Q_{B,2}$ revenues are derived from sales to consumers.

(f) $I_A = P_X X_A + P_Y Y_A$ Each consumer's income is

$I_B = P_X X_B + P_Y Y_B$ derived from selling the factors of production he owns to producers.

(Of course, $I_\alpha + I_\beta = I_A + I_B$.) Although these dependent variables and their determining equations need not be entered explicitly as part of the pricing mechanism for the purpose of determining the allocation of resources, nevertheless they are extremely important and frequently the subject of controversy in economic affairs. All discussions of the question of the *fairness* of the distribution of income pertain to this part of the model and, more particularly, the amendments to this part of the model that are necessary if a successful program of redistribution of income is to be achieved.

One should carefully note at this point that there exists a different solution set, that is, a different set of values for the dependent variables, the prices and quantities, for each possible set of different endowments of resources over which consumers are given ownership. For example, let the factor X represent labor service of one sort or another. Everyone is well aware of the different capacities and capabilities for labor with which each person is born into the world. One may be blessed with intelligence and physical strength; another may be infirm. Infirmities may, of course, also derive from a great variety of environmental forces including physical accidents on one extreme and psychological pressures on the other. Insofar as these affect the capacities of individuals to offer services to the labor market, they affect as well all of the prices and quantities determined by the market mechanism. The ownership of capital and land is also affected by the accident of birth. And in this way the various inheritance customs as well as legal institutions and taxes that impinge upon the rights to inheritances govern in part the ownership of factors of production and therefore the income position of individuals in the society.

Since there exist many solutions to the problem of the allocation of resources, each dependent upon a particular distribution of factor endowments, economists should guard against casual statements that suggest that the pricing system brings about *the* optimum distribution of income as if only one such optimum exists. To speak of an *optimum* distribution of income raises for concern the entire field known as *welfare economics*—a subject to be discussed more fully, but by no means exhaustively, below. But even here the analysis is suggestive of an extremely important guideline for economic policy. It is that welfare programs should be designed to affect individual endowments of factors, or individual incomes, more or less directly. If a government undertakes a program of land reform under which large landholdings are divided among peasants, advocates of the free-enterprise pricing system cannot object on the grounds of interference with the efficient operation of economic affairs. Both before and after the land has been reallocated, from the point of view of economic efficiency, it is appropriate to permit the pricing system to regulate the allocation of resources. But any program of reallocation must itself rest on other than economic criteria. Similarly, a government may introduce programs to provide laborers with better skills through the establishment of technical schools. Insofar as additional skills add to the resource base of the society, such programs clearly have economic implications. But, at base, the decision to tax some individuals in order to provide training in skills for others must rest upon criteria other than that of economic efficiency.

Before the program is introduced, one equilibrium set of prices and quantities would be determined by the pricing system, and after the program has begun, another set of prices and quantities would obtain. Each of these equilibrium sets is optimum from a strictly economic point of view and the choice between them must rest upon social and political factors. In a desire to mitigate the social unrest that stems from unequal educational opportunity, a training program may be very appropriate. But it is on sociological rather than economic grounds that the argument rests. The function of the economist in this case is to provide a *description* of the impact on prices and quantities and income of such a program. This will assist the decision-makers, for they will wish to know the economic implications of their decisions. However, the politicians or citizens must then decide whether or not to implement the program.

The subject of the distribution of income among individuals will arise again in other contexts. It is perhaps the most difficult subject in the realm of economics precisely because economics alone can never provide answers to problems of income distribution. It can, however, provide guidelines on the efficiency of redistribution programs. But the discussion of the problems of income distribution must yield so the analytical framework of general equilibrium can be presented in an abridged graphical form.

4.3 PRODUCTION-POSSIBILITY (TRANSFORMATION) CURVES

The model has far too many equations and variables to be shown in a single graph in its present form, but it can be condensed in an interesting and informative way so that graphical analysis is feasible for some aspects of the model. It will be recalled that the model of the producers' market was portrayed by use of the *Edgeworth-box diagram*. Given the supplies of factors of production, the production functions of the two producers were fitted together in a box and a *contract curve* was generated by points of tangency of production isoquants. At these points, marginal rates of substitution of factors are equal to the ratio of factor prices. But also at each point one can read the amounts of goods 1 and 2 produced each period by observing the labels attached to each of the two isoquants passing through that point of tangency. Thus, the contract curve indicates the various *production possibilities* available from existing factor supplies. By plotting the values of pairs of production possi-

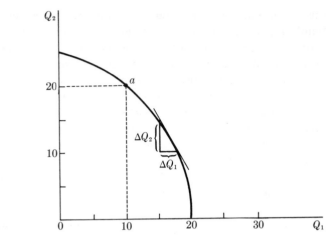

Figure 4.1

Production-possibility, or transformation, curve.

bilities of goods 1 and 2, a *production-possibility curve* can be drawn as in Fig. 4.1.

From the figure, note that if all of the available supplies of factors of production were used to produce good 2, then 25 units of this good could be produced each period. Alternatively, if all factors were used to produce good 1, then 20 units of 1 could be produced each period. If the factors were allocated appropriately to the production of good 1 and good 2, it would be possible to produce 20 units of good 2 and 10 units of good 1, as represented by the position of point a on the curve.

The slope of the *production-possibility,* or *transformation,* curve, as it is sometimes called, is represented by the ratio $\Delta Q_2/\Delta Q_1$. This slope steepens as more of good 1 is produced. This means that the *cost* of producing additional units of good 1 increases the larger the rate of production of good 1. Here, the *cost* of producing an additional unit of good 1 is measured by the amount of good 2 that must be sacrificed. This amount of good 2 is the alternative foregone by the decision to produce more of good 1. In this sense, economists speak of *opportunity* and *alternative* costs. In the final analysis, all costs, however measured, are *opportunity* costs; for if no alternatives are foregone when additional goods are produced, then no costs of production exist.

Since the slope of the transformation curve increases in absolute value as point a on the curve moves rightward down the curve, one may say that good 1 is produced at increasing cost. Similarly, moving up the curve, additional units of good 2 are produced at increasing cost, for more of good 1 must be sacrificed as larger and larger amounts of good 2 are produced. Thus, the concavity of the transformation curve, as viewed from the origin, implies increasing costs of production for both goods.[1]

From the above analysis, one can see why the production-possibility curve may also be called a transformation curve, for in a very real sense one good may be transformed into another good by reallocating the factors of production. The slope of the transformation curve is called the marginal rate of transformation of good 2 into good 1, or $MRT_{1,2} = \Delta Q_2/\Delta Q_1$.

4.4 COMMUNITY INDIFFERENCE CURVES

In order to incorporate the consumers' market in a graphical depiction of general equilibrium, it is useful to introduce the concept of a *community indifference map*. Assume that the preference functions of Mr. A and Mr. B can be expressed as a single function representative of the different amounts of utility that could be received by the community if various different packages of goods were available for community consumption. In making this assumption, it is no longer possible to distinguish between the amounts of utility received by Mr. A and Mr. B separately or between the amounts of goods received by the two members of the community separately; it is possible only to distinguish the totals received by the community jointly. This degree of specificity is being sacrificed, of course, only to enable the presentation to appear in graphic form.[2]

In Fig. 4.2, the transformation curve of Fig. 4.1 and the community indifference map are superimposed. At point *a*, where

[1] An excellent paper for the interested student is Francis M. Bator, The Simple Analytics of Welfare Maximization, *Am. Econ. Rev.*, vol. XLVII, pp. 25–59, March 1957; reprinted in W. Breit and H. M. Hochman (eds.), "Readings in Microeconomics," pp. 385–413, Holt, Rinehart and Winston, Inc., New York, 1968. Bator shows that both production functions may be homogeneous of degree one, but the production possibility curve will still show increasing costs.

[2] *Community indifference curves*, of course, probably do not exist, for individual preference functions are not likely to be of a form such that they can be combined. If we assumed that the welfare of a country were defined by the function identical with that of the identical individuals that live in the country, then we may speak of a community welfare function; but this is a very unrealistic assumption. Nevertheless, the intuitive and pedagogical role of this assumption is helpful.

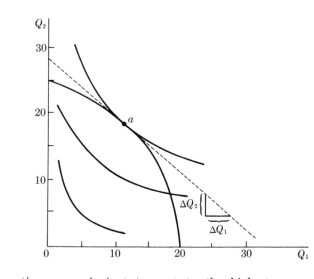

Figure 4.2

the transformation curve is just tangent to the highest community indifference curve, there are designated the equilibrium rates of output of goods 1 and 2 such that community satisfaction is maximized. Hence, it is representative of an efficient allocation of resources. At point a, $MRT_{1,2} = MRS_{1,2} = -P_1/P_2 = \Delta Q_2/\Delta Q_1$. That is, the slope of the transformation curve just equals the slope of the indifference curve, and implicit in this same slope is the rate at which members of the community would be willing to exchange good 1 for good 2; hence, the ratio of the price of good 1 to the price of good 2 is also determined. Absolute prices in units of currency remain undetermined, for this would require additional information on money incomes and rates of turnover of number of nominal units of money in circulation.

This compact graph of a general equilibrium model can be used as an analytical tool in many contexts. Two illustrative examples follow. One concerns an aspect of economic problems in a planned economy. The second describes gains to the community from international trade.

4.5 PLANNED ECONOMIES

Assume that in a planned economy the authorities in charge of production decide to set target rates of output for goods 1 and 2 as designated by point a in Fig. 4.3. Having studied the resource base and economic potential of the country, along with the production functions for both goods, the authorities know that these goods can be produced. Assume also that managers of the production facilities do operate efficiently and the designated rates of output of goods 1 and 2 do take place.

Note, however, that the community indifference curve labeled A *intersects* the production-possibility curve at point a rather than just touching it. Hence, at this point the absolute value of $MRT_{1,2}$ is less than the absolute value of $MRS_{1,2}$, that is, the slope of the indifference curve is absolutely greater than the slope of the transformation curve. This means that consumers, if consuming the produced goods, would gladly give up, say, 5 units of good 2 in exchange for an additional 5 units of good 1; for then at point b the consumers would gain the greater satisfaction as represented by indifference curve B. Furthermore, the package of goods represented by point b could just as easily be produced as that of point a if resources were reallocated appropriately. Thus, if planners decide to produce the package of point a, there will occur an inefficient use of resources.

The planners also face another problem, that of setting prices for goods 1 and 2. If prices are based upon costs of production, then the dashed line tangent to point a represents the equality $MRT_{1,2} = -P_1/P_2$. For this set of prices and incomes, however, the people of the community will wish to consume the package of goods represented by point c, a point on indifference curve C. Thus, in the marketplace there will be a glut of good 2 and a scarcity of good 1. Of the 20 units of good 2

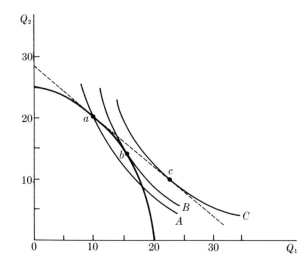

Figure 4.3

produced, consumers will wish to buy only 10 units and the other 10 units will remain unsold on the shelves of the state stores. But 10 units of good 1 produced will be less than half the amount that consumers will wish to buy at the established price. For this good the consumers will queue as each shipment arrives at the store, and before the day is over the shelf will be empty. Some customers will either be turned away with empty hands, or if the good is rationed by coupons they will each leave the store with a smaller amount than they would have bought at the prevailing prices. Conditions such as these give rise to black-market activity. Either the coupons are sold, or else transactions will take place after the customers leave the store. If the black market is allowed to flourish, the price of good 1 will rise in this market relative to the price of good 2, which will cause a de facto price ratio represented by a much steeper price line than the one shown.

If, on the other hand, the pricing authorities should set prices such that the budget curve passes through point a and tangent to indifference curve A, then $MRS_{1,2} = -P_1/P_2$. Consumers will be readily willing to consume precisely the package of goods that the authorities have decided to have produced each period, for under these conditions consumers maximize their position. However, in this case the cost of production of good 1 is less than its price and the cost of production of good 2 is greater than its price. Managers of state enterprises that produce good 1 will observe profits flowing to their enterprises, while losses will occur to those producing good 2.

In a competitive, unplanned economy the profits would encourage new entrants to the market and the losses would force some producing units out of business. Eventually the price of good 1 would fall as more good 1 is produced, the price of good 2 would rise as less good 2 is produced, and factors of production would be reallocated away from the production of good 2 toward the production of good 1 until finally the point of equilibrium, point b, is reached.[1] In the planned economy, however, the central planning authorities may or may not be sensitive to these profit flows; and they may or may not instigate the desirable changes in resource allocation. If they do not and if their objective is to bring about an *efficient* utilization

[1] For a description of problems that arise when planned prices are not equilibrium, see John M. Montias, Price-Setting Problems in the Polish Economy, *J. Pol. Econ.*, vol. LXV, pp. 486–505, December 1957.

of economic resources, they will have failed to attain their objective. If they do respond to pressures that arise when disequilibrium prices exist, they are simply doing what the free-market pricing system would have done in their absence. It is in this sense that economic planners are said to be playing at "mock capitalism."[1]

To raise the terms *mock capitalism* and *profit motive* may mislead the reader because these terms are emotionally charged for certain individuals. The issues are more complex in all their ramifications than this cursory illustrative example portrays. But the purpose of the example is to show that the analytical tools of economic theory can be used as a frame of reference to explain certain observed phenomena in planned economies as well as in unregulated free enterprise economies. There are, of course, certain goods that are unsuitable for production by unregulated free enterprise for one reason or another. But, on strict theoretical grounds planning of economic activity is unnecessary unless a very special case can be made or special circumstances prevail. And when these special criteria do apply, the theoretical tools indicate to the analysts and planners the types of problems that they are likely to face when alternative programs are implemented. Thus, the purpose here is not so much to debate the issues of planning vs. nonplanning but rather to illustrate the usefulness of economic theory.[2]

---

[1] Socialist planning groups have "conservative" and "liberal" elements. In general, conservatives believe rigidly in planning, while liberals wish to decentralize the planning function and make it responsive to disequilibrium forces so that frequent revisions in prices and output targets will bring these into line so as to maximize output and consumer satisfaction. Therefore, only those in the latter group ostensibly play at "mock capitalism." For further discussion of these issues see the selection of readings edited by Morris Bornstein, "Comparative Economic Systems," Richard D. Irwin, Inc., Homewood, Ill., 1965, especially Part II, Models of Economic Systems. For a discussion of planning in the U.S.S.R. see Alex Nove, "The Soviet Economy," revised ed., Frederick A. Praeger, New York, 1966, and the references cited therein.

[2] The author's feeling is that, in general, central planning is an unnecessary and burdensome task, and the special cases in its favor should be scrutinized very carefully before plans are implemented, for the likelihood of error is very great and the costs in terms of the well-being of the populace are likely to be quite great also. The costs of planning involve much more than the mere financing of the planning agency if planners make mistakes. And, unfortunately, the costs of these mistakes are difficult to observe for they are not recordable as such in terms of market values. Mistakes made in private enterprise are also costly, of course, and they are often recorded in courts of bankruptcy as the competitive pressure of private enterprises prevents continued repetition of the same mistake.

4.6 WORLD MARKETS AND GAINS FROM TRADE

The second example to illustrate the analytical usefulness of this compact graph of general equilibrium pertains to international trade. In Fig. 4.2 the transformation curve represents the various amounts of goods 1 and 2 that can be produced in a certain country each period under existing conditions of resource availability. Also, it is assumed that a community preference function may be superimposed. If the economy were in isolation, then the point representing equilibrium rates of output for goods 1 and 2 and maximum satisfaction to consumers is point a. The slope of the dotted price line indicates the relative prices of goods 1 and 2 in isolation. Assume, however, that the ratio P_1/P_2 on the world market differs from that which would exist in isolation.

Let the curve labeled P in Fig. 4.4 represent the negative of the ratio of prices in international markets. Prices determine the *slope* of P, but its *position* is determined by the point of tangency it makes with the transformation curve, that is, the point where $MRT_{1,2} = -P_1/P_2$, which is point b. Since this country can produce the package of goods represented by point b, the optimum solution to its economic problem is to produce at point b and then exchange goods in the world market at going prices so as to consume the package represented by point c. Thus, by producing 8 units of good 1 and 22 units of good 2 (point b) each period and then selling 9 units of good 2 on the world market in exchange for 13 units of good 1, the people

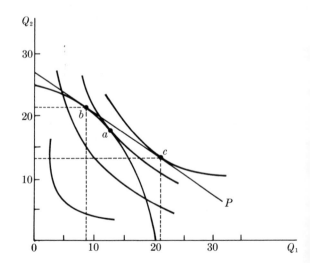

Figure 4.4

of this country can consume 21 units of good 1 and 13 units of good 2 (point c) each period. Since point c is on a higher indifference curve than point a, the members of the community are better off having specialized in the production of good 2, exporting part of it and then importing more of good 1, than they would have been if they had remained in isolation from the world market.

Production-possibility curves can be used to show that world trade not only enables individuals in each economy to increase their levels of satisfaction and hence make better use of the limited resources in the world at large, but also allows the rates of output ,of both goods to be larger than they otherwise would be so as to improve standards of living in this way as well.

In Fig. 4.5 let each graph depict a production-possibility curve for each of two countries. In this example, for ease of exposition the curves are straight lines. Let points a and b represent the equilibrium solutions to production for each country in isolation from the other. Total output of good 1, in this two-country world, is 15 units each period. It is also 15 units each period for good 2. The price of good 1 is relatively low in the first country, as indicated by the slope of the curve. In the second country the price of good 1 is relatively high. One could say that the first country is especially suitable for the production of good 1 for some reason—perhaps because of its climate. On the other hand, the second country is especially suitable for producing good 2. To exploit these *comparative advantages,* assume that the first country produces at a' and the second at b'. Total output of both good 1 and good 2 increases from 15 to 20 units each period. Thus, the world community has 5 more units of each good available for consumption with world trade than it does without world trade.

One can imagine that the phenomenon of expanded world

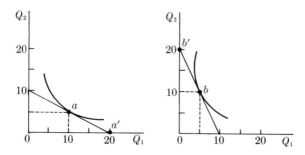

Figure 4.5

production will occur with international trade even though one of the two countries could produce more of both goods than the other country could. That is, imagine that one country could produce along a transformation curve that extended from 50 units of good 2 down to 100 units of good 1. Then it could produce, say, 25 units of 2 and 50 units of 1. This would be more of *both* goods than the second country could produce. Nevertheless, trade would bring advantages to both countries. Thus, it "pays" for large and small countries to trade with each other. With trade, the price of good 1 will rise somewhat in the first country and the price of good 2 will fall somewhat; the opposite will occur in the second country. Thus, an equilibrium set of prices will be established in the world market, with values somewhere within the price ranges taken by each of the two goods prior to the existence of trade. The final world prices would be determined by the preference functions for the two goods.

In Fig. 4.6 the two transformation curves appear in the same graph. The axis of the second country has been rotated 180°, and point b' has been superimposed on point a'. The point of tangency of the community indifference curves, point c, indicates the equilibrium solution for the final price ratio, shown by the slope of the dashed line, and also the final allocation of the two goods that citizens of each country acquire for their own consumption. Exactly where point c lies could, of course, be

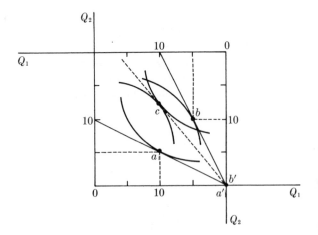

Figure 4.6

described by constructing *offer curves* like those in Chap. 2 on the consumers' market. They are omitted here in order not to clutter the graph.

When the diagrams are drawn with transformation curves that are concave as viewed from the origin rather than straight lines, the gains from trade still exist in the same way. The size of the box still indicates total output of both goods when two concave transformation curves just touch. When they do not touch on the axes, then each country still produces some amount of each of the two goods so there remains diversification of industry in each country as well as some importation and exportation.

These two examples, one of a planned economy and one of international trade, demonstrate the explanatory powers of the general equilibrium framework.. But, of course, the theoretical model is abstract and must be applied to actual problems only with the greatest care. Furthermore, each of the two subjects comparative economic systems and international trade deserves an entire text to be treated with only modest adequacy.

In Chap. 5 the paradigm of the pricing system is extended in two important ways. The first concerns the supplies of factors of production X and Y; these were assumed to be given in the amounts that flowed into the producers' market each period. In the next chapter the possibility that the quantity of X flowing into the market is variable in supply, that is, variable with respect to the price of factor X, will be discussed. The second extension of the paradigm of the pricing system concerns the treatment of capital and its rate of return as well as savings and the inducement to save that is called interest. These extensions of the general equilibrium framework will complete its formal presentation. However, Chap. 6 will be devoted to a brief analysis of the welfare implications of the pricing system and the operational meaningfulness of such a theoretical structure.

EXERCISES

4.1 Describe the connecting links between the producers' and consumers' markets.

4.2 Examine the paradigm of general equilibrium and note all changes that would be required in variables, givens, and equations if another consumer, Mr. C, were introduced into the economy.

4.3 Examine the elements of the model of the pricing system and note all necessary changes in variables, givens, and equations if another good, good 3, were introduced.

4.4 Discuss the implications of the model for changes in the solution values of prices and quantities if some of factor Y were taken from Mr. A and given to Mr. B.

4.5 Using a transformation curve as a frame of reference explain the concept of *opportunity cost*. Also, note the shape that the transformation curve would assume under conditions of *increasing costs of production*.

4.6 Draw a production-possibility curve and indifference maps similar to that of Fig. 4.3, but instead let point a rest on the production-possibility curve below point b rather than above as is now the case. Show that the quantity of good 2 demanded each period by the consuming public exceeds the quantity produced and that the quantity of good 1 demanded falls short of the quantity produced.

4.7 The purpose of this exercise is to construct a production-possibility curve for the world community. Draw concave, as viewed from the origin, transformation curves for two countries α and β. Let good 1 be measured on the horizontal axis and good 2 on the vertical axis. Assume both countries produce *only* good 1. Rotate β's axes by 180° and superimpose β's horizontal axis on α's horizontal axis such that the length of the horizontal axis from α's origin to β's origin equals the sum of α's output and β's output of good 1. Now imagine that a pencil is held by β's origin and as the origin moves the pencil draws a curve. Imagine keeping the two transformation curves tangent to each other and the pairs of axes parallel while you move β's graph to the north and northwest. In this way β's origin will trace the world production-possibility curve that one might call a *grand production frontier*.

Assume a *world community preference function* and draw selected indifference curves to show the optimum world production of goods 1 and 2 by noting the point of tangency of an indifference curve with the grand production frontier. By noting the transformation curves for α and β internal to the grand production frontier indicate the quantities of goods 1 and 2 produced in α and β.

5

Extensions
of
General
Equilibrium

The paradigm of general equilibrium is designed to describe the interrelations of the fundamental forces at work in an impersonal pricing system. These forces operate to determine a solution to the economic problem of the allocation of scarce resources to alternative ends. One of the principal difficulties in the construction of such a paradigm is to decide at what point the elaboration shall stop. Ockham's Razor dictates that concepts or hypotheses should not be multiplied beyond necessity. But William of Ockham did not mean merely that the analyst should omit redundant theorems from a logical framework. The crucial word in his admonition is "necessity," for it implies that there is some problem at hand in solving which the analyst is willing to tolerate some margin of error, and that if he needs further extension of the model to bring the margin of error within predetermined limits of toleration then he may extend the model. Thus, the use to which the model is put determines where Ockham's Razor cuts.

The general equilibrium model that has been developed so far is abstract. For many problems it is as large as necessary, but for others it may not be large enough. One abstraction involves the assumption that the amounts of factors of production that flow into the producers' market each period are fixed. But it is, of course, well known that these amounts can vary in a variety of ways over extended periods of time; birthrates and immigration may affect the amount of labor supplied to the market each period; land may be reclaimed from the sea, or cleared; capital equipment may be constructed by diverting effort away from the production of consumers' goods and toward production of machines and buildings. Therefore, it is important to show how variable amounts of factors of production may be introduced into the model of general equilibrium. First, a variable supply of labor is considered.

5.1 VARIABLE AMOUNTS OF FACTORS OF PRODUCTION: LEISURE AND MONEY INCOME

Let factor X in the model represent labor effort and X_A the number of hours of labor worked per week by Mr. A.[1] An addition can now be made to the model that allows for variability in the labor supply when such variability is the result of changes in the number of hours per week that each worker is willing to work. Each laborer desires leisure time. This is defined as all time not spent on the job. He must have time to eat, sleep, and relax away from his job. If he works 10 hours each day for 5 days of the week, he works 50 hours a week, and since there are 168 hours in the week, he has leisure time of 118 hours. Thus if L_A is the number of leisure hours Mr. A has and X_A is the number of hours he works each week, then $X_A = 168 - L_A$.

If the hourly wage rate is given as P_X, then the more labor hours of work that Mr. A is willing to supply to the market each week X_A, the larger will be his money income I_A. Thus, the next step is simply for Mr. A to compare the value of an additional leisure hour with the value of the additional money income that he would receive if he worked that hour instead. Since it is

[1] Immigration might increase the labor supply by changing the number of workers in the economy. Since each worker is a consumer as well, it would also change the number of consumers, and the model, though unchanged in basic form, would expand in size. However, the basic form of the model would have to be altered somewhat if the rate of immigration were in some *systematic* way related to other economic variables in the system. For the present no attempt will be made to introduce the complicated change in the structure of the model that would come about from changes in the rate of immigration.

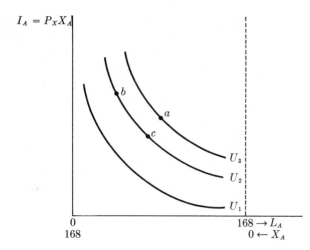

Figure 5.1

possible for him to substitute leisure for money income or money income for leisure, there exist the ingredients for constructing another substitution function. Let money income be measured along the vertical axis, and let leisure hours L_A be measured from left to right along the horizontal axis as in Fig. 5.1. Since there are 168 hours in a week, the maximum length of the horizontal axis is 168. The time Mr. A spends at work X_A can also be measured on the horizontal by reading from right to left beginning at 168.

This substitution function, with indifference curves shaped in the usual way, may be read in the usual fashion. For example, by moving to the right along any indifference curve—say, U_1—the slope of the curve falls in absolute value. This shape indicates that as Mr. A's money income decreases he must be given increasingly larger amounts of leisure time to compensate him for the loss of a unit of income. Or, conversely, moving leftward up U_1, Mr. A is willing to give up an additional hour of leisure time only under the inducement of increasingly larger amounts of money income. Since giving up additional hours of leisure is the same as spending more hours on the job, the shape of U_1 indicates that Mr. A will work additional hours each week only under the inducement of increasingly larger amounts of money income.

If Mr. A has certain skills that producers will buy in the labor market at a going wage rate per hour of work, and if this labor service is Mr. A's only source of income, then his

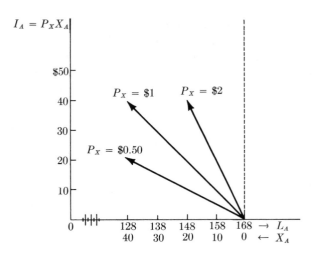

Figure 5.2

wage constraint consists of a straight line originating at **168** with a slope equal to minus P_X. Examples of this wage constraint are shown in Fig. 5.2. As the wage rate P_X becomes larger, the slope of the wage constraint becomes steeper negatively.

Figure 5.3 is formed by superimposing the preference function from Fig. 5.1 on Fig. 5.2. One can now observe selected points of tangency of wage constraint lines with indifference curves for leisure (work) and money income. These points indicate, for a given wage rate, how many hours of work Mr. A will freely supply to the market for labor services. Thus, Mr. A's

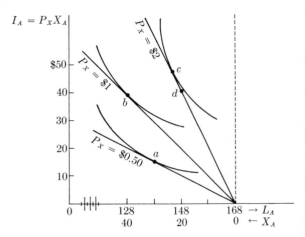

Figure 5.3

willingness to supply labor service depends on the price of labor and on his preferences or desires for leisure and money income. The maximizing principle is that the marginal rate of substitution of leisure for money income, the slope of the indifference curve, must equal the negative of the wage rate.[1] In algebraic terms,

$$_AMRS_{L,P_XX_A} = \frac{\Delta P_X X_A}{\Delta L} = -P_X$$

From the example, as drawn in the diagram, Mr. A will work 30 hours per week if the wage rate is $.50, 40 hours if the wage rate is $1.00, but only 25 hours if the wage rate is $2.00 per hour. By connecting these points one could construct Mr. A's *offer curve* for labor. Thus, depending upon the shape of preference functions, higher wage rates may lead workers to work longer or shorter hours. However, at very low wages, given that preference functions are concave from above, people will work only a few hours each week. This may explain why poor people often appear to lack in willingness to work. This is often construed as laziness, but it is wrong to do so. If, say, an additional 10 cents per day were all the added income one could expect from working an additional hour each day, who could be expected to work the additional hour? Surely the extra hour of leisure would be more valuable than the additional dime so long as the dimes earned from a few hours of work would purchase basic amounts of food and shelter. Similarly, at very high levels of income earned by high wage rates, even higher wage rates may lead to the acceptance of a shorter work week.

5.2 THE SUPPLY CURVE OF LABOR

The foregoing analysis leads economists to believe in the existence of a *backward-bending* short-run supply curve of labor. If the wage rate P_X is plotted on the vertical axis and the number of man-hours of labor service offered to the market X_A is plotted

---

[1] If $X + L = 168$, then $X = 168 - L$ and $dX/dL = -1$. Since income is held to be directly proportional to the number of hours worked each week, $I = P_X X$, then $dI/dX = P_X$. The slope of an indifference curve is $dI/dL = (dI/dX)(dX/dL)$ by the chain rule. Therefore

$$\frac{dI}{dL} = P_X(-1) = -P_X$$

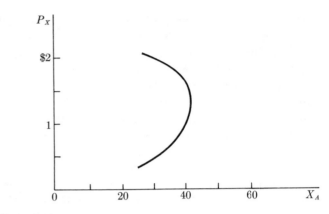

Figure 5.4

on the horizontal axis, the supply curve for labor would appear as in Fig. 5.4.

Reducing the effective rate of wages by imposition of a progressive income-tax structure, for example, may lead to an increase in labor effort on the part of taxpayers (as it will if the supply curve is negatively sloped), or it may reduce labor effort (if positively sloped) as critics of the progressive tax structure claim. There is no clear empirical evidence on either side of this issue, and existing theory alone fails to provide a definitive answer.

If Mr. A had income from sources other than labor service, such as rent from land or interest on capital or even welfare payments, then the originating point for the wage constraints would not be at $L = 168$ as in Fig. 5.3, but would be at the appropriate point vertically above $L = 168$. If workers are paid "time and a half" for overtime (over 40 hours per week), the wage constraint will have a kink in it at $X_A = 40$. The slope of the new part of the wage constraint will be steeper. This wage mechanism may induce Mr. A to work longer hours each week. An elaboration of these and other issues appears in Sec. 5.8.

The prevalence of "moonlighting," working at a second job surreptitiously in defiance of administrative regulations governing the first job, provides empirical evidence that many individuals have leisure–money-income preference functions with properties of the sort just described. If in Fig. 5.3 a vertical line were drawn where $X_A = 20$, and if the wage rate remained at $P_X = \$2$, then Mr. A's satisfaction level would be represented by the indifference curve passing through point d. This is not a maximizing position for Mr. A because he is constrained by the administrative regulation that limits his work to 20 hours a week. In a free society, consumers should be free, not only to choose what they wish to buy and vote for whom they wish to vote, but also to work for whom they wish to work and for as many hours as they wish. Regulations barring effective realization of these freedoms prohibit the maximization of individual satisfaction. It would be best, therefore, if some other means were found to deal with the problems that give rise to the imposition of antimoonlighting regulations, compulsory retirement, etc.

Another example of the use of this analytical tool concerns the social security system in the United States under which, between the ages of sixty-five and seventy-two, eligibility for social security payments is limited. Assume a man would receive $2,000 a year from social security if he did not work. If he took a part-time job and earned $1,000, he would receive social security payments of only $1,000. If he earned $2,000, he would receive no payments. That is, any job earnings he has will reduce his social security payments on a dollar for dollar basis. (Some state welfare payments are made on this basis too.) Under this system, some individuals are induced to retire. That this is so is easily discerned in any casual discussion with a group of men in the sixty-five to seventy-two age bracket. After age seventy-two the individual is eligible to receive his social security and keep any earnings he has as well. Thus, the system tends to induce a 7-year period of retirement. (See Exercise 5.9 for reference to revisions in this law.)

5.3 ADDING TWO WORKERS TO THE MODEL

Leaving the examples and returning to the system as a whole, effort functions for Mr. A and Mr. B can be introduced in algebraic rather than graphic form. In the above analysis, the equilibrium amount of work offered by Mr. A was determined for a given price of X_A, that is, for a given wage rate. But for the system as a whole P_X is one of the dependent variables determined by the interactions of all the forces in the system.

In Chap. 4 it was assumed that X_A and X_B were given in amount. Now, this assumption is relaxed and these two variables become dependent variables. In order to have a determinate solution set for all the dependent variables in the system it is necessary to have two additional functional relations. These can be derived from the utility functions for Mr. A and Mr. B since leisure time is introduced as another variable in each man's utility function. They now appear as

$$U_A = f(Q_{A,1}, Q_{A,2}, L_A, P_X X_A)$$
$$U_B = g(Q_{B,1}, Q_{B,2}, L_B, P_X X_B)$$

However, since $L = 168 - X$, by appropriately amending the form of the utility functions, X_A and X_B can be used in place of L_A and L_B so that

$$U_A = h(Q_{A,1}, Q_{A,2}, X_A, P_X X_A)$$
$$U_B = i(Q_{B,1}, Q_{B,2}, X_B, P_X X_B)$$

In the preceding chapter the variables X_A and X_B were independent variables given for the problem at hand. Here they are dependent variables, and with two additional dependent variables two additional equations are needed in order to have a determinate system. These two equations are derived by imposing the maximizing principle that each individual will freely set the amount of effort he offers to the producers' market each week in such a way that his marginal rate of substitution of leisure for money income equals the negative of the wage rate:

$$_A MRS_{L, P_X X_A} = -P_X \quad \text{and} \quad _B MRS_{L, P_X X_B} = -P_X$$

Having in this fashion allowed factor X to be variable in supply when it represents the amount of labor effort offered for sale in the producers' market each period, the two-person–two-good model now has two more unknowns and two more equations. Hence, the system remains determinate. When X becomes variable in supply, two other equations in the model must be altered. These are the budget equations for Mr. A and Mr. B. Formerly, the incomes of A and B were given; later they were dependent upon an endowment of factors owned by A and B and the prices that these factors would fetch in the producers' market. This step helped to integrate the producers' market and the consumers' market. Now, the budget equations for Mr. A and Mr. B are

$$P_1 Q_{A,1} + P_2 Q_{A,2} = P_X X_A + P_Y Y_A$$
$$P_1 Q_{B,1} + P_2 Q_{B,2} = P_X X_B + P_Y Y_B$$

in which X_A and X_B are no longer independent variables but are now dependent variables determined by the system, while Y_A and Y_B remain independent variables given for the problem at hand.

Some people prefer to work longer hours than others. In a free society if one is permitted to work as much as he likes at prevailing market wage rates, he can maximize his satisfaction. External forces that inhibit this free behavior will prevent this maximization.

5.4 VARIABLE AMOUNTS OF CAPITAL

Let us turn now to another factor of production that is variable in the amount supplied to the market each period, namely, capital goods. These goods are man-made resources; they are produced for use in the production of other goods. It should be clear that the introduction of capital goods into the paradigm of the general equilibrium system complicates the picture in many ways.

First, in the model so far it has been assumed that all of each good that is produced is sold each period. This *market-clearing* assumption is used in the model to give two equations which show that none of the quantities of goods 1 and 2 remain unsold. If we admit that some amounts of goods 1 and 2 are not sold but rather added to the stock of inventories of goods on hand, then there exists some postponement of consumption and these added inventories represent one form of the existence of capital goods. Second, one of the goods being produced may also be a capital good; that is, good 2 may be factor Y in reality and may be bought, not by consumers, but by producers of goods 1 and 2 for use in their production. Third, if some goods are produced but not directly consumed, then those individuals who receive money income from the sale of their ownership of factor supplies must have saved some of their income and lent it to producers, who, in turn, used it to purchase capital goods that flowed into the producers' market. Again both markets are cleared.

Since the paradigm of a market economy becomes so complex when the degree of abstraction is reduced, an analysis is provided here of savings behavior and of capital creation in abstraction from the remainder of the model. One can appreciate the manner in which the model would have to be expanded and altered if explicit account were to be taken of capital and savings.[1]

The successful producer of a commodity must examine a variety of aspects of a piece of machinery before he purchases it for use in the production process. Specifically he must establish the price of the machine, its expected length of life, and some means of allocating the cost of the machine over its lifetime. Depreciation and the means of accounting for it, as well as obsolescence, are matters of concern. For in purchasing a machine he buys a *stock* of services from which he intends to draw a flow of services each period. To measure the cost of the machine, therefore, he must establish the cost of this flow of services each period rather than the price of the machine which embodies this potential flow of services. Thus, in an analysis of production functions when the factor of production Y is thought of as a machine, then P_Y refers not to the selling price of the machine, but rather to the cost of the flow of services extracted from the machine each period. If a machine were leased, then under competitive conditions the cost per period under the leasing contract could be used to represent P_Y. In this case the lessor rather than the producer himself must evaluate depreciation, obsolescence, and so forth. In any case, someone must do the evaluation.

[1] In the model of the consumers' market, the sum of the incomes of Mr. A and Mr. B represents the total income of the two-person community. That is, $P_1Q_{A,1} + P_2Q_{A,2} = I_A$ and $P_1Q_{B,1} + P_2Q_{B,2} = I_B$; therefore, $I_A + I_B = I$. Since the condition was imposed that each consumer spend all of his income on the two consumers' goods, if C represents consumption, one can say that $C = I$. If Mr. A and Mr. B each saves part of his income the new budget equations for consumers might read $P_1Q_{A,1} + P_2Q_{A,2} + S_A = I_A$ and $P_1Q_{B,1} + P_2Q_{B,2} + S_B = I_B$, where S refers to savings. From these two equations one can now note that $I = C + S$ for the entire community. (There is no government and therefore no taxes or government expenditures in this abstract model. Furthermore, it is a *closed* economy, which means merely that we abstract from the existence of international trade as well.)

If, in addition, we note the expenditures of producers on factors X and Y, and if some of the supplies of these factors are devoted to the production of investment or capital goods INV, the producers' budget equations, when added together, become $(P_XX_1 + P_YY_1) + (P_XX_2 + P_YY_2) + (P_XX_{INV} + P_YY_{INV}) = Q_1 + Q_2 + INV = C + INV$. Since the left-hand side of the equation also measures total income I, again we have $I = C + INV$. From the consumers' market with savings behavior we found $I = C + S$; therefore, savings must equal investment. This is an important proposition in macroeconomics. (It is traditional to let Y represent income and I represent investment in macroeconomics, so that $Y = C + I = C + S$; but here we reserved Y to represent a factor of production and have departed from conventional macroeconomic presentation because of this.)

In a static world where machines never wore out or became obsolete a machine would continue to be worth the price that was originally paid for it even after the production period ended. But there still exists a cost of the flow of services from such a machine. It is represented by the interest charges on the funds that are "tied up" in the machine. Thus, if i represents the market rate of interest and P_M is the price of the machine, then $iP_M = P_Y$, which is the cost of the flow of services obtained from the machine.

When the machine has a limited life, however, it is necessary to increase P_Y in order to allow for the depreciation of the machine over its life by one of the methods devised by accountants. Just how this is to be done is a difficult subject that is not directly relevant to the purpose here. It is sufficient to note that certain acceptable methods for evaluation of costs, that is, for the evaluation of P_Y, are available.[1]

Thus, there exists a market in which machines are sold for what they cost to produce if the market is competitive; this price is P_M. But the price of the services of this machine to its *user* is more closely approximated by iP_M, or P_Y. The amount of services of Y that the producers of goods 1 and 2 hire each period will be determined along with other dependent variables by the interaction of the forces in the marketplace. Since P_Y is composed of both i and P_M, these prices must also be determined by the general system. The rate of interest i is a unique sort of price; it is the value of something at a future date expressed in terms of an amount of itself. The term is principally applied to money but may also be applied to units of a commodity.

Given i and P_M, one can determine P_Y; and given P_Y, the production function, and the producers' budgets, one can determine the allocation of scarce machine services among producers who compete for the limited supply. Since i and P_M are determined in the marketplace and are therefore dependent variables in their own right, they too must be explained by the general system. To accomplish this explanation it is necessary to consider another aspect of consumer behavior, namely, savings.

[1] If a machine were to be depreciated over 10 years and if funds were set aside to provide for its replacement at the end of this period, these funds might be invested and thereby earn interest. Therefore, the net interest cost of the machine in money terms would be lowered somewhat.

5.5 TIME-PREFERENCE FUNCTIONS

Assume that Mr. A decides to save part of his income. His budget equation that formerly expressed the principle that he spends all of his income each period is now adjusted to permit part of his income in a given period to be saved. Let this part be labeled S_A, so that the equation reads

$$I_A = P_1 Q_{A,1} + P_2 Q_{A,2} + S_A$$

(There will, of course, be a similar equation for Mr. B.) The variable S_A is a dependent variable in the expanded system of equations. In order to solve for it one must introduce another dimension to Mr. A's utility function. It involves an evaluation of the relationship between his income in the present period and his potential income in following periods. For simplicity it is best to consider only two periods, and since the new dimension carries with it a time period the superscripts 0 and 1 will denote the initial and subsequent periods, respectively.

Thus, the difference $I_A^1 - I_A^0$ indicates the change in Mr. A's income from period 0 to 1. It is assumed that Mr. A has a utility function called a *time-preference function* that reveals his preference for present income over future income or vice versa. These preferences may be illustrated on an indifference map analogous to the ones that have been drawn for commodities, as in Fig. 5.5. On the horizontal axis Mr. A's initial period income

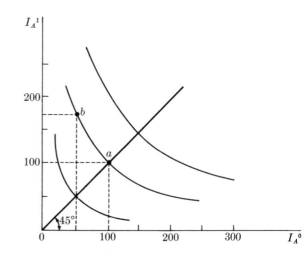

Figure 5.5

is noted $I_A{}^0$. On the vertical axis is $I_A{}^1$, Mr. A's income for the next period. If it is assumed that his income from wages and rents is the same for each of the two periods then these parts of his income stream can be represented by a point on a 45° line drawn out of the origin. Let point a represent his income from these sources for each of the two periods. Whether or not Mr. A chooses to consume his entire income each period in preference to saving some of his income in the initial period and then, with interest returns on these savings, earning a higher income in the second period depends upon his time-preference map. According to the map as drawn Mr. A would be as satisfied with incomes of 100 each period as he would with an income of 50 in the initial period and 170 in the subsequent period since points a and b are both on the same indifference curve in Mr. A's preference map. Any point that lies on an indifference curve above or to the right of his present curve represents a preferred pattern of incomes for the two periods.

5.6 INTEREST RATES AND SAVINGS DECISIONS

As in the case of the consumers' market, in order to illustrate the final position chosen by Mr. A, a budget constraint must be imposed; this appears in Fig. 5.6. It is drawn for a *given* market rate of interest, which determines the slope of the curve, and for a *given* amount of income from wages and rents, which determines the position of the curve. The slope of the curve

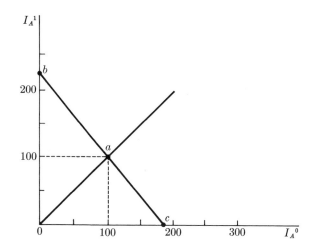

Figure 5.6

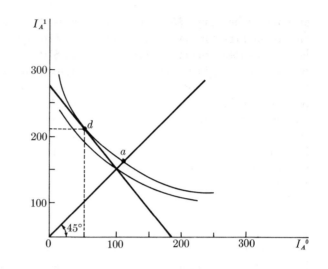

Figure 5.7

is $-(1 + i)$. By examining the intersection points of the curve
with the two axes, one may observe the various alternative patterns of total income open to Mr. A for each of the two periods. If $i = 20$ percent, or 0.20, then by borrowing at discount
$83.33 this period he can have total income of $183.33 this period; but next period he will have to repay his entire next period's income of $100, $16.67 of which will represent interest
on his borrowing.[1] Point c represents this, for at point c in
time period 0 income is $183.33 and next period's income is
zero. Alternatively, if he saves all of this period's income, in
the next period he will have $220, the $100 he earns plus $120
that represents repayment to him of $100 principal and $20
interest on the loan that he made; point b represents this. (To
simplify the arithmetic it is assumed that the periods are 1
year, for this is the typical period used to express interest returns
of certain percentages.) By neither saving nor dissaving, Mr. A
could remain at point a. Thus, a curve with slope $-(1 + i)$
drawn through point a represents the constraint that Mr. A faces
when considering his preference for present over future income.
By superimposing this constraint on Mr. A's time-preference
map, the theory describes Mr. A's savings behavior.

In Fig. 5.7 it appears that he can reach his highest indifference
curve by assuming the position represented by point d. For

[1] Borrowing $83.33 and repaying $100 is, of course, approximately an
interest of 20 percent, for 20 percent of 83.33 is 16.66.

at point d he saves $50 this period, earns 20 percent interest on his savings for an interest return of $10, and in period 1 he realizes total income of $160. Of this, $100 is earnings from wages and rents, $10 is earnings from interest, and $50 is repayment of principal. Point d therefore represents the equilibrium position for Mr. A, for at this point Mr. A is engaging in the optimum level of saving. It is the point where Mr. A's marginal rate of time preference equals the slope of his *budget* constraint. In equation form one may express the principle that Mr. A maximizes his satisfaction from possible adjustments in his time-pattern of consumption:

$$_AMRTP_{0,1} = -(1 + i)$$

Here, $_AMRTP_{0,1}$ represents Mr. A's marginal rate of time preference, that is, the rate at which he is willing to substitute income in the current period for income in the subsequent period. It is, of course, the slope of his time-preference indifference curve. Also, i is a market rate of interest obtainable on lendable funds.

The preference map could as easily be constructed to show a point of equilibrium below the 45° line as above it. If the equilibrium position is below the line, it indicates that Mr. A prefers to borrow rather than save. Although some individuals save and others dissave, in the net there is some positive saving being done in most communities. However, there have been periods in certain communities where exceptions have occurred.

If time-preference functions have indifference curves that are convex as viewed from the origin, then there will be a larger volume of saving each period under a higher level of interest rates. With higher interest rates, individuals who saved some amount will now save larger amounts; others who dissaved will now dissave less than before, with the result that the total level of saving will increase. These conditions hold provided the level of income is affected only to a negligible extent by changes in interest rates.[1] Thus, the policy of a central bank to push up market rates of interest *may not*, in fact, result in higher levels of aggregate saving because these same high interest rates may reduce investment and income so that income receivers will actually save less in the aggregate. Thus, it is necessary to remember that in the final analysis conditions of employment

---

[1] If income is affected significantly, one might derive a backward-bending supply of savings function analogous to the supply of labor function described in Sec. 5.2.

and income are assumed to be determined by the interaction of time preference with all of the other elements of the general equilibrium system.

When legal regulations exist that impose a ceiling on the market rate of interest, then the volume of saving that consumers will do is less than it otherwise would be. For in such a case the effective budget constraint would have a slightly flatter slope. Given convexity of indifference curves the equilibrium rate of saving would be less than otherwise as long as consumers were free to maximize their utility from time preference under this new constraint. However, consumers find themselves in a position of receiving less satisfaction from their savings behavior than they would receive if no such artificial ceiling on rates existed. This can be seen in Fig. 5.7 above if, to represent the ceiling rate, one imagines a budget constraint drawn through point *a* that is *slightly* flatter than the one appearing in the figure. Here, the consumer cannot reach an indifference curve that is as high in utility as the one he attained originally. Therefore, the artificially imposed ceiling on rates prevents the maximization of satisfaction from consumers' savings behavior.[1]

The reader may also imagine the construction of a *savings-offer curve,* that is, a curve that would indicate the various amounts of saving that Mr. A would undertake for each possible different level of the interest rate. From this information it is possible to construct a *supply of savings* relationship. (Because of the close proximity of interest rate budget lines and indifference curves, to graph the savings-offer curve would require an enlargement of the central portion of the graph.)

It is also possible to construct a box diagram under the presumption that there are two consumers, one who saves and the other who lends. The interacting forces of the marketplace will serve to determine an equilibrium market rate of interest such that the amount of lending done by one consumer just equals the amount of borrowing by the other consumer. And any administered interest rate that differs from the market rate could be shown to force both parties to the transaction into a position in which both would be worse off than if the market rate obtained. We may employ the same basic format for box diagrams as used in Chap. 2.

---

[1] If the consumer were a borrower initially, then a ceiling would allow him to reach a higher indifference curve.

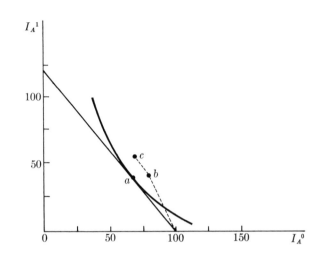

Figure 5.8

The picture of Mr. A's time-preference function provided by
Fig. 5.7 allows one to demonstrate his savings and borrowing
behavior. A similar graph can be used to illustrate investment
behavior. In Fig. 5.8 Mr. A's income in period 0 is $100, and
here, *unlike* the analysis above, it is assumed that he has no
income in the period 1 except what he may carry over from
period 0. Thus, the budget constraint line passes through the
point where I_A^0 = $100, with slope $-(1+i)$. Given that Mr. A
sees no other opportunities for employment of funds, he can
save some part of his income this period, lend it out at interest,
and, given his preferences for present over future consumption,
receive income in period 1 as indicated by, say, point a. In
this way, he maximizes his satisfaction for here he attains the
highest indifference curve within his reach.

Assume, however, that Mr. A is aware of opportunities to
invest his savings in real productive facilities. It comes to his
attention that the purchase of a $20 machine will enable him to
have a return of, say, 100 percent.[1] This is indicated by a
dotted vector from I_A^0 = 100 to point b, which lies above the
point where I_A^0 = $80. The slope of the vector is -2. Thus,
by investing $20 in a machine it is possible for Mr. A to have

[1] The 100 percent figure is arrived at by discounting future net operating
income from employment of the machine by the opportunity cost of capital (approximately equal to the market rate of interest).

income of $40 in period $I_A{}^1$. He may also know of a second investment opportunity for, say, $10, that will yield a return of 50 percent; this rate of return is indicated by the slope of a vector from b to c. He may know of other opportunities for investment as well. In this way one may construct an *investment opportunity curve* for Mr. A. These opportunities have been arrayed so that the highest-yielding investments are listed first and lower-yielding ones follow in order. By assuming that there are a large number of small investments available, with varying yields, a smooth investment opportunity curve can be drawn as the curve labeled IO in Fig. 5.9.

Figure 5.9 now contains enough to suggest how Mr. A can maximize his satisfaction from his combined savings and investment behavior.[1] His income initially is OG. If he sees no investment opportunities, he can move to point a, consuming OE this period and OC next period; here he reaches utility level U_1. However, if certain investments can yield returns greater than the market rate of interest, he can invest his funds (rather than lend them at the market rate of interest), consuming OD this period and OA next period as indicated by point b. But he is not maximizing his satisfaction at b, for here his marginal rate of time preference (slope of the indifference curve through point b) is greater in absolute value than the slope of the budget line. Thus, he is better off if he now borrows DF at the market

---

[1] Time-preference functions and investment opportunity curves were first described by Irving Fisher, "The Theory of Interest," 1930. Reprinted by Augustus M. Kelly, New York, 1961.

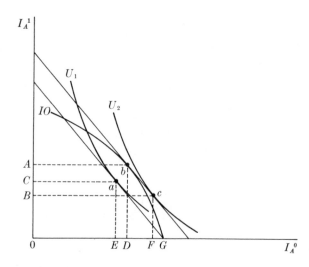

Figure 5.9

rate of interest so that he can consume OF this period and OB next period. In this way, he reaches utility level U_2. Thus, as far as Mr. A is concerned, he borrows and lends at the same time (his investment being a loan to the productive enterprise) in a perfectly rational attempt to maximize his satisfaction.

Note that he invests up to the point where the return on the marginal investment (indicated by the slope of the investment opportunity curve) just equals the market rate of interest (indicated by the slope of the budget constraint line tangent to point b). Thus, in general equilibrium there is a tendency for additional investment to be undertaken until the *real* rate of interest (return to investment) just equals the money rate of interest (the return to saving).

Having provided the picture of Mr. A's behavior, one can now speculate on the behavior of others. Since GD does not equal DF, Mr. A invests (saves) more than he borrows. Others in the economy are willing to borrow and save as well. In final equilibrium the amount of borrowing done altogether must equal the total amount of lending done, for there are two parties to every transaction. An equivalent way to put it is to say that the amount of saving (lending) done altogether must equal the amount of investment (borrowing) undertaken. One must be careful not to confuse *financial* savings and investment with *real* savings and investment at this point. If I buy existing bonds from someone else, then I have saved and he has dissaved; but this transfer of ownership, however important it is in the analysis of financial markets, does not represent any net change in the total of real savings and investment.[1]

In this chapter certain extensions of the general equilibrium model have been considered. It is as if, in constructing the analytical framework, it was decided to finish the attic or add a room in order to have a little more liveable space, that is, in order to be a bit more realistic in the recognition of a few of the numerous interrelationships that tie our economic system together. First, the model was extended to include an *effort* function that represents the willingness of workers to spend time on the job in comparison with their desires for leisure time. Second, the model was extended by a brief consideration of the role of investment, or capital, goods and how the prices of these

---

[1] Several assumptions are implicit in the analysis of Fig. 5.9: that capital markets are perfect, that no transactions costs inhibit the investor, and that riskiness is absent or that all investors are in the same risk class.

goods are determined. Third, the willingness of consumers to save and thereby provide funds for the purchase and production of capital goods was the subject of an extension of the model. In the second and third extensions there was implicit concern with the role of money and capital markets in the multilateral determination of all prices and quantities of the marketplace.

At this point, it is desirable to admonish the reader to recall the discussion in Chap. 1 on the purposes for constructing this theoretical paradigm. It is not to describe reality, but rather to focus attention on those general forces that prevail in any economy and that must be reckoned with. The reader must not personalize the theory. Mr. A and Mr. B are abstractions, not persons. There may be no single person in real life who behaves like either one of these characters, for they are imaginary. The theory's claim to usefulness, then, is that it enhances one's understanding of the nature of forces at work in a pricing system. This understanding helps economists to predict the *general* effects of change in the economic environment: What is the effect on wage rates of an increase in the working force? How will the price of oranges change with a freeze that destroys part of the crop? Economists' answers to these questions are most often in the form of statements of *direction* of change: the price will increase or wage rates will fall. On those occasions when estimates of the magnitude of the change are made, they should be couched in a probabilistic framework. And rarely, if ever, is the economist concerned with the reaction of a single individual or a single productive enterprise. Thus, the reader should always remember that the theory is meant to explain the interaction of the general forces at work and is not meant to describe or explain the behavior of any *specific* price or quantity. The theory does not explain why Joe Smith drives a taxi and Bill Jones cuts hair. It does not explain why a certain record by the Beatles sells for $3.98; but it does help us understand how prices and quantities are related to one another and how they are affected by external or independent forces.

5.8 A DIGRESSION: WORK, INCOME, AND LEISURE

This brief section contains further discussion of the *effort function* and helps to illustrate how it is useful as an analytical tool. The effort function describes an individual's preferences for income (I) and leisure (L). If leisure hours are measured along the horizontal axis and money income is measured on the vertical axis, then a set of convex (as viewed from the origin) indifference curves may be drawn, each of which shows a given level of satisfaction received by Mr. A. A hypothetical map of such indifference curves appears in Fig. 5.1. Point a in Fig. 5.1 is on a higher indifference curve than point c because Mr. A receives a higher level of satisfaction. At point a Mr. A has more income *and* more leisure time. Point b is also less satisfactory than point a even though Mr. A has more income at b. This is because point b also means more work and less leisure for Mr. A. Points b and c are both on the same indifference curve. At b Mr. A has more income but less leisure than at c. The greater income at b gives added satisfaction that just offsets the loss in satisfaction from the additional work demanded of Mr. A at c.

At various wage rates, Mr. A will work various amounts in order to maximize his satisfaction. Thus, in Fig. 5.2 the wage rate P_X is indicated by the negative slope of the straight lines drawn through the point at which $X = 0$ and $I = 0$. Measuring from right to left as the number of hours worked per week increases, then Mr. A's income $P_X X$ also increases. For a given P_X there is a given line that is similar to a budget constraint imposed on usual commodity indifference curves. Points of tangency of these wage lines and Mr. A's indifference curves generate an *offer curve* for effort or work. This offer curve appears in Fig. 5.10.

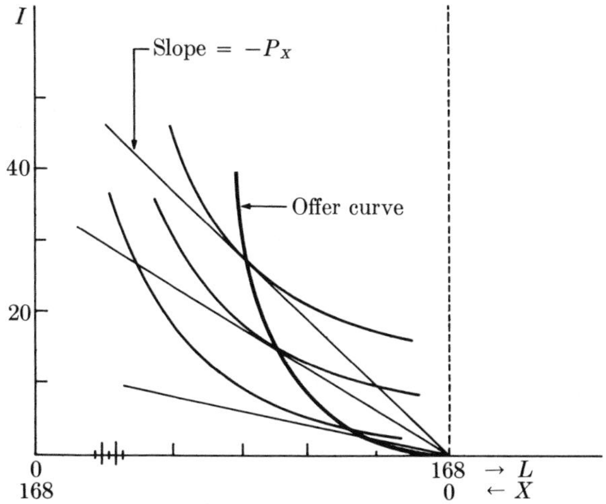

Figure 5.10

I

Slope $= -P_X$

Offer curve

40

20

0
168

168 → L
0 ← X

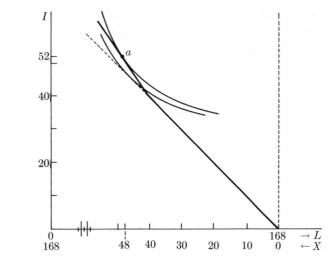

Figure 5.11

The nature of the offer curve is such that it must intersect the origin, where $X = 0$ and $I = 0$. Thus, at very low wage rates, Mr. A will work very few hours per week. This understanding resolves an apparent paradox. In many countries of the world wage rates are very low and the people appear to be lazy and unwilling to work hard in order to improve their lot in life; but if wage rates amount to very little, the value of leisure time is *relatively* great. The offer curve also indicates that after wage rates become very high Mr. A may reduce the hours in his work week. Thus, the amount of labor supplied during the week may fall as the standard of living increases. In the 1860s the work day was typically 12 hours long, 6 days per week. Now it is only 40 hours per week and in some places it has dropped to 35. As wage rates continue to increase, this trend will probably continue as well.

In Fig. 5.11 Mr. A's behavior under "time and a half" for overtime is depicted. For the first 40 hours of work P_X is $1; over 40 hours it is $1.50: the price line has a kink in it. Thus, total income per week $I = \$52$ when Mr. A works 48 hours. The effective average hourly wage becomes $1.0833, which is the absolute numerical value of the slope of a line (not shown) from the origin to point a. As long as the indifference curves are convex from below then "time and a half" induces Mr. A to work more hours than he would be willing to work if the rate of $1 per hour prevailed for all hours worked. Thus, "time and a half" is likely to induce people to work longer hours; this is expected. But what is more astounding is that for the *same* weekly pay check a laborer can be induced by "time and a half" to work *more* hours each week than he would willingly work otherwise. In Fig. 5.12 Mr. A works the hours indicated by point a at wage rate $P_X = \$1$. Under "time and a half" indicated by dotted price lines, he is induced to move to point b, thus working a larger number of hours for the same weekly income. Of course, if a laborer could freely choose between two jobs, one such that he could be at a and the other that would allow him only to reach point b, he would choose the former, for here he is on the highest indifference curve. Thus, the laborer can be induced to move to point b only if he works in a monopolistic labor market—a market in which there is only a single buyer or potential buyer of his labor service.

If the indifference curve tangent to point b is only barely above the point where $X = 0$ and $I = 0$, then the firm has made Mr. A only the slightest amount better off than he would be if he refused to work altogether. This acts as a limit to the extent to which the firm can *exploit* the laborer, for if the indifference curve passed below the point where $X = 0$ and $I = 0$, he would refuse to work at all. Thus, potentially, "time and a half" can be implemented to exploit labor if the employer has monopolistic power, and the exploitation can be greater under "time and a half" than it can be under any single wage rate.

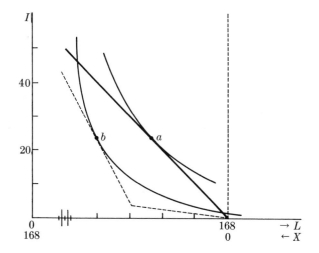

Figure 5.12

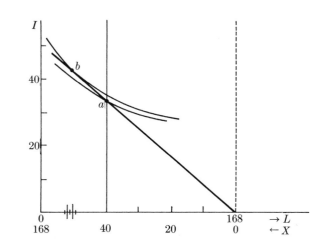

Figure 5.13

0			168 → L
168	40	20	0 ← X

If an administrative rule exists that prohibits an employee from working more than 40 hours per week, some laborers may wish to "moonlight." For example, the vertical line through point a in Fig. 5 13 represents the maximum number of hours in accordance with the administrative regulation; but Mr. A's indifference curve may intersect the price line at point a. Thus, some higher indifference curve may be tangent to the price line at point b, and Mr. A may therefore be induced to moonlight in order to reach this higher curve.

In Fig. 5.14 the price line originates at a position somewhat

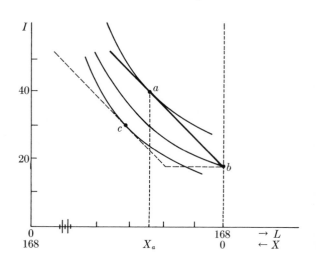

Figure 5.14

0			168 → L
168		X_a	0 ← X

above the point $X = 0$, say, point b. This indicates that Mr. A has income received from rent or interest and that the earnings from work represent an addition to this other income. Thus, Mr. A will move to point a by working X_a hours per week, for at this point he maximizes his satisfaction. If the initial income represented by point b is a welfare payment and if, as is frequently the case, this payment is reduced dollar for dollar for each dollar earned (this is true, for example, under social security for persons who work between the ages of sixty-five and seventy-two), then Mr. A's effective price line becomes the dashed line from b through c. If he works, the highest indifference curve he can reach is the one tangent to point c. But an even higher curve intersects point b. Thus, in order to maximize his position under these conditions, Mr. A will refuse to work and thereby reach the level of satisfaction indicated by the curve through point b. Thus, under any given wage rate, the provision that welfare payments be reduced by the amount of wages received has a tendency to induce people not to work.

EXERCISES

5.1 From an analysis of the supply curve for labor, and assuming that a proportional income tax has simply the effect of reducing the effective wage rate, analyze the likely effect of a higher income tax on the number of hours that people are willing to work each week.

5.2 Draw selected indifference curves derived from Mr. C's preference function for money income and leisure time. Show the wage rate and note the equilibrium number of hours per week that Mr. C will work. Analyze the equation describing the equilibrium solution.

5.3 When adding to the general equilibrium paradigm leisure-income preference functions for Mr. A and Mr. B, what changes must be made in equations, givens, and variables?

5.4 Discuss the relation between the price of an asset (say, a house) and the price (or cost) of the services of the asset.

5.5 Draw a graph with initial period income on the horizontal axis and subsequent period income on the vertical axis. Assume endowed income for Mr. C of $100 each period and draw indifference curves derived from a time-preference function to show that at current market interest rates Mr. C will dissave. Label the graph and note the amounts that he will save and consume in each period.

5.6 Draw a graph with axes as in Exercise 5.5. Let Mr. C be endowed with an income of $100 in the initial period and nothing in the subsequent period.   With indifference curves and varying interest rates derive a savings-offer curve for Mr. C.

5.7   Assume that Mr. A and Mr. B both expect to receive $100 this period and next period.   Draw a box diagram (it will be $200 square) with a point in the middle indicating these endowments. Draw in selected indifference curves reflecting the time-preferences of Mr. A and Mr. B.   Note a *contract* curve and show the amounts of saving and dissaving that Mr. A and Mr. B engage in an equilibrium and the interest rate at which these transactions occur. What is the maximizing principle involved for the two individuals?

5.8   Assume quite low wage rates for Mr. A's labor services.   By law introduce a minimum wage that is larger than the wage he is currently receiving.   Would you expect Mr. A to offer more or less labor time in the market?   What will likely happen to the rate of unemployment?

5.9   Legislation passed in October 1972 states that in retirement up to age seventy-two one can earn $2,100 without loss of social security benefits.   The worker will then begin to lose benefits at the rate of $1.00 for every $2.00 earned over $2,100.   Earnings from interest and dividends are not affected—only wage earnings. Thus the law discriminates against workers.   Use diagrams to show the impact of the law.

6

Welfare
under
General
Equilibrium

6.1 MAXIMUM WELFARE

The term *maximum welfare*, as it is used in formal economics, has a very restricted meaning; it was originally given this meaning by Vilfredo Pareto. Maximum welfare exists when conditions are such that no one person in the community can be made better off *without making some other person* worse off.[1] The reason for such exceptional restraint in the definition in formal economics is that there is at present no possible way to *prove*, say, that a dollar of additional income given to a poor person each period means more to him than it would to a rich person from whom it was taken. Indeed, it can be argued persuasively that an added dollar of income means a great deal to a rich person, and it may even help explain why he is rich, while a poor person may care very little about the income he has. The point is that no one knows for sure, and given the present state of the art there is no way to find out.

The prevalence of graduated tax schedules, under which high

[1] Some authors prefer to let this definition refer to maximum efficiency rather than maximum welfare—allowing the term *welfare* to be used in its popular sense. See, for example, H. T. Koplin, "Microeconomic Analysis," Harper & Row, New York, 1971.

income receivers are supposed to be taxed a larger proportion of their income than low income receivers, may reflect the belief on the part of the public that total welfare is somehow increased if some income is redistributed in the manner of Robin Hood— away from the rich in favor of the poor. Or it may simply reflect the power of the political majority to achieve, in the pursuit of private interest, a better position. The collection of taxes is not the whole story, of course, for one must also consider who receives the benefits of government. In many ways, people who are already rich receive the majority of benefits from the services provided by the government with the money collected. For example, national forests and parks are supported by everyone but are visited principally by persons with above the median income. Owners of private yachts and airplanes can use nautical charts provided by the government at considerable expense for only a nominal fee, and, of course, the poor of the community have little use for such charts. Thus, it is not necessarily true that a graduated income tax does *effectively* redistribute income away from the rich in favor of the poor. However, many, if not most, economists, if their opinions on the matter were sampled, would probably support the graduated tax system.

Economists call the problem of comparing one man's satisfaction from his income with that of another the problem of *interpersonal comparison of utility*. But even if there is no solution in sight for this problem, economists can and do make a number of assertions about welfare in the more restricted sense of making someone better off while making no one else worse off.

6.2 NECESSARY CONDITIONS

In developing this general equilibrium system in earlier chapters the conditions for maximum economic welfare were introduced. Here, they are summarized and specified as such. Think of the following basic components of an economy:

Goods: 1, 2, 3, . . .
Consumers: A, B, C, . . .
Factors of production: X, Y, Z, . . .
Industries (or countries):   α, β, γ, . . .

These conditions are necessary if *maximum welfare* is to obtain:

(1) $$_AMRS_{1,2} = {_B}MRS_{1,2} = \cdots = -\frac{P_1}{P_2}$$

This is the familiar condition, elaborated upon in Chap. 2, that each consumer freely behaves so as to maximize his satisfaction from his consumption behavior. Note that the condition must hold for *each* consumer and for *every* pair of goods. This condition may be stated in terms of the box-diagram analysis of the consumers' market by insisting that the consumers must consume such that each is on the contract curve. No one point on the contract curve is, from the point of view of welfare, better than any other point. The condition does *not* hold whenever two individuals are charged different prices for the same goods or when the free choice of consumers is barred in some way. Examples are easy to find. Students and professors often pay a lower price for tickets to athletic contests than must be paid by other members of the community. That this is an "uneconomic" situation is made evident by the obvious existence of desires to undertake further exchanges of tickets. Employees of transportation companies may often use the facilities of the company at a discount from the price paid by members of the public at large. Again, maximum welfare conditions are not met under these conditions, for if further exchanges of these privileges were permitted, both parties to the exchange would be made better off.

By way of example assume that Mr. A is privileged to purchase good 1 at discount. Mr. A may be a faculty member and good 1 may be football tickets. Assume that Mr. B is a local businessman, and that good 2 is the *numéraire* representative of other goods that sell at competitive prices and that are the same to both Mr. A and Mr. B. Then

$$|_A MRS_{1,2}| = \frac{P_{1,A}}{P_2} < \frac{P_{1,B}}{P_2} = |_B MRS_{1,2}|$$

This means that Mr. A will consume (given that he faces $P_{1,A}$ and P_2 and a certain income) that package that maximizes his satisfaction. Mr. B also consumes to maximize satisfaction. But the absolute value of Mr. A's marginal rate of substitution will be less than that of Mr. B. Thus, Mr. A would be willing to give up some units of good 1 in exchange for good 2, and Mr. B would be willing to give up some units of good 2 in exchange for good 1. Only arbitrary authority of some sort will prevent an exchange of tickets between Mr. A and Mr. B at some price between $P_{1,A}$ and $P_{1,B}$. Such further exchange, of course, puts both Mr. A and Mr. B on higher indifference curves.

$$(2) \qquad {}_aMRT_{1,2} = {}_\beta MRT_{1,2} = \cdots = -\frac{P_1}{P_2}$$

From the analysis of production functions the condition is imposed that the marginal rate of transformation of any good into another good must be the same for each industry (or country) and that they must equal the ratio of the prices of the two products. Note that this condition must hold for *each* industry and for *every* pair of products. A country may have certain advantages in the production of one good as opposed to another, but there are also many countries that produce a variety of quite dissimilar products. In equilibrium, managers of firms within a country are willing to undertake production of a marginal amount of nearly any product, some of which are currently imported as well as being produced at home; but, because of a lack of advantage, it might not be profitable to produce large additional amounts each period. Thus, specialization in production, the stuff of which wealth and income above the barest necessities is made (for without it each family would be self-sufficient and very poor), is noticeable in terms of total output of a good but not in terms of marginal amounts that any firm or country might produce.

The condition simply means that production should be carried on with resources in such a fashion that marginal amounts of resources could be reallocated to expand the production of some other good, and that the loss in physical output of one good each period is to the gain in output of the other good as the price of one good is to the price of the second good. If this condition did not hold, it would be possible to reallocate resources in a fashion such that a dollar's worth of output of good 1 given up would yield greater than a dollar's worth of output of good 2. Thus, this condition must hold for welfare to be maximized. The condition does not hold if certain industries have privileged positions such as those that arise from monopoly power, differential taxation rates, or subsidization programs.

$$(3) \qquad {}_AMRS_{1,2} = {}_aMRT_{1,2} = \cdots = -\frac{P_1}{P_2}$$

This condition is a combination of conditions 1 and 2. It must hold for all consumers and all industries or countries. For if it did not hold, it would then be possible to alter production and thereby enable consumers to substitute more of one good for less of another so as to reach a higher level of total satisfaction. In Chap. 4 the combination of the transformation curve with the community indifference curve provided an elaboration of the necessity for this condition. The condition cannot hold if excise taxes are levied or if tariffs or quotas are imposed on the free flow international trade.

$$\text{(4)} \qquad {}_\alpha MRS_{X,Y} = {}_\beta MRS_{X,Y} = \cdots = -\frac{P_X}{P_Y}$$

This condition is the familiar one discussed at greater length in Chap. 3. It expresses the principle that producers must arrange for the combination of factors for production in a fashion designed to maximize output. Under highly competitive markets, profit-seeking producers will conform to this principle of the maximization of output. If the condition were unfulfilled, then the marginal rate at which managers in one industry were willing to substitute, say, labor for capital would differ from the rate at which managers in the other industry were willing to make such a substitution. By trading factors, one with the other, both industries could then increase output each period. In the box diagram of the producers' market, any point on the contract curve satisfies this condition.

When labor unions are effective in the sense that they are able to command for their members a wage rate higher than the competitive market would otherwise bring, then this condition will not be met. Nor will it be met if firms have monopsonistic power over the factor resources that they purchase so that they can command the employment of resources at a lower price than that which the free competitive market would establish.

$$\text{(5)} \qquad {}_\alpha MP_{1,X} = {}_\beta MP_{1,X} = \cdots = \frac{P_X}{P_1}$$

This necessary condition for the maximization of economic welfare is one which has not been dealt with explicitly in the chapters above. It is called the *condition of optimum factor-product relations*. It must hold for *all* industries, for *all* factors, and for *all* products. $_aMP_1$ is industry α's marginal physical product of factor X in the production of good 1 (or marginal product in terms of physical units of output). If a single industry is observed, say α, then $_aMP_{1,X} = P_X/P_1$. By multiplying through by P_1 the formula reads $_aMP_{1,X}P_1 = P_X$. Its meaning is easier to understand in this form. The left-hand side of the equation is the *value* of the additional output of good 1 that an additional hour of labor service, say, would provide, for it expresses the additional output times the price this output will fetch in the marketplace. It is sometimes called the *value of the marginal product*, or the *marginal revenue product*, and is written as $MRP_{1,X}$. On the right-hand side is the price of the factor (say, the hourly wage paid to the laborer), and it represents the cost of employing this factor. Thus, in equilibrium the marginal *revenue* product of any factor must equal the cost of its employment if economic welfare is to be maximized.

To understand the reason for this more easily, consider the situation in which the equality does not hold; for example, let $_aMRP_{1,X} > P_X$. Translating this inequality into literary form, it reads as follows: The additional revenue obtained from employing an additional unit of labor service is greater than the cost of employment. Thus, managers of maximizing firms in the industry would wish to hire additional labor, for a net increase in profits would accrue to the firm if this were done. Now, as successive additional units of labor are hired, according to the law of diminishing marginal productivity (the law of diminishing returns discussed in Chap. 3), the left-hand side of the inequality will diminish until the inequality is removed. At this point no further reason exists to hire more or less labor, and the amount of labor being hired is, in one sense at least, optimal.

This necessary condition for the maximization of economic welfare is important to the analysis of the behavior of managers of firms under various market structures and is the subject of some elaboration at points in Chaps. 9 to 11. The condition is unlikely to hold in the absence of a highly competitive market, that is, in markets where firms have some degree of monopoly power. It will not hold if labor unions effectively exercise their power to impose make-work restrictions on the activities of their members.

(6) $_A MRS_{L,P_XX_A} = {}_B MRS_{L,P_XX_B} = \cdots = -P_X$

This necessary condition for maximum economic welfare was elaborated in Chap. 5. It relates to the desire for leisure time as compared with the desire for money income. Thus, if Mr. A is unable to work longer hours, produce more product, and thereby increase his money income and his total satisfaction, then he has maximized his position with respect to the possible trade-off between leisure and money income. The condition must hold for all workers if welfare is to be maximized. Artificial infringements on an individual's freedom to work as many hours as he likes each week, sometimes imposed by labor unions and other times imposed by administrative agencies that maintain antimoonlighting regulations, or compulsory retirement rules, all serve to inhibit the attainment of maximum satisfaction by the individual.

(7) $\quad _A MRTP_{I^0,I^1} = {}_B MRTP_{I^0,I^1} = \cdots = -(1 + i)$

For this condition to hold, Mr. A's marginal rate of time preference for present over future income must equal the negative value of one plus the market rate of interest. The same must hold for *all* individuals. Again, an elaboration of the meaning of this condition may be found in Chap. 5. It means that one ought not to be able to refrain from consumption this period, obtain more product to consume in future periods, and attain a higher level of satisfaction. In other words, one ought not to be able to increase his welfare by altering his rate of saving from its present level. For if he is able to increase his satisfaction in this way, welfare is not being maximized.

The interest return that Mr. A can receive is, of course, related uniquely to the price of the factor of production called capital, which has a role to play in conditions 4 and 5. It is this unique relationship among the price of capital, interest rates in the money market, and the rate of savings of individuals that ties together the level of investment and the rate of savings in such a fashion as to provide for the diversion of resources away from consumption and toward the production of investment goods. Taxes levied on investment, such as the interest-equalization tax being levied on purchases of foreign securities by the federal government, will prohibit some individuals from reaching the optimum position on their respective time-preference functions. Similarly, arbitrary limits on the interest that certain banking institutions are permitted to pay on deposit accounts tend to limit the flow of savings into the sorts of investments that such institutions finance, and again optimum savings-investment–time-preference equilibrium position is unattainable.

This completes the list of necessary conditions for the attainment of maximum economic welfare under the restricted definition of the term. There are other ways of stating the same conditions. It was noted, for example, that condition 3 was simply an explicit recognition of the relation between conditions 1 and 2, and could have been omitted. Condition 5 could have been stated in terms of what is called *marginal cost*. Condition 1 could be stated in terms of marginal utilities instead of in terms of marginal rates of substitution. Condition 4 could have been stated in terms of marginal productivity instead of marginal rates of substitution of factors of production. And all conditions could be stated in terms of the mathematics of symbolic logic as well. But the nature of the conditions would obtain regardless of the manner in which they are stated, and one particular frame of reference has been selected arbitrarily here.

Mention was made of the variety of institutional restraints that unions or governments or business trusts might impose that would prevent the maximization of welfare by effectively preventing the realization of the equilibrium equalities. Insofar as such institutional restraints meet with general public approval on noneconomic grounds, then they may or may not serve the ends that the public desires to achieve. But, in any case, to achieve these ends there is very real sacrifice in terms of the loss of economic welfare which, as often as not, remains unmeasurable in terms of market costs and accounting values.

Let us take a brief example to illustrate the point. It is only one of many possible examples. Most trading nations have not only tariffs on some imported goods, but also quotas. Thus, in the United States there is a limit on the number of pounds of Dutch Gouda cheese that can be imported each year, on the amount of sugar that can be imported, and on many other goods. The arguments used in support of the imposition of these restraints are usually spurious, but let us assume that the simplest and most forthright argument, that the quotas are designed for the express purpose of protecting the private interests of ownership in the cheese and sugar industries, is accepted as a desirable aim by the members of the community. What does it cost to administer the program of the customs authorities? This cost can be estimated. But what is the cost in terms of the loss of welfare and satisfaction among the individuals of the community from their inability to equate their marginal rates of substitution with the appropriate price ratios as expressed in condition 1 above? The marketplace does not generate a measure of their losses, but it exists as a cost just the same. Thus, the real cost to the community of supporting such programs is far greater than the out-of-pocket administrative costs. Since these are unknown, the members of the community have no way of determining whether the program is worthy of the costs of implementing it. Indeed, it can be shown that direct income payments provide a means of offering support to private interests that is more *efficient* than support provided by the imposition of quotas or tariffs; it is discussed in Chap. 9. (See also the questions at the end of this chapter.) There are numerous examples, of course, of cases in which optimality conditions cannot hold because of laws or other restraints on the free operation of the market pricing system. The one chosen is particularly onerous because of the multibillion dollar value of costs involved in the total of restraints on free international trade. For this reason, most economists vigorously support measures taken to reduce or remove such restraints.

Most discourse on the subject of maximum welfare concerns these necessary conditions rather than sufficient conditions. Necessary conditions must hold for maximum welfare but may hold even if welfare is not fully maximized. In developing the general equilibrium paradigm of the pricing system, the necessary conditions were made explicit. Here, the purpose was to group them together in order to reveal their fundamental role in the analysis of welfare. They can also be referred to as conditions for *paretian optimality* after Vilfredo Pareto who first began the study of such conditions.[1]

6.3 SUFFICIENT CONDITIONS FOR MAXIMUM WELFARE

The following conditions, if all hold simultaneously, are held to be *sufficient* to ensure the existence of paretian optimality:

1. A given endowment of factors of production, labor skill, etc., held by consumers.
2. A given set of goods; that is, no new goods are introduced.

[1] A recent translation from the 1927 French ed. of Pareto's "Manuel D'Economie Politique" is now available: Alfred N. Page (ed.), Augustus M. Kelley, New York, 1972. (Transl. by Ann S. Schweir.)

3. A given state of technology; that is, no new methods of production are introduced.
4. A given set of tastes; that is, there is no change in the attitudes or desires of people for the packages of goods that are available for consumption.
5. Indifference curves that do not cross, slope downward, and are *convex* as viewed from the origin.
6. Transformation curves derived from production functions that are *concave* as viewed from the origin.
7. Maximizing behavior of producers and consumers.
8. Perfect competition in the markets for goods and factors so no consumer or producer has unusual bargaining power.

The first four conditions are often assumed to exist implicitly, while the last four are elaborated upon. Tastes may change, of course, and so may technology; but when such changes occur, the pricing system seems to accommodate them quite rapidly through the process of adjustment that is inherent in it.[1] The direction of economic activity is, of course, greatly affected by changes in tastes and changes in technology. But these changes derive from noneconomic forces, and the economic system is merely one which provides a form of adaptability to such changes, whatever they may be. To predict the course of economic activity it is necessary to predict changes in tastes and technology as well as changes in prices and quantities. But to predict these changes one must rely on sociologists, psychologists, and other scientists. If sociologists were to provide a framework of analysis which could be attached to the general equilibrium framework of economics, then perhaps the formal integration of two social sciences could be realized.

Many questions with respect to welfare analysis remain unanswered. There are important moral and ethical questions. There are also questions concerning the positive content of the theory of general equilibrium. For example, the interdependencies of the relations in general equilibrium models leave certain questions regarding the *stability* of the equilibrium solution set of values in doubt. By stability, of course, is meant the direction of movement of a variable when a shock occurs that moves

---

[1] A theoretical process of adjustment in which repeated recontracting was allowed until equilibrium is reached was called *tâtonnement* by Leon Walras, the creator of the formal general equilibrium system.

it from its equilibrium position. If it continues to move farther away from its original position, the solution is said to be unstable. Forces that shock the economic system arise repeatedly in everyday life: a crop failure, a war, an invention or discovery, and so forth. Whether or not shocks to the system that result from the changes cause large divergences from equilibrium because the system is basically unstable or whether they only cause temporary· aberrations so that a rapid return to an approximation of the original solution set occurs are questions for which economists at present have no certain answers. Formal theory as yet gives no clear guide to answers for these questions. Thus, the welfare criterion, so intimately tied with properties of general equilibrium, is also left in a state of some uncertainty.

6.4 DISTRIBUTION OF INCOME

Maximum welfare and *paretian optimality* exist under conditions of perfect competition, and each owner of factors of production receives income equal to the marginal revenue product of the factors he owns, so that his income equals the value of what his factors produce. Chapter 4 above contains a brief discussion of the determination of income and of the distribution of income among individuals under general equilibrium, and there it was noted that a change in the original endowment of resources of individuals in the society brings about a change in the solution of prices, quantities, and incomes. In this context one can discuss the *ethical* question of the *best* income distribution and the attendant *welfare* questions. Is the distribution of income, under a given general equilibrium solution, the best distribution just because conditions of paretian optimality obtain? Although, as noted earlier, there is no way to know the answer to this question, it is nevertheless true that people can observe a particular distribution of income and say whether they like it or not.

As an extreme example, assume that someone is born without the physical or mental capacity to produce anything of value. Then his income simply must be provided by some means other than his earning power in a free pricing system. The ethics and morality of our society dictate that he must be assisted. Alongside this strong ethical standard is another nearly as strong. It is that each person should be rewarded in proportion to his contribution; that is, presumably, in terms of our economic jargon, he should be paid the value of his marginal product, for since he produced it, this is what he "deserves." The strength of this ethical standard is so paramount that it even provided the basis for Marx's principal criticism of capitalism. According to Marx, the workers produce all of the goods of society but receive only part of them. Of course, our theory holds that the workers share with capital and land in the production effort and that there is a return to capital and a return to land in the form of marginal revenue productivity just as there is a return to labor in the same form. Who is to receive the return to capital and who is to receive the return to land?

Property ownership is control over a stream of services. Income can be used to buy food for today's consumption or to buy a house and garden—assets that will provide a stream of services over time. If one is free to spend income as he sees fit to maximize his satisfaction, then he must be free, not only to make choices between different items of current consumption, but also to choose between these items and assets that provide consumption streams. If he is not free to own property, then he does not have freedom to spend his income as he sees fit. If he cannot bequeath his assets to his children, he again lacks freedom to dispose of his income in the manner of his choice. Thus, property ownership is intimately tied to the effective operation of the pricing system. However, when all is said and done there still remains the ethical question: Do you like the distribution of income the system generates or not? If you do not, then a redistribution of the ownership of land or of the ownership of capital or a redistribution of income through income taxes and welfare payments can help achieve the distribution you wish. Having made this redistribution, the pricing system, if free to operate in a competitive environment, will generate an *efficient* solution set of prices, quantities, and incomes. This discussion merely emphasizes that the ethical and normative issues of welfare will always remain whether the economic system is a competitive pricing system or any other system.

6.5 SECOND-BEST SOLUTIONS

A disquieting feature of general equilibrium concerns the way this system is affected when, for one reason or another, one of the welfare-maximizing conditions is unobtainable. In searching for the *second-best* solution it may be necessary to depart from other maximizing conditions. If so, it is difficult to know with certainty whether a policy designed to remove, say, a restriction on free trade will in fact leave members of the community economically better off than they would be if the existing impediment to free trade were retained. Although several economists had recognized the possibility of this outcome, little attention was paid to it until James E. Meade coined the phrase "second-best" in a lengthy discussion of the impact of customs unions.[1] Lipsey and Lancaster later provided a mathematical proof that the existence of second-best solutions does not involve competitive behavior in the *rest* of the economy.[2]

An example may help clarify the concept of second-best. If all paretian welfare conditions are met, then presumably the solution set of prices and quantities represents a particular *first-best* solution set. However, if a tariff exists on importation of a good for, say, political reasons and there exists no realistic opportunity to have this tariff removed—and so the people must live with it—then the second-best solution set of prices and quantities may involve departing from paretian optimality in other ways as well, perhaps by imposing another tariff on a complementary good. The precise nature of the secondary departure from paretian optimality is something about which economists are uncertain, but that a secondary departure is required to achieve a second-best solution in certain cases has been demonstrated.

An illustration in graphic form that is suggestive, but not conclusive, may be found in Fig. 6.1. Let curve AB represent a production-possibility frontier, and let I_0 be a community indifference curve. The curves are just tangent at point a. This figure is like Fig. 4.2 in Chap. 4. It is recalled that in country α the maximizing condition that $MRT_{1,2} = MRS_{1,2} = -P_1/P_2$ is satisfied at point a. By producing and consuming the package of goods represented by point a the community of individuals reaches the highest possible level of total satisfaction, and the goods exchange for each other at a relative price indicated by the slope of the curves at point a. Assume now that good 1 is woolen clothing and that it is produced with raw wool that

[1] J. E. Meade, "Trade and Welfare," Oxford University Press, London, 1955.

[2] R. G. Lipsey and R. K. Lancaster, The General Theory of Second Best, *Rev. Econ. Studies*, vol. XXIV(1), pp. 11–32, 1956–1957.

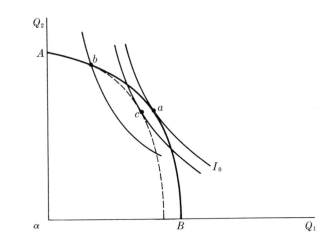

Figure 6.1

is imported. Assume further that an annual quota exists on the imports of wool and that after the quota is filled all further imports of raw wool can enter only after the payment of a tariff. Thus, as the quantity of good 1 produced increases from zero, producers can move along the curve from point a until they reach point b. As even more of good 1 is produced, however, the more costly (in terms of the amount of good 2 that must be foregone for additional amounts of good 1) it is to produce because of the tariff that now must be paid on raw wool imports. Hence, producers are constrained in their behavior and can only move along the dotted curve from b toward c. Recall that each point on the production-possibility frontier AB is derived from the contract curve in the box diagram, and for each point on the contract curve the condition $_1MRS_{X,Y} = {_2}MRS_{X,Y} = -P_X/P_Y$ holds. This is the condition that marginal rates of substitution of factors are equal whether they are employed in the production of good 1 or 2, and in this way production of the two goods is maximized in the sense that if the condition did not hold, more of both goods could be produced by reallocating factors X and Y in their employment appropriately. This maximizing condition does hold in the range from a to b, but it does not hold in the range from b to c. By producing at point b, this maximizing condition could be retained; but here consumers would be on a lower indifference curve than they would be at point c, where this maximizing condition is not met. Thus, a departure from the condition that $_1MRS_{X,Y} = {_2}MRS_{X,Y} = -P_X/P_Y$ is required in order to reach the second-best position, point c. If the tariff were removed, of course, the community could reach point a, the first-best solution. Given that the tariff cannot be removed, then one should no longer insist upon maintaining the condition for maximizing output, for at point b satisfaction is less than it is at point c. But the example is only suggestive, not definitive, for it merely shows how one should make the best of a bad and constrained situation and does not show how one bad situation requires another in order to make the best of it.

There is, as yet, no general theory of the second-best, but the possibility that one could be developed raises many questions about the promotion of economic policies that press toward the attainment of paretian optima. Can these policies be carried out in a "piece-meal" fashion without considerable loss of welfare in the process?[1] Presumably, the potential loss in welfare could be avoided if progress toward optimum conditions could be made simultaneously on all fronts. But this is not politically feasible in a world in which most problems are likely to be attacked successfully only one at a time. Thus, the second-best issue will doubtless persist as a cloud over the general equilibrium paradigm and its prescriptions for economic welfare for a considerable time to come.[2]

6.6 EXTERNALITIES AND PROPERTY RIGHTS

One final and widely recognized concern over welfare under general equilibrium is called the problem of *externalities*. If my neighbor spends a great deal of money to paint his house and maintain his lawn, I benefit from his expenditure. If a local factory pollutes the air with smoke, I suffer. These social benefits and costs are not measured in the marketplace. I am not required to pay my neighbor for the external benefits I receive from his efforts, nor is the owner of the factory required to reimburse me for the discomfort of impure air. Thus, there are social costs and social benefits that are not priced in the market.

[1] See O. A. Davis and A. B. Whinston, Welfare Economics and the Theory of Second Best, *Rev. Econ. Studies*, vol. XXXII, pp. 1–13, January 1965; and further discussion of these issues and bibliography in articles by McManus, Lipsey, Lancaster, Davis, Whinston, Negishi, and Bohm in *Rev. Econ. Studies*, vol. XXXIV, pp. 301–331, July 1967.

[2] For discussion of the policy implications of second-best, see William J. Baumol, Informed Judgment, Rigorous Theory and Public Policy, *Southern Econ. J.*, vol. XXXII, pp. 137–145, October 1965.

Some of these benefits and costs stem from the incompleteness of property rights. By its very nature the air we breathe must always be a common property. Another example of a common property resource is the fish in the sea. Social control of fishing, air pollution, and other activities involving common property resources is required in the interest of promoting the general welfare. To have efficient social control over these extramarket activities one must appropriately evaluate the effects of different instruments of social control on the general equilibrium system. This topic is discussed further in Chap. 11.

With this brief discussion of welfare, we conclude our discussion of general equilibrium.[1] The general equilibrium system is a logically consistent framework that economists use to rationalize the pricing system as a means for rationing goods and services among consumers and factors of production among producers. This system may be used to solve the problem of the allocation of scarce resources among alternative ends in an efficient or economical way. At least in one pertinent respect, one can say that if permitted to operate fully and freely, it would provide a *best* or *optimum* solution to the economic problem. But even if it does not operate fully, if planners are to plan effectively, they must understand the way in which the pricing system does operate, for the economic forces that the general equilibrium system describes are real and must be reckoned with in any economy.

EXERCISES

6.1 Using maximizing Eq. (2) from the text, assume that country α places a tariff on good 1 so that $P_{1,\alpha}$ is greater than $P_{1,\beta}$ while P_2 is the same for both α and β. Discuss why both countries could have more of both goods if the tariff were removed. Draw a box diagram showing the production-possibility curves for α and β when the tariff exists and describe the potential increase in output by both countries.

6.2 Using maximizing Eq. (4) from the text assume that factor X is labor and that unions have power to set $P_{X,\alpha}$ above $P_{X,\beta}$, that is, that the α industry is unionized and the β industry is not. Show by any technique you like that total output of goods 1 and 2 is below

[1] For further reading see: N. F. Laing, A Diagrammatic Approach to General Equilibrium Analysis, *Rev. Econ. Studies*, vol. XXX, pp. 43–55, February 1963; and Ronald W. Jones, The Structure of Simple General Equilibrium Models, *J. Political Economy*, vol. LXXIII, pp. 557–572, December 1965.

the maximum possible indicated by the production-possibility curve.

6.3 On a graph with the quantity of good 1 measured on the horizontal axis and the quantity of good 2 measured on the vertical axis draw an indifference curve and a budget line tangent to it. Label the point of tangency a. Assume that good 1 is housing and good 2 is a composite good representative of the purchasing power of Mr. A's income. Label the origin O, and the point on the horizontal axis directly below point a as H. Then to maximize his satisfaction Mr. A will purchase OH of housing. Label the point of intersection of the budget line with the vertical axis A.

Assume now that a rent subsidy is offered to Mr. A. Thus, for him the price of housing falls. Show a new budget line indicating this lower price of housing. Draw another indifference curve that is tangential to this new budget line and label the point of tangency b. Note the amount of housing that Mr. A will now consume by Hs. On the vertical axis, moving down from point A, show how much of good 2 (representative of money income) Mr. A gives up to buy housing. Indicate also the amount of good 2 the housing authority must contribute to assist Mr. A in the purchase of Hs amount of housing. This is equal to the vertical distance between point b and the original budget line. Does Mr. A buy more housing? Does he spend more or less on housing when he receives a subsidy? (Would this answer be different if the position of the indifference curves were changed?)

Now assume that the contribution made by the housing authority toward Mr. A's rent were given directly to Mr. A. This is accomplished by raising point A to a height equal to the vertical distance between b and the original budget line. Call the new point A'. Draw a budget line from A' through point b. This indicates that the original price of housing prevails and that the subsidy has been made in the form of a lump-sum payment to Mr. A rather than in the form of a lower price of housing (rent) to Mr. A. Is Mr. A now able to reach a higher level of satisfaction than he could have under the rent subsidy? Discuss, in general terms, the welfare implications of the analysis and your normative impressions of the two possible means of subsidizing housing.

6.4 Having worked through Exercise 6.3, now apply the same technique of analysis to show the difference in impact of a lump-sum income tax and an excise tax levied on good 1. The excise tax will *raise* the price of good 1. The vertical distance between the new point of equilibrium and the old budget constraint will indicate the tax revenues received by the government. Alternatively, this amount of revenue could be obtained directly from Mr. A and point A would be lowered accordingly. Given the original price of good 1, show that Mr. A can now reach a higher indifference curve than he could under the excise tax.

6.5   The purpose of this exercise is to illustrate that a proportional income tax may be less efficient than a lump-sum income tax because of the effect of the proportional tax upon the leisure–money-income position of the worker. The format is similar to that used in the two previous exercises.

Draw a figure like Fig. 5.3 showing only $P_X = \$1.00$ and $P_X = \$.50$. Equilibrium position b shows the appropriate X hours worked per week in the absence of a tax on income. Assume that the proportional income tax rate, t, is 50 percent. Thus, the pay rate to the employer is P_X; but take-home pay for the employee is tP_X, or $.5P_X$, and the lower price line represents the pay situation faced by the employee. Hence, he moves to equilibrium position a. Now draw a vertical line from point a to the line representing $P_X = \$1$. This distance represents the tax receipts of the government.

Now assume that the government levies a lump-sum tax of this amount. Show this by extending the vertical axis *below* the point at which $X_A = 0$ by the appropriate distance. From this point below axis draw a straight line through point a. This line should be parallel with the line showing $P_X = \$1.00$. Since this new price line intersects point a, it also intersects Mr. A's indifference curve that is tangent to point a. The new price line will therefore be a tangent to some indifference curve lying somewhere between points a and b. Show such a curve and label the point of tangency as point c.

At c the government receives the same tax revenue as before, and Mr. A reaches a higher level of satisfaction. If it were administratively possible to observe the vertical distance between a and the $P_X = \$1.00$ line, the government could simply levy a lump-sum tax of this amount and allow Mr. A to keep whatever wages he wished to earn in the market for his labor and he would be better off than he is at point a. In the absence of such administrative feasibility the proportional tax is probably the best that can be devised. What would the price line look like if marginal tax rates increased with income?

7

Demand
and
Supply

When a freeze in Florida destroys one-third of a season's orange crop, the price of oranges rises. This rise is sufficient to bring about a reduction in the consumption of oranges by several million tons. While any single individual may raise, lower, or leave unchanged his consumption rate, many individuals will consume less. In general equilibrium analysis it was shown that all prices and quantities were determined interdependently. Thus, failure of an orange crop in Florida would have an effect on the amount of fruit-processing machinery that would be produced and therefore on employment in the capital-goods industry in, say, Indiana, on the migration of labor to California, etc. The reverberations would permeate the economy. But the effects of an orange crop failure in Florida on the production of aircraft in Seattle may be so slight that for practical purposes they may be ignored when analyzing the economics of aircraft production. Similarly, the price of oranges may be insignificantly related to the consumption pattern of any given individual. That is, although interdependence is known to exist, for many purposes and problems it is convenient to ignore these forces that are insignificant. Of course, whether they are significant or insignificant depends upon the particular problem faced. The analyst must use his judgment, and this is not always easy to do.

When certain interdependencies are ignored, the economist is dealing in partial equilibrium analysis. Much of the analysis of the previous chapters has been partial equilibrium as, for example, when the consumers' market was subjected to detailed examination. For then the supplies of goods entering the market each period were assumed to be given by activity in the producers' market, as though the two markets were independent of each other. The most widely used framework of analysis in economics even today, some eighty years after its inception, is that of demand and supply, with which every reader is doubtless already familiar. Analysis of demand and supply is partial equilibrium analysis, for it is presumed that the forces that determine the position and the shape of the demand curve for a product are independent of those forces that determine the position and shape of the supply curve. Moreover, it is presumed that price or quantity can change with no residual effect on any of the other variables that serve to form the position and shape of the curves.

7.1 DERIVATION OF DEMAND CURVES

A partial equilibrium demand curve may be derived from the information of the consumers' market. The reader may return to Fig. 2.9 where the derivation of the *price-consumption curve* appears; it shows the quantities of good 2 that Mr. A will purchase for alternative prices of good 2. If one were to measure the price of good 2 on a vertical axis and the quantity of good 2 that Mr. A buys on the horizontal axis, then the *individual consumer demand curve* for good 2 can be constructed from the information gathered from the price-consumption curve; similarly, Mr. B's *individual consumer demand curve* could be constructed. By adding the individual demand curves for Mr. A, Mr. B, and other individuals in the economy, one could construct a *market demand curve* for good 2.

In this construction it is assumed that money income and prices of other goods remain unchanged. However, when the price-consumption curve was analyzed in Chap. 2 it was pointed out that a reduction in price had both substitution effects and real income effects associated with it. A reduction in price allows a consumer to move to a higher indifference curve and thereby realize a higher level of *real* income. Thus, implicit in the market demand curve constructed from the aggregation of individual demand curves is the relation between price and real income while money income remains unchanged.

Another demand curve can be derived from the analysis of the consumers' market. It differs from that derived by the aggregation of individual consumer demand curves. Readers may recall the eight-equation-model analysis of the consumers' market in Chap. 2. There, the quantity of good 1 and the quantity of good 2 flowing into the market each period were assumed to be given. One of the dependent variables was the price of good 1. By assuming a variety of values for the quantity of good 1 flowing into the market (i.e., letting Q_1 vary) and solving for the various values of P_1 that result from assuming different values of Q_1, a *market demand* schedule showing the relation between Q_1 and P_1 can be constructed: $P_1 = f(Q_1)$. In implicit form the function becomes $Q_1 = g(P_1)$, and the equilibrium price that is observed becomes that price at which the market is cleared, or the price that will just induce consumers to purchase all of the available quantity offered into the market each period. This demand function, however, implicitly allows for variation in the price of good 2, as well as for variation in real income, and because of this it differs from the demand curve constructed from the aggregation of individual demand curves under the assumption of a given price of good 2.

For example, assume that two goods are substitutes for each other. An increase in the rate at which one good is supplied to the market will lead to a reduction in its price. But there will then be a reduction in the demand for the second good and its price will also fall. Thus, the price of the first good will fall even further than it would have fallen if the price of the substitute had remained constant. To illustrate refer to Fig. 7.1. The rightmost demand curve in the figure illustrates the relation between the quantity of good 1 purchased and its price when the price of good 2 is given as $\bar{P}_2$. Assume that point a is the initial equilibrium position inasmuch as Q_a is the quantity forthcoming. Now let quantity increase to Q_b. The initial response will be a reduction in price as the new equilibrium point, point b, is reached. However, because of a relation between P_1 and P_2, the new lower P_1 leads to a lower P_2 and the curve shifts to the left to be consistent with $\bar{P}_2$. Thus, the new equilibrium is point c, and the demand curve that allows for variation in P_2 is the dashed

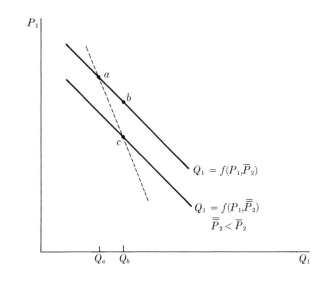

Figure 7.1

$$Q_1 = f(P_1, \overline{P}_2)$$

$$Q_1 = f(P_1, \overline{\overline{P}}_2)$$

$$\overline{\overline{P}}_2 < \overline{P}_2$$

line through points a and c. In constructing this demand curve one has simply moved a step further away from partial equilibrium analysis and closer to general equilibrium analysis. One could continue to take more steps that allow for more *feedback* from other parts of the general equilibrium model, but each step greatly impairs the clarity with which relations can be understood.

The shape of the different demand curves depends upon Mr. A's and Mr. B's preference functions. The *law of demand* holds that P_1 and Q_1 are negatively related. There are a few recognized exceptions to this law, but they are not generally believed to be so numerous as to weaken the law significantly. One exception was described earlier, that of the Giffen good (see Fig. 2.12). Another exception could conceivably occur, and some economists hold that it occurs quite frequently. Generally stemming from the writings of Thorstein Veblen, it is that the price of a good may itself be a variable in Mr. A's preference function. That is, if sold at a high price, a good may acquire prestige value and Mr. A's demand for it may increase with an increase in the price of it. This is supposed to typify goods that are "fashionable," especially among individuals in relatively high income brackets. However, the empirical evidence of this effect is somewhat hazy. In 1966 the makers of the £6,000 Aston Martin faced a decline in sales along with the rest of a depressed British economy. They reacted by reducing the price to £5,000, and sales began to boom again under the influence of this change in price. Thus, the conventional pattern does appear to hold, even in this case. And one can hardly think of a good that is more illustrative of a "prestige" good than this or a society more concerned with prestige than the European society in which this automobile is normally sold.

On the other hand, examples of what appear to be positively sloped demand curves for fashionable goods can be found. A reduction in the cost of producing mink coats may have led to a lower price *and* a reduction in the quantity of coats sold each year.[1] And since the theory of such an effect is logically consistent, the question of the existence of positively sloped demand curves is principally an empirical question—one to be tested by the evidence. How important it is to the effective operation of a pricing system is still in doubt. Veblen and many of his followers believe it to be very important, but most economists do not agree.

Another rational argument for the existence of positively sloping demand curves concerns the question of health and safety. A person undergoing an operation may seek out a doctor whose fees are high in the false belief that the successful outcome of the operation is more assured in this case. Also, in purchasing equipment that might jeopardize someone's life if it were to fail, the person responsible for the purchase may be likely to purchase the more expensive of two items even though they are, in fact, of identical quality. But these phenomena exist precisely because, as a *general* rule, a higher-priced item does imply a different item of higher quality. On occasion one may pay $100 for a $50 suit, or $50 for a $100 suit—but most often for $50 you get a $50 suit and for $100 you get a $100 suit. But, lack of information regarding quality may impart a perverse (positive) slope to a demand curve on rare occasions.

Thus, within the framework of partial equilibrium models, one may examine the several incidental forces that are unique to the determination of the particular price of a particular good, while at the same time ignoring most of the interdependencies with the rest of the economic system on the presumption that these are of negligible importance for the problem at hand.

[1] See: Dwight E. Robinson, The Economics of Fashion Demand, *Quart. J. Econ.* vol. LXXV, pp. 376–398, August 1961.

7.2 DERIVATION OF SUPPLY CURVES

Just as demand curves can be derived from the consumers' market, supply curves may be derived from the model of the producers' market. In a competitive world producers of good 1 have certain revenues obtained from the sales of this good to Mr. A and Mr. B. If the demand for this good increased and its price increased, revenues to the producers would also increase. For a time producers might pocket the extra revenues as profits, but soon competition would lead other producers to enter the market and these extra revenues would be spent on factors X and Y. Thus, output of good 1 would increase. By assuming different prices for good 1 and observing the different amounts of good 1 that are produced each period as a result, one can express the relationship between the quantity supplied and price as $Q_1 = f(P_1)$. The relationship between the two variables is held to be positive in most cases, so that an increase in price results in a larger output of good 1. An extended description of the relation of production functions to cost curves and supply curves is deferred until Chap. 8.

Demand and supply curves are only single examples of tools used in partial equilibrium analysis. The analysis of costs and revenues of a firm, of imperfect competition, of indifference curves, and of production functions are all partial equilibrium tools when used independently of the other elements in the general equilibrium model. It is to the use of these partial equilibrium tools that the remaining chapters of this book are devoted.

The simplest form of a demand curve is expressed in the formula $Q_d = f(P)$, where Q_d represents the quantity of the good that people will purchase each period and P is the price of the good in question. For some reason, in drawing a demand curve it became the convention among economists to place the variable P on the vertical axis, even though it is held to be the independent variable in the equation, and the variable Q on the horizontal axis. This is the opposite arrangement from that in mathematics where the convention is to place the independent variable on the horizontal axis.

In Fig. 7.2, a straight-line demand curve has been drawn from one axis to another. At price P_0 consumers will purchase Q_0 units of the good each period, and so forth. The aggregate tastes of consumers are reflected in this curve and it is a behavioral function derived in the case of any particular good from empirical evidence. It is frequently said that as the price falls the

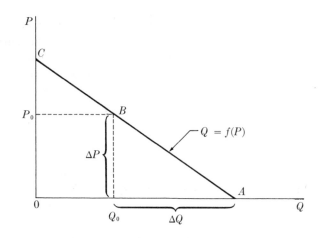

Figure 7.2

demand increases. Although everyone understands what is meant, it would be more appropriate to say that as the price falls the *quantity demanded* each period will increase. For an increase in demand means that at *each* and *every* price more will be bought each period than was bought before. Thus, an increase in demand implies a rightward shift in the *entire* curve.

7.3 THE COEFFICIENT OF ELASTICITY

The letters have been placed on the curve to assist in illustrating the meaning of the term *coefficient of elasticity* ϵ defined as the percentage change in quantity demanded divided by the percentage change in price. Thus

$$\epsilon = \frac{\Delta Q/Q}{\Delta P/P}$$

Here, $(\Delta Q/Q) \times 100$ represents the percentage change in quantity, and $(\Delta P/P) \times 100$ represents the percentage change in price. Since the 100s cancel, there is no need to include them in the equation. Most economics books follow the lead of Alfred Marshall, who defined elasticity as the *negative* of the ratio of the two percentages.[1] But it should be kept in mind by anyone working with actual measurement of demand that the negative slope of the curve implies that one of the Δ's will be negative so that the ratio will also be negative unless one defines the elasticity as the negative value of the ratio or as the absolute

---

[1] Alfred Marshall, "Principles of Economics," 8th ed., Mathematical Appendix, note 3, p. 839, The Macmillan Company, New York, 1949.

value of the ratio. Here, the minus sign will be left out of the definition of elasticity; hence, demand elasticity coefficients will carry a negative sign.

The formula for ϵ may also be written

$$\epsilon = \frac{\Delta Q}{\Delta P} \frac{P}{Q}$$

Since the curve is a straight line, the slope of the curve may be estimated geometrically by any right-angle triangle such as ABQ_0. Thus $\Delta Q = AQ_0$ and, thinking of a fall in price from P_0 to O, $\Delta P = -BQ_0 = -OP_0$. Since $P = OP_0$ and $Q = OQ_0$, substitution of the relevant geometric measures in terms of line segments in the equation for elasticity yields

$$\epsilon = \frac{\Delta Q}{\Delta P} \frac{P}{Q} = \frac{AQ_0}{OP_0} \frac{-OP_0}{OQ_0} = -\frac{AQ_0}{OQ_0}$$

By the laws of similar triangles it is also true that

$$\epsilon = -\frac{AQ_0}{OQ_0} = -\frac{AB}{BC} = -\frac{OP_0}{P_0C}$$

The value assumed by the ϵ coefficient holds for a *single* point on the demand curve. At some other point, the coefficient would assume a different value. If the demand curve is not a straight line, then the elasticity of demand at a single point on the curve can still be estimated by drawing a tangent to the curve at that point so as to intersect both axes. With this tangent line, the value of ϵ can be estimated in the above fashion.[1]

The term *elasticity*, as used in engineering, refers to the stretching of a material that follows from the application of a force. The analogy is appropriate here if one thinks of a price as a force, and the quantity of a good purchased as the material subject to stretch. Thus, if a small percentage change in price leads to a relatively large percentage change in quantity

---

[1] If the formula for a demand curve were given in place of a graph, the derivative of the function could be evaluated at a particular price (which would give the reciprocal of the slope as viewed in the graph since the axes are reversed) and this information on the slope, together with knowledge of P and Q, would enable one to compute ϵ mathematically.

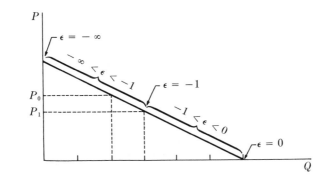

Figure 7.3

bought, the demand for a good is held to be elastic. If, on the other hand, it takes a relatively large percentage change in price to bring about even a small percentage change in the quantity bought, the demand for a good is held to be *inelastic*. To be exact the following inequalities define the ranges for the different types of elasticity of a demand curve:

$\epsilon = -\infty$	Perfectly elastic[1]
$-\infty < \epsilon < -1$	Elastic
$\epsilon = -1$	Of unit elasticity
$-1 < \epsilon < 0$	Inelastic
$\epsilon = 0$	Perfectly inelastic

The ranges for which these types of elasticities hold can be shown easily in a graph with a straight-line demand curve, as in Fig. 7.3.

Analysts are concerned about the shape of the demand curve because it indicates what happens to total revenue as a result of a change in price. Price times quantity equals total revenue—the total value of sales of the good each period. The area of one of the boxes drawn in with dotted lines represents total revenue from the sale of a certain quantity of this good. Knowledge of the elasticity coefficient indicates what would happen to total revenue if price were to change by a small amount. Thus, if the price were to fall from P_0 to P_1, the size of the box subtended by the relevant points on the line increases when

---

[1] Strictly speaking, mathematics does not permit us to define elasticity at points on the axes. The values there are called *indeterminate forms*.

$\epsilon < -1$; that is, total revenue increases. Therefore, when the price falls

1. If total revenue increases, demand is elastic.
2. If total revenue remains constant, demand is of unit elasticity.
3. If total revenue decreases, demand is inelastic.

A demand curve that is horizontal is perfectly elastic throughout; one that is vertical is perfectly inelastic throughout; and any rectangular hyperbola is of unit elasticity throughout since, for a rectangular hyperbola, PQ = constant. Other hyperbolic functions have constant elasticities throughout, for example, the function such that $\epsilon = -2$ at every point on the demand curve.

7.4 INCOME ELASTICITY

An extended version of a demand curve incorporates, not only price, but also income as a variable that is important in the determination of the quantity of a good that is bought each period. In the paradigm of the consumers' market, Mr. A's income as well as the price of a good was shown to be a significant determinant of quantity bought. Thus, let $Q_0 = f(P,Y)$. (Here, to conform to general usage, Y represents income rather than a factor of production as in previous chapters.)

To show this function in a graph with two dimensions, assume two values for income Y_0 and Y_1 and then draw the two curves variable in P and Q as in Fig. 7.4. In the figure it appears

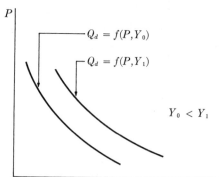

$$Q_d = f(P,Y_0)$$
$$Q_d = f(P,Y_1)$$
$$Y_0 < Y_1$$

Figure 7.4

that, for any given price, the higher the level of income the larger the quantity of this good purchased each period. This is the case of a *normal* good; but if the good were an *inferior* good, then the curve would have shifted leftward rather than rightward, and for any given price less of it would have been bought at the higher income level. It is assumed that all other prices are unchanged.

Including an income variable in the demand curve allows the introduction of the concept of the *income elasticity* of demand, in contrast with the previous discussion of *price elasticity* of demand. The definition of income elasticity of demand ϵ_Y is analogous in nearly all respects with price elasticity in that

$$\epsilon_Y = \frac{\Delta Q/Q}{\Delta Y/Y} = \frac{\Delta Q}{Q}\frac{Y}{\Delta Y}$$

Here, the *force* of concern is income rather than price, and the coefficient of income elasticity indicates the relative percentage change in quantity bought in response to a percentage change in income.

When concerned with the slope or elasticity of a simple demand curve such as $Q_d = g(P)$, the analyst simply operates under the assumption that the level of income is given. Similarly, one may assume that price is given and examine the function $Q_d = h(Y)$ for its characteristics such as slope and elasticity. One may draw examples of this function with Y measured on the vertical axis as shown in Fig. 7.5.

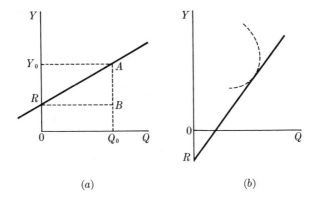

Figure 7.5   (a)   (b)

Using geometric line segment measures for the slope of the hypotenuse of the ABR triangle, $RB = OQ_0$ and is a measure of ΔQ as well as Q in the formula for income elasticity. Thus, $\Delta Q/Q = 1$. In the figure $Y = OY_0$ and $\Delta Y = AB = RY_0$ so that

$$\epsilon_Y = \frac{\Delta Q}{Q}\frac{Y}{\Delta Y} = \frac{OY_0}{RY_0}$$

where R is the intersection point of the curve with the vertical axis. If the curve is flat, point R is also point Y_0; therefore, RY_0 is zero while OY_0 remains positive so the elasticity coefficient is infinite, or perfectly elastic. As long as R is between Y_0 and the origin, for any point on the curve $\epsilon_Y > 1$, or is elastic. If R lies below the origin, $RY_0 > OY_0$, and $\epsilon_Y < 1$, or is inelastic. If R is on the origin, then $\epsilon_Y = 1$ for a curve with *any* slope.

When the function $Q_d = h(Y)$ is not linear but has curvature in it like that of the dotted line in Fig. 7.5b, a geometrical estimate of ϵ_Y can be made for any particular point by drawing the tangent to that point and noting where it intersects the vertical axis. If, as Y increases, the function turns back on itself so that it has a negative slope, the ϵ_Y coefficient becomes negative and is measured in the same way that the price elasticity coefficient is measured. It was shown in Chap. 2 that when less of a good was bought each period after an increase in income, this good was called an inferior good. Here, if ϵ_Y is negative, the good is inferior.[1]

7.5 CROSS ELASTICITY

In empirical estimation of demand curves, one must allow all of the nonnegligible variables to enter the equation. This is in keeping with the approach of partial equilibrium analysis. It is often a mistake to estimate demand simply as a function of price. Besides income, other important variables are the prices of close substitutes. For if the price of a close substitute varies greatly, it will have an important influence on the quantity of a good purchased each period. Thus, let the demand function for good 1 be $Q_1 = j(P_1, Y, P_2)$, where P_2 is the price of a good believed to be an

[1] If the demand function $Q_d = f(P_1 Y)$ is given mathematically, to find elasticities one simply takes the partial derivative of Q with respect to the relevant variable to find the proper slope and then evaluates this for given values of the other variables and substitutes it in the appropriate elasticity formula.

important substitute for good 1.   Then

$$\epsilon_{P_2} = \frac{\Delta Q_1/Q_1}{\Delta P_2/P_2} = \frac{\Delta Q_1}{\Delta P_2}\frac{P_2}{Q_1}$$

evaluated in the usual way.   It measures the responsiveness of the quantity of good 1 bought each period to a percentage change in the price of a second good.   The coefficient is called the coefficient of *cross elasticity* of demand.

If ϵ_{P_2} is positive, then a rise in P_2 leads to an increase in the quantity of good 1 bought, which is the case if goods 1 and 2 are substitutes for each other.   If $\epsilon_{P_2} = \infty$, the goods are perfect substitutes for each other.   (However, if one uses discrete values for ΔQ and ΔP as approximations in place of the infinitesimally small values used in calculus, computations in the above formula for ϵ_{P_2} may not yield a value of infinity even for perfect substitutes because of the error in approximation.)   If $\epsilon_{P_2} = 0$, the price of good 2 has no effect on the quantity of good 1 purchased.   In this case it may be possible to drop P_2 as a variable in the demand function.   Finally, ϵ_{P_2} may be negative instead of positive.   This occurs if a fall in the price of good 2 leads consumers to purchase, not only more of good 2, but also more of good 1.   Presumably a strong complementarity between goods 1 and 2 would lead to a negative value for ϵ_{P_2}.*

* It should be remembered that money income is assumed to be constant when ϵ_{P_2} is evaluated.   Our strict definition of *complementarity* offered in Chap. 3 required, not only money income, but also real income to remain constant.   Since the change in price used to evaluate ϵ_{P_2} implies a change in real income as well, it is not possible to use negative or positive cross elasticities as *certain* evidence of complementarity or substitutability.   However, strong positive elasticity is suggestive of substitutability and strong negative elasticity is suggestive of complementarity.

Mathematically, the concept of elasticity is perfectly general.   It measures the response of one variable, the dependent variable, to a change in another variable, an independent variable.   In the case of price elasticity of demand the coefficient describes the response of the quantity of the good that consumers will purchase each period to a change in the price of the good.   In the case of income elasticity the independent variable, or *force*, is income rather than price.   In the case of cross elasticity the force is the price of some other good rather than of the good in question.   If *own price* is the only argument in the demand function, e.g., if $Q = f(P)$, then the elasticity coefficient is simply

$$\epsilon = \frac{dQ}{dP}\frac{P}{Q}$$

If the function is linear, say, $Q = a + bP$, then $dQ/dP = b$ so that

$$\epsilon = b\frac{P}{Q}$$

7.6 HOMOGENEITY OF DEGREE ZERO AND THE MONEY ILLUSION IN DEMAND

For a moment assume that there are only two goods in the economy. Then if the prices of these two goods change by a given proportion and if individual incomes also change by the same proportion, it is assumed that the quantity of good 1 will not change. This is the assumption of the *absence of money illusion* on the part of the consumers. The demand function is said to be *homogeneous of degree zero*. (The reader may

---

According to the *law of demand*, the slope of the function is negative and hence $b \leq 0$; therefore $\epsilon \leq 0$. [Note that the slope of the function $Q = f(P)$ is the reciprocal of the implicit function $P = g(Q)$. Graphically, P appears on the vertical axis and Q on the horizontal axis.] If one computes the elasticity of supply the elasticity coefficient, as computed by the very same formula, will most often be positive. But, supply curves may be negatively sloped in some instances; there is no *law of supply* comparable to the law of demand. Most often, however, the quantity supplied each period is thought to increase when price increases. The elasticity coefficient can range in value from minus to plus infinity.

An example of an important nonlinear form of the demand function is $Q = aP^b$. Hence, $dQ/dP = abP^{b-1}$, and

$$\epsilon = \frac{dQ}{dP} \frac{P}{Q} = \frac{abP^{b-1}P}{Q} = \frac{abP^b}{Q}$$

Since $Q = aP^b$, everything cancels except b; therefore $\epsilon = b$. Elasticity is unchanged regardless of values assumed by P and Q.

Statisticians often use logarithmic transformations of the variables Q and P. The function $Q = aP^b$, transformed to logarithms, becomes $\ln Q = \ln a + b \ln P$, a function *linear in logarithms*. From this formula elasticity is simply $d \ln Q / d \ln P = b$. Plotting original values of P and Q for such a function on double-log graph paper gives a straight line, the slope of which is b.

If the demand function is of the form $Q_1 = f(P_1, P_2, Y)$, where P_2 is the price of a related good and Y is income, then three elasticity coefficients can be computed, one for each independent variable. These are *own-price elasticity*, *cross-price elasticity*, and *income elasticity*. The formulas are, respectively,

$$\epsilon_{P_1} = \frac{\partial Q_1}{\partial P_1} \frac{P_1}{Q_1}$$

$$\epsilon_{P_2} = \frac{\partial Q_1}{\partial P_2} \frac{P_2}{Q_1}$$

$$\epsilon_Y = \frac{\partial Q_1}{\partial Y} \frac{Y}{Q_1}$$

If $\epsilon_Y < 0$, good 1 is inferior; if $\epsilon_Y > 0$, good 1 is superior. For a demand curve ϵ_{P_1} should be negative. For a supply curve ϵ_{P_1} can be either positive or negative, but most likely will be positive. It will be negative only in special cases where there exist *economies of scale*.

recall the discussion of *homogeneity of degree n* in Chap. 3 as he follows through this example.) Assume a demand function $Q_1 = f(P_1, P_2, Y)$. Assume P_1, P_2, and Y each double in value. If there are no other prices then Mr. A, whose income has doubled, will buy precisely the same quantity of good 1 as before and so will Mr. B and all the other consumers; hence Q_1 remains unchanged. For the function *homogeneous of degree n*

$$\lambda^n Q_1 = \lambda^n f(P_1, P_2, Y) = f(\lambda P_1, \lambda P_2, \lambda Y)$$

and when $n = 0$, no change in Q_1 occurs because $\lambda^0 = 1$. Thus, when $\lambda = 2$, it assumed that P_1, P_2, and Y are each doubled, but the function shows that the quantity of good 1 purchased each period is unchanged; hence the function is homogeneous of degree zero.

If Q_1 did change under these conditions, one would suspect that the buyers were subject to a money illusion. They may feel or think, for example, that since their incomes have increased, they are richer then before and thus might attempt to increase their purchases of good 1 even at its higher price. Thus, it is generally assumed that demand functions are homogeneous of degree zero with respect to money prices and income, that is, that consumers are not misled in their purchasing behavior by changes in money values in which transactions take place. The subject of money illusion and its possible existence is most relevant to the study of the effects of changes in the money supply on income and will not be pursued further here.

In the construction of a demand curve it is evident that the determining variables should be, not only price, but also income, the prices of substitutes and complements, and indeed all other variables that significantly affect the quantity of a good purchased each period. If the period in question is a month, then a seasonal influence may be at work. The amount of ice cream sold may be affected by the average monthly temperature so that even *noneconomic* factors such as temperature may systematically affect tastes for a particular commodity. Population growth will also affect the quantity sold. Hence, in the empirical analysis of demand curves it is very rare to consider price as the *only* determining variable, and instead a more generalized form of a demand curve must be used.

To permit many variables to enter a demand curve illustrates at once both the strengths and the weaknesses of partial equilibrium analytical techniques. Strength lies in the wider applicability of the demand curve as a tool in practical affairs. But the weaknesses have two strands, and at base these often outweigh the strengths. The first is that as additional variables are introduced the analysis rapidly becomes more complex. A useful theory is a simple theory, and increasing complexity can, if carried too far, impair its usefulness so that what is a strength at the outset becomes a weakness. The second weakness is of greatest importance to the scientific merit of the demand curve as a tool of analysis.

If one sets no arbitrary limit to the number of variables that can be included in a demand function, in other words, if one leaves the demand curve *open-ended,* then whenever a prediction that is made on the basis of the demand curve fails to conform to reality, the scientist can always excuse his failure to predict by alluding to some *other* unaccounted-for variable that was "inadvertently" omitted. Analytical tools that are open-ended in this way are called *nonoperational,* meaning *nontestable,* for there is no way to disprove the theory in question. There is no way to disprove it because any disparity between prediction and subsequent events can always be attributed to some other originally unaccounted-for variable. The question of the necessity for a scientific hypothesis to be capable of refutation is still debated among philosophers who study the epistemological aspects of the scientific method. The arguments cannot be presented here, but it is desirable to draw attention to the questionable foundation of theoretical tools that lack well-defined limits.

It is best, therefore, to let the quantity demanded be a function of price, income, and prices of close substitutes and complements and leave it at that. If seasonal factors exist, they should be accounted for in the compilation of data. There is no theoretical justification for including other variables, and if the theory does not predict adequately for the purpose at hand when limited to this range of variables, then it should be rejected. The theory should be retained as long as it remains useful, but it should not be allowed to hinder the search for better theories.

7.7 SUPPLY CURVES AND THE ELASTICITY OF SUPPLY

Supply curves may be derived from the information contained in the theoretical description of the producers' market in Chap. 3. Practically every aspect of demand has its counterpart in supply. The supply function $Q_s = g(P)$ relates the amount of a good that will be offered for sale each period to the price paid for the good. The function is thought to be positively sloped in the short run and perhaps of zero slope in the long run for almost all commodities.

How many taxicabs, barbers, restaurants, are there in your home town? If customers offered a higher than current price for these services, would not more services be offered for sale (provided licensing arrangements were not inhibiting)? This is the essence of supply analysis—that a higher price will evoke a larger quantity supplied each period. The elasticity of supply ϵ_s is defined in precisely the same way as the elasticity of demand. Since the usual supply curve is positively sloped, the presentation of Fig. 7.5 showing elasticity in graphic form for a positively sloped curve could be interpreted as a presentation of the elasticity of supply by letting price replace income on the vertical axis.

The quantity of a good that producers are willing to supply each period will be affected, not only by its price, but also by costs of production; and these, in turn, are affected by labor contracts, licenses, some types of taxes, as well as rainfall, availability of raw materials, and so forth. Whenever someone wishes to look empirically at a supply curve, he should examine a healthy set of factors of this sort. But again, as in the case of the demand curve, primary emphasis should be given to prices and availability of factors of production, for otherwise the theory behind the inclusion of another variable becomes open-ended and is weakened to that extent.

When demand and supply schedules are combined for a single good, its equilibrium price and output are determined. In both functions $Q_d = f(P)$ and $Q_s = g(P)$ the variable P is the independent variable to which the forces giving rise to demand and to supply respond. If the supply function is positively sloped and the demand function is negatively sloped throughout, then there exists at most only one value for P and one value for Q consistent with both the forces of supply and the forces of demand.

Since, in the absence of taxes or other artificial restraints, the price paid by the purchaser is the same as the price received by the supplier, a nonequilibrium price reveals itself by the existence of two different quantities in the equations for demand and supply and empirically by the building up or the depletion of the stock

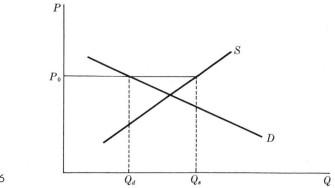

Figure 7.6

of the good as the rate of flow to consumers differs from the rate of production. In Fig. 7.6, at price P_0 the quantity purchased each period is only Q_d while the quantity produced is Q_s, and a glut of the good will soon cluster on the suppliers' shelves unless the price falls nearer to equilibrium. There is only one price for which Q_s and Q_d will be the same.

7.8 UNIT TAXES

If a unit tax were placed on the sale of a good and collected from the supplier, the effect on price and output can be shown easily with the help of another diagram. In Fig. 7.7, P_d is the price that the consumer pays for the good, P_s is the amount the supplier receives, and the difference between the two P's is the amount per unit that the government receives in taxes. The shaded area is the total tax bill from this one revenue source.

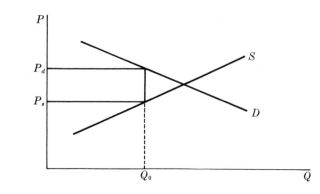

Figure 7.7

If the demand function were vertical, the price would rise by the full amount of the tax and there would be no change in the quantity sold each period. Suppliers would have little objection to such a tax in this case. If the supply function were vertical while the demand function remained as it was originally, then the price would not rise the slightest amount above the equilibrium price. Instead the suppliers would be forced to accept a lower price by an amount just equal to the tax. Again there would be no change in the quantity sold. Here, buyers would have little objection to the tax. If the supply function were horizontal, then a tax would result in an increase in the price of the good by the exact amount of the tax, but there would also be some reduction in quantity sold so that revenues to the government would be affected. Revenues might have been anticipated to equal tax times quantity, but, if quantity falls, revenues will be smaller by this amount. Buyers would complain and so would suppliers, for some suppliers would either cut output rates or abandon the business.

A government employee may not believe in the pricing system as an effective means of economic regulation, but were an excise tax proposed he would be foolish not to make some attempt to estimate the shapes of the demand and supply curves so that the likely impact of the tax could be evaluated. Indeed, a forecast of the effect of a tax is only possible if one implicitly believes that the pricing system works effectively as a rationing device.

7.9 PRICE-SUPPORT PROGRAMS

An excise tax, of course, is only one of many platforms available to show the usefulness of demand and supply as analytical tools. Another worthy of mention is a subsidy program such as that sometimes applied to certain agricultural crops. If government sets a price for, say, cotton higher than otherwise would prevail and maintains this price by purchasing any amounts produced in excess of what can be sold to the public, then the graph in Fig. 7.8 can be used to show the effects of this subsidy program on cotton.

In Fig. 7.8, for simplicity, the supply function has been drawn vertical in order to indicate that the amount of cotton offered for sale each period is inflexible, or insensitive, to price changes.

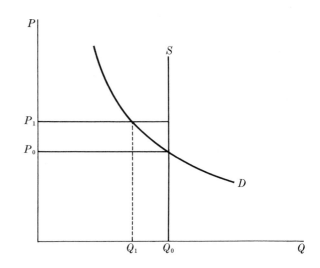

Figure 7.8

The market equilibrium price would be P_0, and people would purchase Q_0 cotton each period at this price. However, for some reason, the government finds it appropriate to support the cotton producers by setting the price somewhat higher at a level of P_1. At this price, consumers will purchase only Q_1 each period, leaving the government to purchase the remainder of the output perhaps for storage. Of course, if the supply curve were positively sloped rather than vertical, the government would have to store even larger amounts. (Under programs of this sort the United States government has stored vast quantities of commodities such as cotton and wheat and even butter.)

Although the partial equilibrium analysis implicit in the figure is simple and straightforward, nevertheless it provides an excellent example of a case in which a partial approach to a problem is unsatisfactory, except as it offers a very temporary palliative. For a single season the outcome is much as prescribed in the analysis, but as time passes other problems begin to arise. First, to keep domestic textile producers from going to the world market in search of a lower price, a tariff wall must be erected to keep out foreign-produced cotton. Later, the textile manufacturers will find shirts and sheets entering the country because they can be produced more cheaply abroad. Therefore, managers in the textile industry will either seek and receive higher tariffs on shirts and sheets, or they will cut back on production. A change in output of cotton shirts will also have some effect on the volume of production in the synthetic fiber industry. As time passes and the government's stockpiles of cotton increase, there will be pressure for legislation restricting output of cotton. Cotton producers may then be saddled with acreage restrictions and other administrative regulations. Thus, as the demand for cotton falls and more and more legislation and regulation are required, what began as a simple attempt to help cotton farmers brings with it a number of damaging side effects—so many that one wonders if the farmers are better off in the final outcome than they would have been if no attempt had been made to help them *initially*.

The analytical tool of supply and demand can be looked upon only as a first approximation. In its simple form it may be grossly misleading. However, if a limited but significant number of other nonnegligible variables, in addition to price and quantity, can be introduced to the analysis, the tool may serve quite well in many instances.

7.10 LONG- AND SHORT-RUN SUPPLY CURVES

The shape and position of supply curves may differ in the *short run* from what they are in the *long run*. The short run is defined to be that period of time for which at least one of the factors used in producing the good in question is *fixed* in supply. Thus, the law of diminishing returns discussed in Chap. 3 holds in the short run; that is, it holds when one factor of production is varied in amount while another factor is held fixed. Short-run supply curves are typically thought to be upward-sloping because of the diminishing marginal productivity of the variable factor of production as more of it is used in the production process to expand output. More will be said about this in Chap. 8. Here it is sufficient to note simply that long-run supply curves may be horizontal, as they are likely to be if industry production functions are homogeneous of degree one, or they may even be negatively sloped. It is the negatively sloped supply curve that creates a concern in the minds of economists about the *stability* of the equilibrium of the price and quantity determined by supply and demand.

7.11 WALRASIAN AND MARSHALLIAN STABILITY

As long as the demand curve falls downward to the right and the supply curve rises to the right then the equilibrium price is *stable*

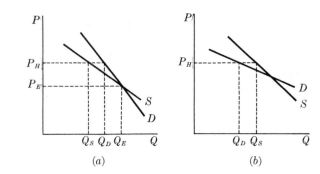

Figure 7.9   (a)   (b)

(a) Walrasian unstable; (b) walrasian stable.

in the sense that a movement of the price away from equilibrium sets in motion forces that lead to a return to the same equilibrium. However, when both demand and supply curves are falling downward to the right, the supply curve may intersect the demand curve in either of two ways: from below, as in Fig. 7.9a, or from above, as in Fig. 7.9b. In these cases the equilibrium price denoted by the intersection of demand and supply may be stable or unstable depending upon the reaction of forces set in motion by a shock that creates a departure from the equilibrium price.

Consider, for example, Fig. 7.9a. Here, P_E is the equilibrium price. Assume that somehow a higher price P_H is set on this good. Under this condition $Q_S < Q_D$; that is, the quantity supplied is less than the quantity demanded. In this case *buyers* may bid competitively for the limited supply and push the price up even higher. Every increase in price causes the divergence between the quantity demanded each period and the quantity offered for sale each period to become even greater than before; this may be called the condition for *walrasian instability*. Note that when the supply curve cuts the demand curve from above, as in Fig. 7.9b, at the price P_H, the inequality $Q_S > Q_D$ holds. Given this excess of supply over demand, *sellers* may react by lowering the price toward its equilibrium value. Thus, the condition is one of *walrasian stability*. In the walrasian cases, then, buyers bid up prices if demand exceeds supply and sellers cut prices if supply exceeds demand.

However, it is possible to interpret the reactions of buyers and sellers in a different way. Considering Fig. 7.10a, let Q_E be the equilibrium output and assume that supply is restricted to Q_L. Under this lower quantity note that $P_D > P_S$. When the demand price exceeds the supply price, assume that sellers offer more for sale. This leads to a reduction in price and return to equilibrium and may be called the condition for *marshallian stability.* In Fig. 7.10*b*, $P_D < P_S$ and sellers may reduce their output and push the price even higher and further away from equilibrium. This may be called *marshallian instability.* Thus, in the walrasian cases the responses of *buyers* and *sellers* to divergencies in *quantity* are the crucial determinants of stability. In the marshallian case it is the response of *sellers* to divergencies in *price* that is the determinant of stability.

Whether or not instability conditions arise frequently in real-world pricing situations is an empirical question. Although theoretically feasible, unstable price behavior does not appear to be widespread in the eyes of a casual observer; but perhaps this is simply because most casual observers only observe short-run situations, and short-run supply curves are positively sloped so that conditions for instability do not hold.

Very often an analyst may refer to long-run conditions when he wishes to discuss *changes* that occur over a rather long period of time but that will not occur in a short period of time. This type of analysis has important uses, but it is not what the economist has in mind when he speaks carefully. In the short run it is assumed, for example, that certain adjustments in price and quantity will occur in response to a *given* change in the location of the demand curve. Similarly, in the long run it is assumed that certain adjustments will occur in response to a *given* change in the location of the demand curve. Sometimes one must speak of a demand curve that is expected to change its location over time. Thus, for example, as population grows or as income increases, period by period, one would expect that

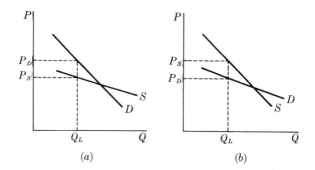

Figure 7.10   (a)   (b)

(a) Marshallian stable; (b) marshallian unstable.

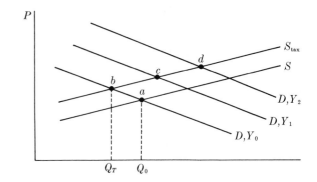

Figure 7.11

the demand curve would shift to the right, period by period, while essentially retaining its shape. This type of long-run analysis has its uses but is not the static analysis of demand and supply that is defined in terms of fixity of a factor resource.

To illustrate, assume that a heavy excise tax is levied on tobacco. Tobacco sales might fall sharply in the wake of the tax, indicating a relatively flat demand curve. However, after a few years of income growth tobacco sales might surpass their previous level. Would one conclude that the demand curve showing the relation of price and quantity was steep in the long run? Probably not. Rather, one would conclude that a relatively flat demand curve for tobacco shifts to the right as income increases. The purpose of this example is to note that the concept of the long run must be treated carefully and that dynamic analysis involves the extra element of attaching a time sequence to changes in some variable. Here the variable with time attached was income.

The analysis is depicted in Fig. 7.11, where the demand curve $Q = f(P,Y)$ shifts to the right as income increases from Y_0 to Y_1, to Y_2, and so on, over time periods 0, 1, 2, ... The tax initially raised the long-run static supply curve to S_{tax} and the equilibrium price and quantity moved in the pattern represented by points a, b, c, d.

7.12 THE COBWEB

A somewhat different time sequence of events is found in the *cobweb* analysis of demand and supply that is sometimes used to explain the rather larger variability in prices of farm products than exists for manufactured products. Assume that farmers plant and supply corn on the basis of last year's price of corn. Thus, the quantity supplied today is a function of yesterday's price, or $Q_{s,t} = f(P_{t-1})$. Assume, however, that the quantity demanded today is a function of today's price, or $Q_{D,t} = g(P_t)$. If, as shown in Fig. 7.12, the price is initially P_0, farmers plant a large crop and supply Q_1 in the following year. But then prices fall to P_1 and farmers now plant only Q_2. The price changes year after year until it converges upon the equilibrium price. If the supply curve were flat relative to the demand curve, of course, this process would lead to even larger divergencies from equilibrium rather than convergence.

Having introduced a lag structure into the analysis it is possible to trace the time path of price and the time path of quantity. This is *dynamic* analysis. It is offered in contrast with earlier examples in which a given change in the location of, say, the supply curve generates a new equilibrium of price and quantity, that is, a change from one equilibrium position to another. This is called *comparative statics* inasmuch as a comparison is made between initial equilibrium values and subsequent equilibrium values. Comparative statics is dynamic in the limited sense that it can be used to evaluate discrete differences in price and quantity at two points in time, but it does not trace a time path over many points in time.

Theoretical analysis based upon intuitive feelings about the position and shape of demand and supply curves can provide

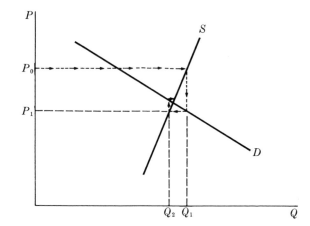

Figure 7.12

rough solutions to most real problems that policy-makers and businessmen face. Marketing specialists face the task of predicting the quantity of a good that will be sold each period at different prices. This is especially difficult in the case of a new product just being introduced to the consuming public, and many businesses fail because the judgment was faulty. The job is easier if the product is an "old" one, that is, one for which the price has long been known and for which a historical pattern of different prices has appeared in response to different sets of conditions of demand and supply. Policy authorities, when imposing an excise tax, want to have some idea of the revenues that the tax will bring in. To estimate revenues they must use intuitive judgments about the shape, position, and possible shifts in the demand and supply curves. Mistakes in judgment often form the bone of contention in political battles waged in election years.

7.13 THE IDENTIFICATION PROBLEM

The desire to have more than intuitive judgment about conditions of supply and demand has led to the expenditure of large sums to discover them. But the observation of historical prices and quantities does not, in most cases, enable one to know the shape or position of either the demand or supply curve. The problem faced by the analyst is known as *the identification problem*. If the demand function is $Q_D = f(P)$ and the supply function is $Q_S = g(P)$, and if data on P and Q are collected, how does one know whether or not these data depict the demand curve or the supply curve? For simplicity assume that the functions are linear. Assume also that the quantity demanded is a function of income as well as price. Demand and supply consist, therefore, of the following equations:

$$Q_D = a + bP + cY$$
$$Q_S = a' + b'P$$

For selected values of the parameters in these equations the graph of demand and supply might appear as in Fig. 7.13. Remember that the dependent variable is quantity and is measured on the horizontal axis. This is contrary to conventional usage in mathematics in which the dependent variable is generally

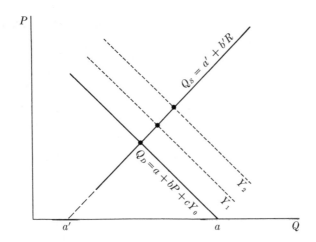

Figure 7.13

placed on the vertical axis. Thus, the intercepts a and a' are for the demand and supply curves, respectively, and the slopes of the functions are the reciprocals of the observed slopes in the graph. The demand curve shifts with changes in income, as illustrated by the dashed curves in the graph. If the analyst, having observed data on prices and quantity, knows that the supply curve has been stable in its location over the period for which the observations were made, then the points of intersection of demand and supply generate sets of prices and quantities that represent points on the *supply* curve. Thus a shifting demand curve generates the supply curve.

The reader can easily imagine the converse of the above situation. Rather than having income in the demand curve, let the supply curve have an extra variable, say, Z, which might represent rainfall in the case of an agricultural good. The two equations are

$$Q_D = a + bP$$
$$Q_S = a' + b'P + c'Z$$

The graph of these equations appears in Fig. 7.14. If the analyst knows, for some reason, that demand conditions have not changed over the period of observation but that rainfall has varied with a significant effect on yields, then the data on price and quantity describe the shape of the *demand* curve as the graph clearly indicates.

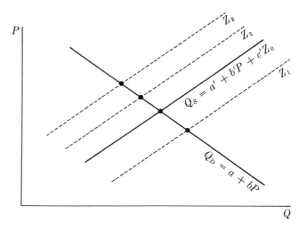

Figure 7.14

If *both* the demand curve and supply curves are subject to shifting—the demand by income changes and the supply by rainfall—then by imagining the two graphs superimposed it is clear that the sets of prices and quantities created by intersections would form a general scatter of points about the graph. It is not likely that this scatter would indicate anything about the shape or position of either the demand curve or the supply curve; but, of course, the points reflect values, not only of P and Q, but also Y and Z. By sorting out the impact of various Y's on the demand for the good the supply function appears, and by sorting out the impact of various Z's on the supply of the good, the demand function appears. Thus, the *structural* parameters in the demand function a, b, and c can be *identified*, and the structural parameters of the supply function a', b', and c' can also be identified. The equations, as they now stand, are *just identified* on *a priori* grounds. If more exogenous variables such as Y and Z are included, say, V and W, in the two-equation system of equations, then the model would be *overidentified*. In the original case in which the only exogenous variable was Y, one of the two equations was not identified and the model would, therefore, be called *underidentified*. When the system is underidentified, the analyst has insufficient information to. sort out the structural parameters. When the system is *just identified*, he has just enough information; and when it is *overidentified*, he has more information than he can use and so must discard surplus information.

It is sometimes evident that bureaucratic management, either private or public, prefers bad numbers to no numbers at all, but, if the numbers come from an underidentified system, they can easily be totally wrong and misleading. It is not intuitively obvious that a bad number is always better than no number at all. With improved statistical methods designed to ensure that parameters that fix the position and shape of demand and supply curves will be properly identified, businessmen and policy-makers should get better numbers from future studies. As this happens, demand and supply analysis should become even more useful, but the analyst should never forget that the tool concerns only partial equilibrium and should always carefully consider all the possible ramifications that are suggested by general equilibrium analysis.

EXERCISES

7.1   Assume the demand curve $Q = 20 - 2P$. Draw a graph of this curve. Using geometric line segments in the formula for elasticity of demand, what are the coefficients of price elasticity for the points at which $P = 8$, $P = 3$, and $P = 10$? Using the algebraic formula for elasticity, calculate the elasticity coefficients again to check your answers.

7.2   Sketch the demand curve $Q = 10/P$. At the point for which $P = 5$, what is the price elasticity of demand? Use algebra and also make an estimate of the coefficient by using a tangent to the curve and the line segment formula.

7.3   Draw the supply curve $Q = 2P - 10$. Using the line segment formula, compute the coefficient of elasticity of supply for the points at which $P = 10$, $P = 15$, and $P = 5$. Compute each of the coefficients again using algebra. Draw the curve $P = 2P + 10$ and repeat the computations for the three price elasticities for this supply function.

7.4   The object of this exercise is to illustrate the computation of the price elasticity of demand from an indifference map for a consumer. Draw an indifference map for Mr. A with two indifference curves, and draw a budget constraint tangent to the leftmost curve. Let the quantity of good 1 purchased each period be measured on the horizontal axis. Assume the price of good 1 falls so that a new budget constraint is just tangent to the rightmost indifference curve. Label the intercept of the initial budget constraint with the horizontal axis Q_0 and the intercept with the subsequent budget constraint Q_1. Now the difference between these two quantities is $Q_1 - Q_0$ and the original quantity is OQ_0. Thus, the ratio $(Q_1 - Q_0)/OQ_0$ represents the proportional *reduction* in *price* of good 1 because under the initial price the quantity OQ_0

can be bought and under the subsequent price the quantity OQ_1 can be bought. If the price falls by 50 percent, then the quantity that Mr. A can buy with a given income increases by 50 percent. Thus, the ratio $-(Q_1 - Q_0)/OQ_0$ is $\Delta P/P$ in the formula for the elasticity of demand. Drop a vertical line from the point of tangency of the first budget constraint with the indifference curve to the horizontal axis and label the point A; drop another from the second point of tangency and label the point B. Then the proportional increase in the quantity that Mr. A will purchase each period is $(B - A)/OA$. In the elasticity formula this ratio is $\Delta Q/Q$. Now an approximation to the elasticity of demand can be estimated by using the relevant discrete intervals along the horizontal axis in the elasticity formula. From the graph you have drawn what is this estimate of the elasticity coefficient?

7.5 Following a procedure similar to that of Exercise 7.4 estimate a discrete approximation to the income elasticity of demand. Let the budget constraint shift in a parallel fashion to the right and denote the proportional increase in income by observing the proportional increase in the quantity of good 1 that Mr. A could purchase if he spent all his income on good 1. Then note the actual proportional change in quantity that Mr. A would buy by observing the points of tangency and the vertical intercepts from such points. If, with an increase in income, Mr. A increases the quantity of good 1 he buys, then the elasticity coefficient is positive; this is called a *superior* good. Indifference curves might be drawn so that the income-expansion curve bends up and back to the left. Mr. A will then reduce the quantity of good 1 he buys as his income increases. In this case the good is inferior and the income elasticity coefficient is negative. Illustrate the two cases of superior and inferior goods and estimate respective elasticity coefficients.

7.6 Assume a demand function $Q = 20 - 2P$ and a supply function $Q = P + 5$. Solve for equilibrium values of P and Q. Now let an excise tax of 3 per unit be levied on the suppliers of this good. What is the new equilibrium price to the consumer? What price do suppliers receive? How much revenue is collected by the government?

7.7 Let a demand function be $Q = 3P^5$. What is the price elasticity of demand? Does this elasticity coefficient hold for any price? Explain.

7.8 Draw an indifference map and budget constraint for Mr. A showing a point of tangency. Assume that P_1 doubles and note the change in the budget constraint. Now draw the same original graph again. Let, not only P_1, but also P_2 and income double. Note what happens to the budget constraint under these conditions, and what happens to the quantities of goods 1 and 2 that Mr. A purchases. Explain in your own words the statement "In the absence of a money illusion demand functions for consumers will be homogeneous of degree zero."

7.9 Draw a set of figures similar to Figs. 7.9 and 7.10 and describe walrasian and marshallian stability conditions using prices *below* equilibrium as the frame of reference rather than prices above equilibrium as in the text.

7.10 Illustrate the case in which the cobweb analysis of demand and supply shows divergence from equilibrium (instability). Can you express the conditions for stability in terms of the elasticities of the demand and supply curves?

7.11 What is the identification problem?

8

Production Functions,
Cost Curves,
and the Theory
of the Firm
in Competition

The tools of analysis developed in the paradigm of the producers'
market in Chap. 3 are relevant to the discussion that follows
here. In Chap. 3 a producer played the role of an automaton
whose function it was to maximize output each period by spending all of the industry's revenues on factors of production. But
industry production is generally the result of the activity of
a number of firms. In this chapter and the next the motives
of the manager of a firm are examined in greater detail. It
is assumed that managers seek to maximize money profits. Although this may not be true in many instances, it is an assumption that enables one to predict the economic activity of a very
large proportion of all the managers in Western societies and
is therefore a useful assumption and descriptive of forces that
exist *in artificial isolation,* whether or not the assumption is
"true" in some empirical or absolute sense.

8.1 THE ENGINEER, ACCOUNTANT, AND SALESMAN

The manager of a firm may be thought of as the individual
who hires the services of three specialists: an engineer, an ac-

countant, and a salesman or marketing specialist. Although, in fact, the manager himself may perform one or more of the functions of the specialists it is convenient to think of these functions as separate from one another.

The engineer's function is to provide the manager with the relevant information about the production function. If $Q_1 = f(X,Y)$, where Q_1 represents the rate of output of good 1 each period and X and Y are factors of production, the form taken by the function depends upon existing technology, which is under the purview of the engineer. What inputs does it take to get a certain level of output? Can alternative rates of input be used to achieve the same level of output, or if not, what output can they be used to achieve? These are the sort of questions the manager will put to his engineer. The accountant's job is to measure prices and quantities. It is from the accountant that the manager acquires information on the costs of inputs or the expenses of production. Finally, the salesman's job is to inform the manager about the market for the output of the firm. He should be able to estimate the probable level of sales for various possible prices of the commodity; that is, he should have some knowledge of or ability to estimate the demand curve for the product. All these jobs are difficult. Nevertheless, production goes on only if some knowledge on these subjects, even if imperfect, is conveyed to the manager of the firm.

When the market is *perfectly competitive*, the role of the salesman is quite simple. He merely sells all of the output of the firm at the going market price. No one would buy any of the product at any higher price, and there is no reason to take any price lower than that for which other producers sell their output. Producers of wheat, feed grain, certain raw materials, and other commodities exist in an environment of perfect competition in that they have no influence over the existing price. For example, farmers will assist each other in harvesting their crops, for competition is so great that no one farmer feels that he is "in competition" with his neighbor. Certain industrialists, for example, automobile manufacturers, often speak of the "highly competitive" market in which they sell their wares. But although the market seems competitive because of the clear recognition of interdependencies of pricing and advertising policies, in fact, it is not nearly as competitive as that of many farm products in which producers are simply *price-takers*.

When the price of a good is given to the firm, a schedule may be constructed that shows the total revenue received by the firm each period for each different rate of output. If the price of the good is $1.00, then the total revenue curve labeled *TR* is a straight line as shown in Fig. 8.1. If 10 units of output are sold by the firm each period at a price of $1.00 per unit, then total revenues are $10.00 each period, and so forth.

From the engineer the firm's manager learns the quantity of factors of production that are required to produce each rate of output. From the accountant he learns the costs of these factors. By combining this information, the manager can ascer-

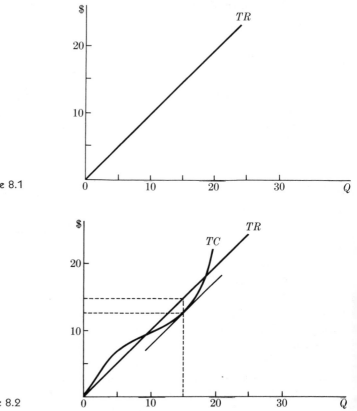

Figure 8.1

Figure 8.2

tain the total cost of producing each rate of output, and a total cost curve can be superimposed on the total revenue curve as in Fig. 8.2. From the figure as drawn it is evident that for any rate of output the vertical distance between the TR curve and the TC curve is a measure of the profits per period earned by this firm, for profits are defined as $TR - TC$. Profits are positive in the uppermost cigar-shaped area, and they are maximized each period when Q is 15. When Q is 15, total revenue is $15.00 and total cost is $12.50, leaving profits of $2.50 per period.

8.2 MARGINAL COST, AVERAGE COST, AND TOTAL COST

When the total revenue curve is a straight line and the total cost curve is smooth and of the general shape depicted, then the maximum vertical distance between the two curves will occur at the rate of output for which the slope of the TC curve, indicated by the slope of the lightly drawn tangent to the TC curve, is the same as the slope of the TR curve.

Marginal cost is defined as the slope of the total cost curve $MC = \Delta TC/\Delta Q$, or, for a continuous function using the calculus, $MC = d(TC)/dQ$. Marginal cost may be evaluated for each point on the total cost curve. Glancing at Fig. 8.3, it appears that the slope of the total cost curve decreases as one moves along the curve from the origin rightward until a rate of output

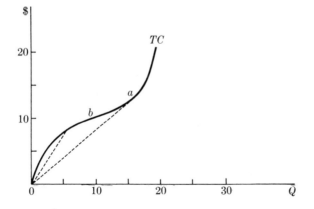

Figure 8.3

of 10 units per period is reached. Beyond this point the slope (marginal cost) increases as Q increases. Thus, when Q is 10, marginal cost is a minimum; this point, point b, is called the *point of inflection* on the total cost curve.

Average cost is simply total cost divided by the rate of output $AC = TC/Q$. But average cost also may be thought of in terms of a slope. In this case the slope of concern is the slope of a vector (a straight line) from the origin to the relevant point on the total cost curve. In Fig. 8.3 two vectors serve to illustrate the way in which average cost appears as a slope in a graph. When Q is 15, total cost is approximately 12 and the slope of the vector to point a is .8, indicating an average cost of 80 cents per unit for 15 units of output each period.

In this diagram this vector appears to be tangent to the total cost curve at point a, and such tangency indicates that this is the minimum average cost for which this product can be produced by this firm. The slope of a vector to any other point on the total cost curve is greater than the slope of the vector to point a. At minimum average cost it is also true that average cost is equal to marginal cost, for the slope of the vector is equal to the slope of the total cost curve at point a.

For the entire range of the curve from the origin up to point a average cost is greater than marginal cost, and beyond point a average cost is less than marginal cost. This is seen by comparing the slope of the curve at any point with the slope of the vector to the same point. Thus, if average cost is falling, marginal cost is less than average cost; and if average cost is rising, marginal cost is greater than average cost. If average cost is constant, average cost and marginal cost are the same. From the origin to point b, marginal cost is falling and so also is average cost. Between b and a marginal cost is rising even though average cost continues to fall. Beyond point a both average cost and marginal cost are rising. Marginal cost may be constant while average cost rises, falls, or stays constant. These propositions hold for smooth or continuous functions.

8.3 FIXED AND VARIABLE COSTS

In some cases the analysis is more straightforward if certain costs are assumed to be *fixed*, such as in the case of a lease on certain plant or equipment where a long-term agreement has been entered into and the obligation to pay exists whether or

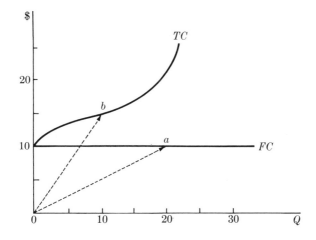

Figure 8.4

not any production goes on. In Fig. 8.4 fixed costs are separated from other costs which are variable with the rate of output.

Since average fixed costs equal fixed costs divided by output $AFC = FC/Q$, again the slope of the vector from the origin to the relevant point on the FC curve will give the average fixed costs. At point a fixed costs are 10 and output is 20 per period, so that $AFC = .5$, or 50 cents, per unit; the slope of the vector is .5. The slope of the vector to the TC curve is, again, a measure of average total costs.

If one wishes to estimate average variable costs, he need only use the slope of the vector from the point where the TC curve emerges from the vertical axis to the relevant point on the TC curve. (This vector is not shown in Fig. 8.4.) Average variable cost will fall, reach a minimum, and begin to rise as the rate of output increases in the same way that average total cost does. However, AVC reaches a minimum at a lower Q than does ATC.

Marginal cost, the slope of the TC curve, will equal AVC when it is a minimum and will equal ATC when it is a minimum. Thus, if one draws a single TC curve and can visualize MC as a slope and ATC, AVC, and AFC as slopes, he can easily "see" the relations existing among these various useful concepts. The average and marginal functions appear in Fig. 8.5, but it is more difficult to visualize the relations existing between them in this multiple-curve graph than it is when the simpler TC function is drawn.

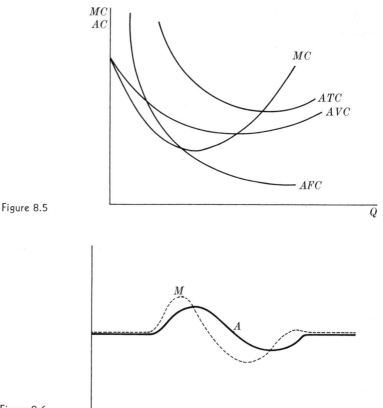

Figure 8.5

Figure 8.6

The *ATC* curve is the sum, vertically, of the *AFC* and *AVC* curves. The *MC* curve is below both *AVC* and *ATC* when they are falling and is above them when they are rising; thus, the *MC* curve intersects the minimum points on both the *AVC* and *ATC* curves. One may illustrate the relation between an *average* and a *marginal* function by drawing a curve showing all of the various shapes an average function can assume, as in Fig. 8.6. The solid curve labeled *A* is representative of any average function, and the dotted curve labeled *M* is the relevant marginal function. Here, it is easily seen that if *A* is rising, *M* lies above *A*; if *A* is falling, *M* lies below *A*. Thus, *M* intersects *A* when *A* is either a maximum or a minimum. Also, *M* equals *A* whenever *A* is unchanging.

With these tools, one can now analyze the behavior of a maximizing firm in a perfectly competitive market.

8.4 PROFIT MAXIMIZATION

In Fig. 8.7, two TR curves appear along with the firm's TC curve. Considering only TR_0 initially one may visualize the price of the good as the slope of TR_0. The maximizing firm will produce a rate of output of Q_0 for which $AC = MC = P = MR = AR$, where MR is marginal revenue or the slope of the total revenue curve at Q_0 rate of output. All the relevant slopes are equal. The firm is producing at minimum average cost, and the price of the product just equals what it costs to produce it. Managers of the firm have no motivation to move away from this rate of production for here profits are maximized even though they are zero. Remember that *all* costs of production, implicit and explicit, are being covered under these conditions, including the manager's salary and/or the imputed value of the proprietor's salary based upon his opportunity cost (the highest salary he could earn by offering his services in the market) as well as other items sometimes called *normal profits* such as interest and dividend returns to the owners of bonds and equities in the firm. All costs are fully covered and all who contribute to the firm's operations are earning a competitive return in comparison with other alternatives. This is the

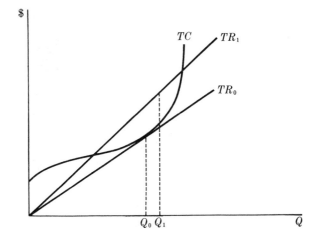

Figure 8.7

picture of the firm in perfect competition when the market is in long-run equilibrium.

Suppose that for some reason the price of the product should increase. This will be reflected in the new total revenue curve TR_1. How will maximizing managers of this firm react to this change in market environment? First, the rate of output will increase to Q_1, for here the largest vertical distance exists between the TR and TC curves; hence, at rate of output Q_1 profits are maximized. Incidentally, this is also the rate of output for which MC, the slope of the TC curve, equals MR, the slope of the TR curve. At rate of output Q_1 the average cost of production is slightly above the minimum, and the price, of course, is considerably above the average cost of production.

When a firm makes profits, remembering that profits are returns in excess of *all* costs of production, both implicit and explicit, the evidence of these profits will attract others into the production of this good. If the market is free so that no barriers to entry exist, new supplies of the good will appear for sale and the price will fall. It will continue to fall until no further profits are being made and the old equilibrium price is established. Thus, there may be only one producer of a good, and yet if many potential entrants are at hand with no restrictions on their behavior, the firm may be said to exist in a perfectly competitive environment. The number of firms in an industry, therefore, is not always an accurate index of the extent of competition, although if there already exist a large number of independent and unregulated firms that produce this good, it is a fairly good indication that competition approximates perfectly competitive conditions.

The above paragraphs describe, in theory, the way in which Adam Smith's laissez faire economy is supposed to operate. By considering the possibility of a decline in demand, a lower price for the good, and firms leaving the industry since to remain in production involves losses, one can show how the exit of firms will bring about the situation in which price will again equal average cost of production. Thus, an increase in demand will lead to greater output, and a decline in demand will lead to smaller output, with price approximating cost in the final analysis.

It is often ironical to watch some of the most vocal defenders of "free enterprise" do their best to get government assistance to prevent the entry of other firms into markets for their goods—witness pressure for tariffs, fair-trade legislation, and restrictive licensing arrangements. Restrictive legislation can be very damaging. What would America be like today if the government had staunchly protected candle makers and black-smiths—perhaps everyone would be burning candles and riding horses. The competitive system is effective only if it is permitted to work. It is, of course, unfair to allow blacksmiths to be forced out of business unless you also freely permit them to become mechanics. In order to accommodate change fairly the system must be open and free in its commercial aspects.

8.5 PRICE EQUALS MARGINAL COST

Maximizing managers of a firm operating in perfect competition will push the rate of output to the point where marginal cost of production equals the price of the product. Thus, in a competitive world, the price of a product that you buy just equals the additional cost involved in producing it. In a certain sense, then, no one is exploited as a consumer; he must pay for what he receives but he pays no more than the amount required to bring forth the production of an additional unit. This is sometimes called the *principle of marginal cost pricing*. It is equivalent to the fifth principle for maximum welfare discussed in Chap. 6; in that chapter it was called the *optimum factor-output relationship*

$$_aMP_{1,X} = \frac{P_X}{P_1} \quad \text{or} \quad _aMP_{1,X}P_1 = P_X$$

This optimum welfare criterion is equivalent to the criterion that $P_1 = MC_1$. To illustrate equivalence:

Since
$$MC_1 = \frac{\Delta TC_1}{\Delta Q_1} \quad \text{and} \quad \Delta TC_1 = P_X \Delta X_1$$

then
$$MC_1 = P_X \frac{\Delta X_1}{\Delta Q_1}$$

But since
$$_aMP_{1,X} = \frac{\Delta Q_1}{\Delta X_1}$$

then
$$MC_1 = P_X \frac{1}{_aMP_{1,X}}$$

By imposing the condition that $MC_1 = P_1$, which is true of the maximizing firm in a perfectly competitive market, it follows that $P_1 = P_X/_aMP_{1,X}$, which may be written $_aMP_{1,X}P_1 = P_X$. Thus, to state that $MC_1 = P_1$ is another way of stating that $_aMP_{1,X}P_1 = P_X$, and this must hold, not only for X, but also for all other factors of production as well.

The reader will recall that when this maximizing principle was discussed in Chap. 6 it was noted that the owner of factor X received P_X in payment for sales of the factor to producers, and that this just equaled the value of the additional output attributable to the employment of the factor. Thus, in a competitive market under conditions approximating equilibrium, a consumer paying a dollar for an item would be paying just that amount necessary to bring forth its production, and that dollar would accrue as income to factor owners who would receive an amount just equal to the value of what was produced. If, however, firms are able to earn profits, so that total revenues exceed total costs, then the firm may pay each factor its marginal product and yet have revenues left over. Profit-making firms are the subject of Chap. 9.

8.6 PRODUCTION FUNCTIONS AND FIXED FACTORS

In Chap. 7 on demand and supply we presented an analysis of short- and long-run supply curves in which it was noted that in the short run at least one factor of production is fixed in supply to the firm. If a firm has a manufacturing plant, for example, it may have sold bonds in order to finance the construction of the plant, and the interest charges on this outstanding indebtedness payable each period represent costs that the firm incurs regardless of the level of output that the firm produces each period. Thus, fixed factors imply fixed costs and both imply short-run analysis; on the other hand, in long-run analysis there is no fixed factor nor any fixed cost of production. To clarify the relation between short- and long-run analysis it is desirable to trace more carefully than heretofore the manner in which cost curves are derived from production functions.

Figure 8.8 contains the graph of a two-factor production function of the type described at length in Chap. 3. Each isoquant represents a particular rate of production; the budget constraints are drawn for a given ratio of prices P_X/P_Y and for three different levels of total expenditure on factors X and Y each period.

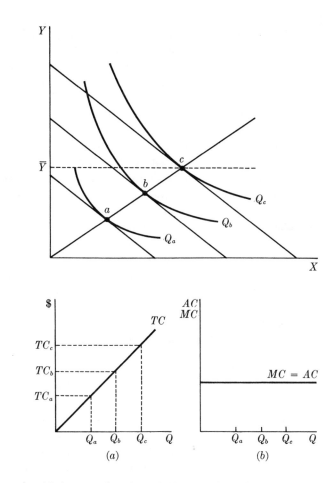

Figure 8.8

Figure 8.9   (a)   (b)

(The reader should ignore the dotted line at this point.) For any given budget for production of good 1, a budget constraint line is determined by the formula

$$TC = P_X X + P_Y Y$$

The right-hand side of this equation represents total expenditures (costs) on factors X and Y at going market prices for factors. Maximizing points a, b, and c in the graph represent least-cost combinations of factors X and Y that can produce outputs Q_a, Q_b, and Q_c each period. By reading the total expenditures and comparing these with relevant outputs, one can construct a total cost curve for the production of good 1, as in Fig. 8.9a. The TC curve as drawn is a straight line. It comes out of the origin which indicates there are no fixed costs. It is, therefore, a long-run total cost curve.

8.7 EXPANSION RAYS AND FACTOR/PRICE RATIOS

If factor prices are fixed so that budget constraints for different budgets are parallel, and if the production function is homogeneous (of any degree), then the expansion path drawn on the map of production isoquants will be a straight line. Expansion of the rate of output by maximizing managers of the firm will involve proportional expansion in the rate of utilization of each input. If, *in addition,* the production function is homogeneous of degree *one,* then proportional increases in all factor inputs lead to equiproportional changes in output (constant returns to scale). Also, with fixed factor prices the formula for the budget constraint shows that proportional changes in all inputs lead to equiproportional changes in total costs. Thus, output varies directly with total costs $TC = kQ$. Since k is fixed and represents the slope of the TC curve, $k = TC/Q = AC$ and also $k = \Delta TC/\Delta Q = MC$, for all rates of output; this is illustrated in Fig. 8.9b. Constant costs of production refers to constant average costs of production as output varies. Thus, with factor prices fixed, constant returns to scale imply constant costs of production.

Since expansion rays are generated by points of tangency of budget constraints and production isoquants, a different ray is generated for each possible different set of price ratios showing the relation of the price of factor X to the price of factor Y. Cobb–Douglas production functions that are homogeneous of degree one are such that for *any* given price ratio the expansion ray will show constant returns to scale and constant costs of production.[1] Assuming constant factor prices, if a Cobb–Douglas form of production function were homogeneous of a degree greater than one (implying increasing returns to scale throughout), then the total cost curve would rise at a decreasing rate as does TC_0 in Fig. 8.10a. This total cost curve

---

[1] If factor prices should increase as output increases, then a production function showing constant returns (in terms of the number of units of real output) to scale might nevertheless show increasing (rather than constant) costs of production because factors become more expensive as output increases. Therefore, constant returns to scale imply constant costs of production *provided* prices of factors are fixed.

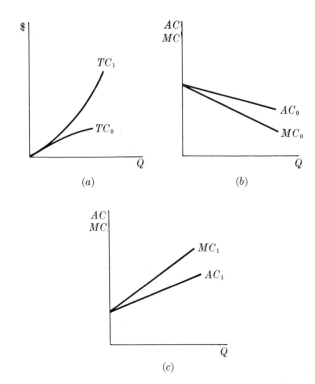

Figure 8.10   (c)

implies decreasing average and marginal costs of production as output expands. Similarly, a Cobb–Douglas production function that is homogeneous of a degree less than one implies decreasing returns to scale throughout, a total cost curve that rises at an increasing rate as does TC_1, and increasing average and marginal costs of production. Average and marginal cost curves derived from the two total cost curves are described in Fig. 8.10b and c, respectively. Since the TC curves have some positive slope throughout, that is, they leave the origin with a positive slope, then marginal and average costs are both positive and equal when $Q = 0$.

Total cost, average cost, and marginal cost curves are all *minimum* cost curves, for they indicate the minimum periodic expenditure required to produce any one of many particular levels of output each period. Each curve is a long-run cost curve because each is derived under the assumption that all factors are variable in supply and so there is no constraint on managers of the firm that hinders their selection above many alternative packages of factors in order to minimize the cost of production of whatever output is finally selected.

8.8 SHORT-RUN COST CURVES

Short-run cost curves can be constructed from the same basic information used to construct long-run cost curves. Return to Fig. 8.8 and note the dotted line; this line might be called a *short-run* expansion line in contrast to the original expansion line. It is a short-run expansion line because it indicates a *fixed* supply of factor Y. A movement rightward along the dotted line intersects with isoproduct curves which indicate the outputs obtainable by hiring various amounts of factor X to work with the fixed supply of factor Y. Again, the formula $TC = P_Y Y + P_X X$ applies, except in this case $P_Y Y$ is fixed. By assuming various amounts of X employed (given the price of X) one can read the maximum quantity that can be produced and from the formula calculate the minimum cost of producing this rate of output. When adding this information about total cost to that provided in Fig. 8.9a, the graph appears as in Fig. 8.11.

In Fig. 8.8 the dotted short-run expansion line intersects the original long-run expansion line at point c. Thus, in Fig. 8.11 c is the point at which the short-run TC curve is just tangent to the long-run TC curve, for the same package of factors is employed in either case. It should be clear that there exists an entire *family* of short-run curves, one for each level of Y

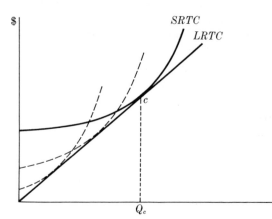

Figure 8.11

assumed to be fixed in supply to the firm; these are indicated by the dotted curves. The *envelope* of these curves, that is, the *frontier*, or border, that would be generated if a very large number of short-run cost curves were drawn in the graph, would make up the long-run TC curve.[1] The short-run TC curve does not have a hump in it as did those presented early in this chapter. This short-run curve has the proper shape to conform with the assumption that the production function is Cobb–Douglas and is homogeneous of degree one throughout. From Chap. 3 the reader may recall the example showing that the marginal productivity of X falls with increases in the employment of X when production functions are of Cobb–Douglas form. If marginal productivity falls, given the price of X, the marginal cost of producing good 1 increases. Hence, the upward-curving TC curve indicates increasing marginal costs of production as output increases.[2]

---

[1] At any point on the long-run total cost curve the maximizing condition that $MP_X P_1 = P_X$ holds for each and every factor of production. Thus

$$MC = P_X/MP_X = P_Y/MP_Y = \cdots \qquad \text{for all factors}$$

To show this mathematically, note that for $Q = f(X,Y)$, $MP_X = \partial Q/\partial X$ and $MP_Y = \partial Q/\partial Y$. Therefore, for maximization $P_X = MC\, \partial Q/\partial X$ and $P_Y = MC\, \partial Q/\partial Y$. Since $dQ = (\partial Q/\partial X)\, dX + (\partial Q/\partial Y)\, dY$ and, if $TC = P_X X + P_Y Y$, then $dTC = P_X\, dX + P_Y\, dY$, and

$$\frac{dTC}{dQ} = \frac{P_X\, dX + P_Y\, dY}{(\partial Q/\partial X)\, dX + (\partial Q/\partial Y)\, dY}$$

Substituting for P_X and P_Y we have

$$\frac{dTC}{dQ} = MC\, \frac{(\partial Q/\partial X)\, dX + (\partial Q/\partial Y)\, dY}{(\partial Q/\partial X)\, dX + (\partial Q/\partial Y)\, dY} = MC$$

If the short-run maximizing position is not on the long-run cost curve, then the marginal productivity of the *fixed* factor will not equal its price divided by the price of the product; but if the factor is fixed in amount then although there exists a marginal productivity for this factor, the concept of a price of the factor is cloudy. The amount of the factor employed is not sensitive to its price.

[2] A production function may be homogeneous of degree one and still have ranges in which short-run total cost curves have a hump showing falling MC at low rates of output and then increasing MC as output expands, e.g.,

$$Q = e\, \frac{ax^3 y^2 + bx^2 y^3}{cx^4 + dy^4}$$

where a, b, c, d, and e are positive constants, is such a function. See C. E. Ferguson, "Microeconomic Theory," rev. ed., p. 128, Richard D. Irwin, Inc., Chicago, Ill., 1969. Such a function, of course, is not Cobb–Douglas, which is of the form $Q = aX^\alpha Y^\beta$.

If the production function is not of Cobb–Douglas form but rather shows increasing returns to scale at low rates of output, then constant returns to scale, and finally decreasing returns to scale at high levels of output, the long- and short-run TC curves will appear as in Fig. 8.12a. At low output levels the rising TC curve indicates *falling* MC because the slope of the TC curve diminishes for a time. Then, as output increases a further rightward movement along the TC curve indicates rising MC as the slope of the TC curve increases. Relevant AC curves appear in Fig. 8.12b.

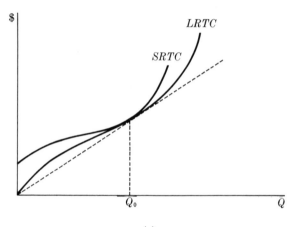

(a)

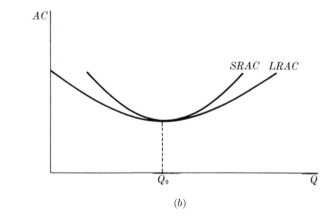

Figure 8.12   (b)

8.9 RIDGE LINES ON PRODUCTION FUNCTIONS

The exact shape of a cost curve and of a production function depends upon technology and prices of factors. The economist calls the shape an *empirical question;* it is a question of fact not of theory. However, it is crucial at this point to distinguish carefully between a production function for a firm, and a production function for an industry. In the discussion of production functions in Chap. 3, the reader was admonished to think of the output of good 1 as if it were produced by a representative group of competitive firms. If all firms in a representative group were approximately the same size and were operating at minimum average cost as they would under competitive conditions as described earlier in this chapter, then it would be likely that an expansion of output of the industry would occur through duplication of the facilities of existing firms by existing or new firms. If there were 100 such firms and demand increased then the hundred-and-first firm would enter the market, output would increase by $\frac{1}{100}$, and the quantity of each factor employed in producing this good would also increase by $\frac{1}{100}$. The logical extension of this duplication process leads to the belief that *industry* production functions are homogeneous of degree one, at least roughly so for reasonable ranges of output around the existing level of output, and so this assumption is often made.[1]

However, a firm's production function, in contrast to that of an industry, may not be so neatly formed. Some economists like to draw a production isoquant map such as that in Fig. 8.13. The ridge lines are formed by points at which the isoquants are either vertical or horizontal. When the isoquant is vertical, as at point a, it means that the marginal productivity of factor Y is zero; and when it is horizontal, the marginal productivity of X is zero and the marginal rate of substitution of X for Y (the slope of the isoproduct curve) is also zero. Thus, the area between the ridge lines contains the set of pack-

---

[1] Moroney reported on estimates of coefficients in production functions and found support for the reasonableness of this assumption for firms as well as industries: John R. Moroney, Cobb–Douglas Production Functions and Returns to Scale in U.S. Manufacturing Industry, *Western Econ. J.*, vol. VI, pp. 39–51, December 1967. For a comprehensive bibliography on the subject of production and cost functions containing 345 items, see: A. A. Walters, Production and Cost Functions: An Econometric Survey, *Econometrica*, vol. 31, pp. 1–66, Jan.–April 1963.

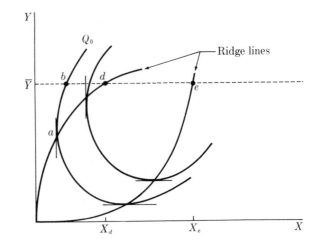

Figure 8.13

ages of factors X and Y that are economically efficient. To produce output Q_0 the firm would never freely choose to use the combination of factors denoted by point b, because the same output could be produced more cheaply with less of *both* X and Y, as at point a.*

According to the law of diminishing returns the marginal product of a variable factor of production may increase for a time as its employment and output increase but eventually its marginal productivity will decrease. If factor X represents labor and factor Y represents capital equipment then by moving along the dashed line to the right of $\bar{Y}$ in Fig. 8.13 the average productivity of X will increase until point d on the ridge line is reached. As output expands with the employment of more labor both the average and the marginal productivity of X will decrease. Beyond point e the marginal productivity of X becomes negative. These results can be described by the total product function in Fig. 8.14.

By reading the measures of output from the isoquants in Fig. 8.13 along the dashed line that indicates a fixed amount of Y, and by plotting output, Q, on the vertical axis and the rate of employment of X, labor, on the horizontal axis, the total

---

* If the firm's manager has no choice but to use $\bar{Y}$ of factor Y, then he might operate at point b. For example, to homestead 160 acres of land and acquire ownership one must be prepared to live on it and use it for a certain time period. Thus, the homesteader *may* be forced to produce with an inefficient package of factors under legal constraint. Even then he would be tempted to allow part of the land to lie in fallow if he could do so and still meet his legal responsibilities.

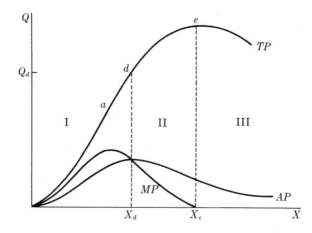

Figure 8.14

product curve of Fig. 8.14 may be constructed. Point d on the ridge line in Fig. 8.13 shows the rate of employment of X_d of labor, and this is the same rate of employment as that associated with point d in Fig. 8.14. Similarly, point e in the two graphs indicates a rate of employment of factor X of X_e.

8.10 STAGES I, II, AND III

These rates of employment of X define the boundaries of what is called *Stage II* of the production function. It is somewhere in Stage II, where employment may vary in the range from X_d to X_e, that production will be carried on. The line of sepa-ration between Stage II and Stage III is called the *intensive margin*, for here the fixed resource is being used most intensively; that is, large amounts of the variable resource are being *applied* to the fixed factor in the production activity. The line separating Stage II from Stage I is called the *extensive* margin.

Note that the marginal productivity of X increases up to the rate of utilization indicated by point a on the total product curve. This is the *point of inflection* and the marginal productivity of X is a maximum at this point. Between points a and d MP_X falls but the average productivity of X is still increasing. Thus, in this range the law of diminishing returns is in operation with respect to factor X. However, in this range the MP_Y is *negative*. (Remember that the MP_X varies when X varies *and* when Y varies; similarly, MP_Y varies when Y varies *and* when X varies.) Returning to Fig. 8.13, to the left of the ridge line on which points

a and d lie, MP_Y is negative. In a sense, too much Y is being employed with too little X. For example, at point b, if X were fixed in amount and if the amount of Y increased beyond $\bar{Y}$, then output would fall. Hence, the contribution to output from an increment in the employment of Y would be *negative*. The MP_Y is negative at every point along the dashed line from $\bar{Y}$ to b to d. Beyond d the MP_Y is positive. Thus, point d on the ridge line marks, not only the *extensive* margin for the employment of X, but also the *intensive* margin for the employment of Y. That is, to the left of point d the small amount of labor employed is so little that it may be thought of as being employed *intensively* by the large amount of equipment that it works with.[1]

Assume that the rate of output desired by managers of the firm is Q_0 in Fig. 8.13. The managers would desire to produce at point a. If Y represented a building or land, part of which could simply be left idle—closed off or abandoned—then operation at point a indicates that managers are not *forced* to use all of the fixed factor. If a horizontal line were drawn through point a, then an entirely different set of product curves would have to be drawn in Fig. 8.14 to accord with this level of fixed input of Y. Thus, it would seem at first glance that operation at point a would be rational. However, this is not likely to be the case. The rate of output desired might be at least as large as that indicated by an isoproduct curve through point d (not shown) or else no output at all will be produced. This is because the firm's variable costs will not be covered (or will just barely be covered) if it operates either at points a or d. The following discussion should clarify this point.

8.11 TOTAL PRODUCT AND TOTAL COST

By a simple mechanism the TP function of Fig. 8.14 can be transformed into the total cost function. To simplify, assume $P_X = \$1$. Then the horizontal axis in Fig. 8.14 measures, not only the number of units of X employed each period, but also the dollar value of expenditure on factor X, or total variable costs of production. Output in Fig. 8.14 is measured on the vertical axis. Now let us reverse the axes and measure output on the horizontal axis and P_X, or TVC, on the vertical axis, as in Fig. 8.15.

---

[1] For further discussion see C. E. Ferguson, *op. cit.*, p. 136.

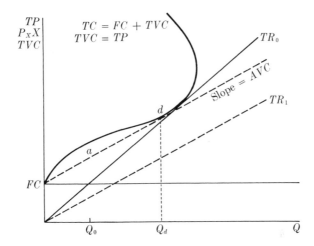

Figure 8.15

Point d, which earlier denoted the rate of employment of X at which average product was a maximum, now represents the rate of output at which average variable cost is a minimum (the slope of the dotted vector is a minimum). In equilibrium, the price of the product equals the slope of TR_0. If the price of the product fell to equal the slope of TR_1, it would also equal AVC, indicated by the slope of the dotted line. At rate of output Q_d the firm would be making losses just equal to its fixed costs. Therefore, managers of the firm would be indifferent to whether it operated and produced Q_d each period, or whether it ceased operation, produced no output at all, and suffered losses equal to all of its fixed costs each period. The losses in either case would be the same. Thus, if a firm does not earn enough to cover all of its variable costs plus some part, however small, of its fixed costs, it might as well cease production altogether, otherwise its losses would be even larger.

If the firm were forced to use all of the fixed factor ($\bar{Y}$ in Fig. 8.13) then any rate of output less than Q_d would mean $AVC > P$, and losses would exceed FC. However, if a firm could abandon part of its fixed equipment and operate at point a in Fig. 8.13, then a new total product curve for the appropriate amount of Y would give a new TVC curve. This new curve would be tangent to the AVC (slope) vector in Fig. 8.15 at point a, the point where AP is a maximum and AVC is a minimum. Thus, restricting output to Q_0 would still leave the firm with losses as great as it would suffer if it ceased production altogether. Hence, no rate of output between Q_d and zero would enable the firm to avoid losses equivalent to its fixed costs. Thus, if a firm is free to abandon any part of its fixed equipment that managers see fit to abandon, its TC curve for the short run should be a straight line from the vertical axis along through point a and point d and then up along the TC curve as drawn in Fig. 8.15. However, if it must use *all* of the fixed equipment to carry out *any* level of production, the original short-run TVC curve is the appropriate one.

This lengthy return to discussion of production functions enabled the construction of cost curves of both short- and long-run varieties. These cost curves provide the basis for constructing short- and long-run supply curves for an industry.

8.12 SHORT-RUN SUPPLY AND MARGINAL COST

Short-run supply curves are comprised, principally, of the upward-sloping part of the marginal cost curves of existing firms engaged in producing the good. It was noted early in this chapter that a maximizing firm in a perfectly competitive market environment would choose that rate of output for which price equals marginal cost. Thus, for each price, the supply of the good offered for sale will equal the sum of outputs of all firms, and each firm's output is set by marginal cost. The summation process appears in Fig. 8.16.*

In the short run some factors are fixed in supply, and therefore only variation in output on the part of existing firms will change output of the industry; i.e., new firms do not enter or leave the industry under this analysis because it would involve varying *all* factors of production. The short run is sufficiently short that new firms cannot be established in the time available.

8.13 SHORT-RUN SUPPLY AND FACTOR-PRICE VARIATION

When adding the marginal cost curves together it is assumed that factors of production can be bought at going market prices for factors without affecting their prices. The wage rate is the going price of labor, and a firm or any set of firms in an industry can buy as much labor as it likes at the going wage rate. However, the production of some commodities may involve a unique material or ingredient. Thus, attention to general equilibrium analysis suggests that an increase in the output of a

---

*At the price indicated in Fig. 8.16, firm α produces 17, firm β produces 10, and so forth, for all firms so that total output for the industry is 150, as noted in Fig. 8.16c.

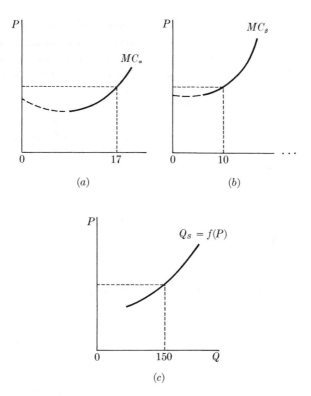

Figure 8.16

(a) Firm α; (b) firm β; (c) all firms in industry.

particular industry may, because of the derived demand for this unique resource, drive up the price of this resource. A 10 percent increase in the demand for aluminum might be expected to drive up the price of bauxite—and hence also drive up the MC that each firm faces in purchasing this factor of production necessary to the production of aluminum. In this case the short-run curve for the industry would be more steeply sloped than the curve derived by simply adding up the MC curves for firms under the assumption of no change in factor prices. Such is the nature of the criteria used in construction of short-run supply curves. Analysis may be incomplete without attention to general equilibrium aspects.

The construction of long-run supply curves allows for variation in *all* factors of production, and therefore for the entry and exit of firms as well. Since many firms in many industries can simply be duplicated, the long-run supply curves of goods in many industries are believed to be horizontal. Increases in factor prices as output increases may give rise to long-run supply curves with increasing slope in these instances.

If the demand for a good increases, in the short run the price will increase and output will increase; then profits are being made in the industry, and new firms will enter. Existing firms will expand their producing facilities. The price will gradually fall toward a new equilibrium of long-run supply and demand. Classical economists argued that the costs of production determine price or value of the good. Neoclassical economists introduced demand as a partner along with supply (costs of production) in determining price. If the long-run supply curve is horizontal, then demand can shift but the price will stay the same—only the quantity sold will vary. In these cases it is true that costs of production alone determine price.

8.14 CONSTANT COST, FIRM SIZE, AND OUTPUT RATES

If the firm's marginal cost curve is constant (horizontal) for some range of rates of output, then there is no optimum rate of production for the firm; that is, there is no optimum *size* of firm. If there were an optimum size, then the strength of demand would determine the number of firms in an industry; but if there is no optimum size of firm, then the number of firms in the industry is indeterminate. In some industries the firms seem to be roughly of the same size. In others, large and small firms are found competing with each other successfully.[1] In any case, however, the number of firms in an industry is not likely always to be a good indication of the degree or extent of competition. If there is a large number of firms, then the degree of competition is doubtless very high; but if there are only one or two firms, competition may still approximate perfect competition because extremely easy entry of new firms will prevent existing firms from raising their prices. Imperfect competition is the subject of Chap. 9.

To derive a cost curve for a firm, the firm's budget was varied, and in this way the minimum total cost for a variety of levels of firm output was calculated. Managers of the firm must decide which specific level of output can be sold at a price that will maximize the firm's profits, and this level of output will require an appropriate budget. Thus, managers of a firm do

[1] See Moroney, *op. cit.*, p. 50.

not face a *budget constraint* in quite the same way that a consumer does. A manager is free to vary his budget to fit his prospective level of sales, but a consumer must maximize subject to a budget given by his earnings.

In the analysis of the consumers' market there is considerable discussion of the way in which consumers respond to variation in product prices as well as to variation in budgets. But the response of firms to variation in factor prices is *not* analogous to consumer behavior. This is one important respect in which the partial equilibrium analysis of the two markets differs—firms do not respond to changes in factor prices in the same way that consumers respond to changes in goods prices. This is because, when the price of a factor of production changes, this change will also affect the marginal cost of output and therefore the rate of output that managers of the firm will choose to produce in order to maximize profits. If the price of a factor increases, marginal cost will increase and output will be reduced; and if the factor price falls, marginal cost will fall and output will be increased. Thus, any change in the budget constraint that results from a change in (one or more) factor prices implies that a change in the rate of output is in order.

Reference to Fig. 8.17 may help clarify this point. In Fig. 8.17a let the budget constraint tangent to the isoquant labeled Q_1 at point a be the original equilibrium position. Now let the price of factor X fall so that the budget constraint rotates until it is tangent to the isoquant labeled Q_2 at point b. Given this lower price of X, the firm will find its marginal cost has fallen and managers will no longer maximize profits if they produce only Q_1 each period. Instead, they may expand output to Q_3. In Fig. 8.17b two marginal cost curves are shown: MC_1, which corresponds to the original situation, and MC_2, which exists after the price of X has fallen. The maximizing output is now Q_3. This merely illustrates the proposition that a change in factor prices implies a change in marginal cost and therefore a change in output level that may or may not correspond to the level of output produced under the same dollar budget as before. Depending on the demand for the product and the production function, managers of the firm *may* want to produce Q_2, or Q_3, or some level of output greater than Q_1 but less than Q_2. It all depends on the extent of the fall in MC that occurs as the price of X falls (and whether MR falls as output increases). But there is no particular reason to suppose that point

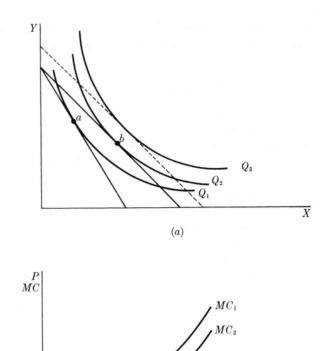

(a)

Figure 8.17   (b)

b in Fig. 8.17a will be the appropriate equilibrium position for the firm. Thus price changes for factors of production imply output changes as well; whereas, in the consumers' market, prices of commodities do not imply changes in incomes for it is assumed that the feedback effect on consumer income is negligible in partial equilibrium analysis.

8.15 FUNCTION COEFFICIENTS

Elasticity concepts are perfectly general in application. For any relation one can compute the ratio of the percentage change in a dependent variable to the percentage change in one of the independent variables. Thus, from a production function $Q = f(X,Y)$, one can define *output* coefficients for X and for Y as

$$\epsilon_X = \frac{\Delta Q/Q}{\Delta X/X} \quad \text{and} \quad \epsilon_Y = \frac{\Delta Q/Q}{\Delta Y/Y}$$

ϵ_X represents the percentage change in output that results from a given percentage change in the employment of factor X (similarly for factor Y). For example, the output coefficient for X could be calculated for any point along the dashed line in Fig. 8.8 where the amount of Y employed is fixed. If, on the other hand, a fixed amount of X were to be assumed, the output coefficient for Y could be computed.

The expansion line in Fig. 8.8 is also subject to analysis by an elasticity coefficient called the *function coefficient*. Along any straight line from the origin the proportional increase in X equals the proportional increase in Y; that is, $\Delta X/X = \Delta Y/Y$. If we let the ratio $\Delta\lambda/\lambda$ refer to the proportion by which each factor of production changes, then the function coefficient is

$$\epsilon_F = \frac{\Delta Q/Q}{\Delta\lambda/\lambda}$$

Recall that one characteristic of production functions that are homogeneous of degree one is that a given proportional change in all inputs leads to an equiproportional change in output. Hence, the function coefficient would be 1 in this case of constant returns to scale. It would be greater than 1 in the case of increasing returns to scale and less than 1 in the case of decreasing returns to scale.

EXERCISES

8.1 (a) Draw total cost and total revenue curves to show the case of a firm in long-run equilibrium operating in a perfectly competitive market environment.

(b) What is the relation between price, marginal cost, and average cost?

(c) Draw the same TC and TR curves again and show how an increase in market price leads to a change in the rate of output of this firm.

(d) Now express the relation between price, marginal cost, and average cost under the new equilibrium conditions.

(e) Is this firm now making a profit? If so, show the amount of profit on the graph.

(*f*)   On a new graph, with price and marginal cost both measured on the vertical axis and quantity on the horizontal axis, show that the firm's marginal cost curve is its supply curve for the relevant range of rates of output.

8.2 (*a*) Draw the TC and TR curves as shown in Fig. 8.15. Assume an increase in wage rates so that the TC curve is shifted upward. (Since the wage bill increases with output, the vertical spread between the original and subsequent TC curves will increase with larger rates of output.)

(*b*) As you have drawn the new TC curve, will the firm continue in business or not? That is, compare the minimum loss incurred from maintaining production with that incurred if the rate of output is zero and decide which alternative results in the least loss.

(*c*) A manager sometimes says, "If I can just cover my overhead (fixed costs), I'll stay in business." Discuss the error in his reasoning.

8.3 (*a*) Assume that you are considering establishing a firm to provide helicopter service from downtown to a suburban airport. If 1 helicopter carries 20 passengers, requires 1 pilot and a given amount of fuel and service regardless of the number of passengers carried, draw the total variable cost function for rates of output per trip of from zero to 80 passengers (that is, 4 helicopters).

(*b*) Draw a linear total revenue function that just touches the total variable cost function at rates of output of 20, 40, 60, and 80 passengers per trip. If the slope of this function equals the price per trip charged each passenger, is the number of helicopters to be purchased by the firm indeterminate?

(*c*) Add to the TVC function the fixed costs of constructing a landing port. Assume, furthermore, that *if* you operate *more* than 4 helicopters you incur a very large license fee. Show that if you are to have a profitable business you will not operate more than 4 helicopters.

8.4 Draw a graph similar to Fig. 8.8 of four isoproduct curves with factor X measured on the horizontal axis and factor Y on the vertical. Label each isoproduct curve to indicate the total output the various packages of factors can produce. Draw a set of budget constraints, each of which is just tangent to one of the isoproduct curves, assuming the prices of factors X and Y are given. Note that the points of interception of these budget constraints with the X axis can be used as a measure of the number of dollars spent on factors to produce the relevant output. (Or, interception points on the Y axis could be used instead.) From the formula $TC = P_X X + P_Y Y$, if TC is given for any budget constraint, if all expenditure were made on X above (assuming $Y = 0$), and if P_X

is a given, then TC is strictly proportional to X. If X is the *numéraire* in this market treat P_X as equal to unity. Now plot values of Q on the horizontal axis, and the relevant TC (or X) on the vertical axis for each value of Q thereby constructing a long-run TC curve from the information contained in the production map.

8.5 After briefly reviewing the material on homogeneous functions in Chap. 3, show that homogeneity of a degree greater than one implies increasing returns to scale and decreasing costs of production.

8.6 Figure 8.12b has short- and long-run AC curves but does not have the related MC curves. Draw a graph that shows both MC and AC curves for the short and long run to obtain some perspective on their relation. The long-run average cost curve is sometimes called the firm's *planning* curve. If you were just starting a business in a perfectly competitive market environment, why would knowledge of the long-run average cost curve be of concern to you in making plans?

8.7 Construct a short-run supply curve from the marginal cost curves of three firms by estimating numerical values for output at various prices. Use your own numbers and scales in the graphs you draw.

9

Theory of Monopoly and Its Regulation

The theory of the firm operating in a market characterized by perfect competition is simple and capable of explaining and even predicting a wide range of behavior of those two classes of economic variables, prices and quantities. In the short run, prices will equal marginal cost; in long-run equilibrium, prices will equal marginal costs and output will be produced at minimum average costs while economic profits will be zero. But in case the market is imperfect so that managers of the firm no longer treat price as a parameter (take price as given), the range of behavior of prices and quantities becomes much less certain and predictable; the theories do not explain the determination of prices and quantities nearly so well. The theory is quite well developed in the case of monopoly, but, as the following paragraphs indicate, even here a wide range of outcomes is possible. Nevertheless, the theory is capable of providing considerable enlightenment on the question of monopoly. In the case of. duopoly, oligopoly, and monopolistic competition the state of the theory is even less satisfactory, although there are a few meaningful statements that can be made about prices and quantities even under these market structures.

In the first several paragraphs of this chapter the theory of monopoly is developed. In later paragraphs the manner and effects of regulation over monopoly are surveyed and final paragraphs of the chapter concern other types of market structure, especially duopoly.

9.1 TOTAL COST AND TOTAL REVENUE CURVES

A monopolist, unlike the manager of a perfectly competitive firm, must rely heavily upon the estimates of the demand situation provided to him by his marketing specialist, a man with a difficult task. For under monopoly managers of the firm have price-setting discretion. And the demand curve for the *industry* is now identical with the demand curve for the firm since there is, by definition, only one firm in the industry producing the good in question and there are no *potential* entrants to the industry. The most clear-cut cases of monopolies might be those in which patents or licenses protect the single supplier from competition by other firms. Other monopolies such as public utilities exist under licensing arrangements, but these are most often also subject to regulation, and discussion of regulatory behavior is deferred.

Following the total-cost–total-revenue outline of the competitive firm in the previous chapter, Fig. 9.1 illustrates the "typical" monopoly in operation. The profit-maximizing rate of output is 100 units per period. The difference between TC and TR is the measure of profits accruing to the firm. The maximizing price is the slope of the radius vector (not shown) to the relevant point on the TR curve, and average cost is the slope of the

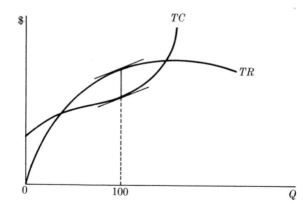

Figure 9.1

vector to the relevant point on the TC curve. The maximum vertical distance between the two curves in the cigar-shaped area occurs where the slope of the TC curve itself (marginal cost) just equals the slope of the TR curve (marginal revenue) when output is 100 units per period.

This picture differs from that in the case of perfect competition only in that the total revenue curve is concave as viewed from below rather than a straight line. This shape of total revenue curve is derived from the downward-sloping demand curve faced by the firm, since $TR = PQ$. For different prices, customers will purchase different amounts each period, and P times Q will yield the total sales revenue that the firm receives each period.

9.2 TOTAL REVENUE AND ELASTICITY

Keeping in mind the discussion of the relation between TR and elasticity in Chap. 7, it is clear that as TR is increasing $\epsilon < -1$ and therefore demand is elastic. When the peak of the TR curve is reached, demand is of unit elasticity $\epsilon = -1$ and the downward-sloping part of the TR curve indicates falling TR so that demand in this range of the curve is inelastic $-1 < \epsilon < 0$.

9.3 CHARACTERISTICS OF MONOPOLY

We shall now state the first of many points to be made about monopolistic behavior: As long as marginal costs are positive (the total cost curve is rising, indicating that additional output per period is produced at some positive additional cost), a maximizing monopolist will always set a price and quantity such that demand for the product at that price is elastic. In common discussion it is often said erroneously that monopolists have inelastic demand for their goods, but what is meant is surely that a monopolist will push price up until the demand is no longer inelastic. Of course, it is assumed here (and until otherwise noted) that the monopoly in question is unregulated. In perfect competition, the price of the good may be such that the demand for it is elastic or inelastic, but this is not so for maximizing, unregulated monopolists.

A second point concerning monopolistic behavior is that there is no necessary tendency for the monopolist to produce at a rate of output such that average cost is a minimum. In Fig. 9.1 one can see that minimum average cost would prevail at that rate of output where a vector from the origin would be just tangent to the total cost curve, approximately where $Q = 110$. This vector would have the lowest possible slope, indicating minimum average cost of production. Firms in perfect competition might, if making profits or losses, produce at some point other than at minimum average cost, but there is always a tendency for prices to adjust in these cases so that the long-run equilibrium rate of output is produced at minimum average cost. No such tendency exists for monopolists, although it is possible that demand and cost conditions could be just so for a monopolist so that when he maximizes he will just happen to be producing at minimum average cost. (The interested reader can show such a case more easily if he draws curves showing a rather larger profit position.) But there are no forces that push him to this position. If production at minimum average cost is a measure of economic efficiency in some general sense, then a monopolist *may* be very "efficient" but not necessarily.

A third point concerning monopolists is that in the short run they can be operating at a loss. By simply imagining a TR curve that stays below the TC curve and the point of minimum vertical distance between the two, one can see how this comes about. As in the case of perfect competition, revenues must be large enough to cover variable costs plus some part of fixed costs. In the long run, of course, the firm will cease to exist; but it is not true that simply because a firm is a monopoly it is necessarily able to earn positive profits.

A fourth point concerning the monopolist's pricing and output policies concerns his reaction to a change in demand. Let an increase in demand be depicted by the shift in the total revenue curve from TR_0 to TR_1 in Fig. 9.2, where TR_0 represents the

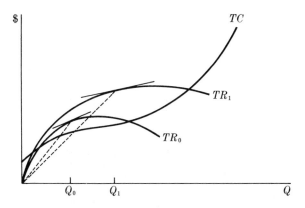

Figure 9.2

initial demand situation and TR_1 represents demand in subsequent periods. This shift in the TR curve represents an increase in demand in that a larger output per period may be sold after the shift at each and every possible price. The graph has been rigged to show that with larger rates of output Q_1 the price represented by the slope of the vector to the TR_1 curve is now lower than it was before. Thus, an increase in demand *may* lead to an increase in output and a *lower* price. Under perfect competition an increase in demand always results in a higher price in the short run.[1]

The converse of the above would be that monopolists might be observed raising the price of the product in the face of a declining demand, a situation very unlikely to occur in highly competitive markets. Cases in which this does occur are sometimes observed in the business world, and these cases strongly suggest that the firms in question do have significant monopoly power—it is evidence of an independent ability to set prices within certain ranges rather than simply responding to changes in prices imposed by the marketplace.

A fifth characteristic of monopoly is that there exists no supply curve for the industry over which the monopolist has control. A supply curve is usually written $Q_s = f(P)$, so that for various prices there exist various rates of production of the commodity as dictated by the form of the function. The function is generally considered to be upward-sloping in the belief that most industries face conditions of increasing cost, at least in the short run. That no function such as this exists for a monopolist becomes immediately evident whenever one attempts to construct one. By assuming a relatively high price in the form of a rather steep vector to point a on the TR curve in Fig. 9.3, the monopolist, if faced with this price, will produce Q_a each period. If the price is lowered, then the monopolist will produce Q_b and if lowered further Q_c. But these three points, if plotted in a graph with price and quantity on the axes, will merely trace out the demand curve for this good. Finally, if price is indicated by the vector to point d, a maximizing monopolist will produce Q_d and the quantity produced is insufficient to satisfy consumer

---

[1] In the long run, under perfect competition, the price may remain unchanged in the case of a constant cost industry. In the case of a decreasing cost industry, the long-run price could fall because of the nature of costs. Here, a monopolist may lower price even though he faces increasing costs of production in either the short or long run.

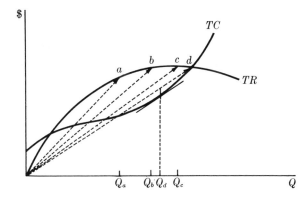

Figure 9.3

demand for the good at this price. Although the specific rate of output undertaken by a monopolist under the constraint of a given price is determinate in most cases, there is certainly no industry supply curve of the sort one presumes to exist for perfectly competitive industries. The amount a monopolist will supply depends, not simply on price, but on the *entire* shape and position of the demand curve.

A sixth point concerning monopolists, often quoted among laymen, is that they raise prices and restrict output. Presumably this means that monopoly prices are higher and output per period lower than would be the case if the industry existed in a perfectly competitive market. This proposition is generally accepted as true by economists, but it is not easily shown. Given the existence of a large number of firms in an industry that are more or less duplications of each other, the long-run total cost curve for the industry is a straight line indicating constant returns to scale as shown in Fig. 9.4.

The TR curve reflects the demand for the good in question. In perfect competition price will equal average cost, and Q_0 will be produced and sold each period at this price. If the members of this industry now form a trust, and agree among themselves on a price and output policy to maximize profits, output per period will be restricted to Q_1 with the higher price reflected in the slope of the vector to the TR curve. The case here clearly shows that the *introduction* of monopoly power leads to restricted output and higher prices. However, to show that a monopolist, in his present state, restricts output and charges higher prices is difficult, for at the outset we have a graph of

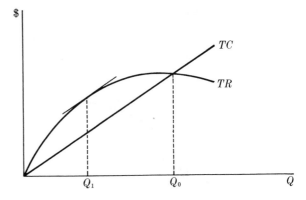

Figure 9.4

his TC and TR curves. Just what shape the TC curve for the industry would take if his monopoly power were suddenly removed is not always clear. If there are economies of scale in production, then perhaps one firm undertaking the output formerly produced by 100 firms may produce this output at lower cost, and hence output *may* be higher and prices lower under monopoly. The upshot is simply that if one is permitted to draw a different cost curve in the case of monopoly from the one drawn in the case of perfect competition, then there is no way to assert unequivocally that, in fact, monopolists do restrict output. Indeed, it has been suggested that what often appears to be a tendency for large firms to grow larger and gradually take over control of a market is due precisely to the existence of economies of scale, which implies that the aggregate of several small firms' costs of production is greater than the cost of production of a given output when it is undertaken by one large firm. Thus, one must take care in condemning monopoly power on the ground that monopolists restrict output and raise prices. It is more appropriate to refer to the abuse of conditions of welfare maximization outlined in Chap. 6, which will be discussed at greater length later in this chapter.

A seventh point concerning monopolists is that it is often said on the basis of economic analysis that the managers of a firm, especially a firm with some monopoly power, should set prices and output rates so that marginal costs equal marginal revenues if their desire is to maximize profits. The trouble is that $MC = MR$ is a necessary condition for profit maximization; it is not a sufficient condition, for MC may equal MR when

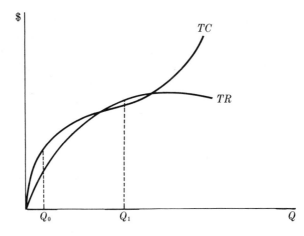

Figure 9.5

Q_0 Q_1 Q

losses are maximized. This is the case for rate of output Q_0 in Fig. 9.5.

Sometimes economists argue that $MC = MR$ is, of course, only a first-order condition for profit maximization and they say that a second-order condition is also necessary. It is the condition that MC be increasing. (Formally stated, it is that the second derivative of the TC curve be positive.) These two conditions will suffice to ensure profit maximization provided the short-run total cost curve is the smooth, reversed S-shaped curve drawn in the figure, and that the total revenue curve is smooth (with no humps) and concave from below.[1]

---

[1] If $\pi = TR - TC$, then $\pi = PQ - f(Q)$ since $P = g(Q)$ and $\pi = g(Q)Q - f(Q)$.

$$\frac{d\pi}{dQ} = g(Q) + Q\frac{d[g(Q)]}{dQ} - \frac{d[f(Q)]}{dQ}$$

since

$$MR = \frac{dTR}{dQ} = g(Q) + Q\frac{d[g(Q)]}{dQ}$$

and

$$MC = \frac{dTC}{dQ} = \frac{d[f(Q)]}{dQ}$$

then

$$\frac{d\pi}{dQ} = MR - MC$$

For maximization set this derivative equal to zero and the condition is that $MC = MR$. The second-order condition is that $d^2\pi/dQ^2 < 0$, for a maximum, or that $d(MC)/dQ > d(MR)/dQ$, which means that marginal cost must be increasing more rapidly (or decreasing less rapidly) than marginal revenue is increasing.

Having always drawn short-run cost curves of this shape it may not seem cricket to introduce a different shape at this late point in the game. But until our discussion reached this point, a curve of the usual shape sufficed. Consider, then, a short-run total cost curve of the sort depicted in Fig. 9.6. The step-like humps can easily exist in true-to-life cost curves. Think of a trucking firm. When the rate of output increases at some point, it becomes desirable to add another truck to the fleet or trade in smaller trucks for larger ones. When this occurs, a more or less sharp jump in total costs will take place. How many helicopters should be in service carrying passengers from the top of the Pan Am Building to John F. Kennedy International Airport (a service no longer offered)? A maximizing monopolist will set output Q_0 and the concomitant price. However, both first- and second-order maximizing conditions are met at point b as well as at point a. Thus, the best advice to give a monopolist or any manager who wishes to maximize profits is that he should look at his *entire* TR and TC curves and choose the rate of output at which the difference between them is greatest and set the appropriate price. Profit maximization is sufficient to ensure that $MC = MR$, but $MC = MR$ does not necessarily ensure maximum profits.

Eighth in the list of points to be made about monopolistic behavior also entails a TC curve that is altered from its normal shape. What would the manager of the monopoly do if his cost accountants and engineers combined their information and

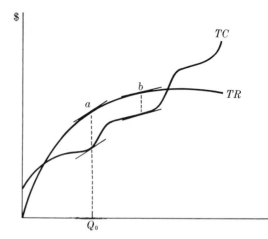

Figure 9.6

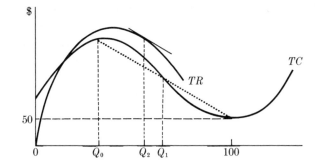

Figure 9.7

provided him with a total cost curve of the sort depicted in Fig. 9.7? (The humped figure is exaggerated for ease of illustration.) His first inclination would be to draw a horizontal line (dotted) cutting off the hump in the curve, arguing that if 100 units of output per period could be produced for $50, then surely 70 or 80 units could also be produced for no more than this sum by simply producing 100 units and disposing of the rest. The manager might be inclined to dismiss the team of specialists who gave him the original TC curve under the presumption that some error must have been made in the team's analysis. And he might be right in this a large part of the time. But, upon reflection, it might be that disposal of the extra units could not be made without some positive costs. Thus, disposing of 20 units of output per period might cost an additional $5 so that the minimum cost for 80 units would be $55 instead of $50. If the average cost per unit of disposal were constant, the dotted straight line would represent the total cost when an allowance for disposal costs was introduced in the range of output from Q_0 to Q_1. Thus, the true TC curve would be that drawn originally except for the portion lying between Q_0 and Q_1 where the cost of disposal played its role. For example, the cost of atomic-powered electricity plants requires the costly disposal of atomic wastes. The declining portion of the original cost curve might have come about if, say, some raw materials could be purchased under discounts for large quantities or if production could be carried on more cheaply somehow under a large scale of operations. Under these circumstances, therefore, a monopolist might operate to maximize his profits at Q_2, and be actively engaged in disposing of some of his output, carrying on production in a range where MR and MC were both negative.[1]

These eight considerations of monopolistic behavior hardly exhaust the possible list. They are enough to show, however, that our theory of monopoly is more complex than our theory of the competitive firm in the singular sense that monopolistic behavior is far more difficult to predict. Nevertheless, the theory is quite informative. For if the price of a good is observed to be rising when demand for it has fallen and cost conditions have remained unchanged, this is surely evidence of monopoly power, and the theory of monopoly helps us to understand events like this.[2]

9.4 PRICE, ELASTICITY, AND MARGINAL REVENUE

Before proceeding to a discussion of the regulation of the prices charged by certain monopolists under the supervision of certain regulating authorities, it is propitious to note the unique relation between elasticity, marginal revenue, and price that exists for maximizing monopolists. Since a monopolist is the sole producer of a good and no potential exists for other firms to produce it, the demand curve for the good is the monopolist's average revenue curve. The quantity that consumers will buy each period depends upon the price placed upon the good, and the monopolist can set any price he likes. It happens that, for the relevant range of possible prices, there exists a unique relation among price, marginal revenue, and the elasticity of demand. To illustrate how this relation is derived, refer to Fig. 9.8. Measure quantity per period on the horizontal axis, and measure price, average revenue, and marginal revenue all on the vertical axis. For simplicity, assume a straight-line demand curve (average revenue curve). Choose a price OP_0 and bisect the distance from A to P_0. Draw a line from point P through the bisecting point and extend it below point A. Then point B becomes a point on the marginal revenue curve. Thus, BQ_0 is marginal

---

[1] Demand would be inelastic in this case. Above it was noted that demand would always be elastic if marginal costs were positive and if the monopolist maximized profits. Here, since marginal costs are falling over a range, demand can be inelastic at the maximizing rate of output.

[2] A steel firm once raised prices when operating at 65 percent of capacity; three months earlier it had been operating at 85 percent of capacity. Thus, demand fell and afterward prices were raised.

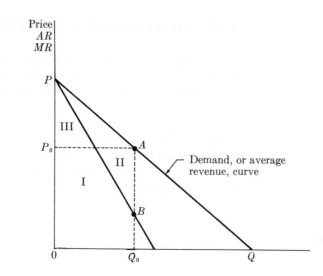

Figure 9.8

revenue when OP_0 is price. This is because areas I and II, when added together, equal total revenue $(TR = PQ)$. Also, areas II and III are identical because two angles and one side are equal for each of the two triangles. Thus, areas I and III also equal total revenue. Since these areas represent total revenue and the area under the marginal revenue curve also equals total revenue, point B is a point on the marginal revenue curve.[1]

In the case of a straight-line AR curve, the straight line from P through B is the MR curve; however, in the case of a *curved*

---

[1] The calculus student will recognize the integral of the marginal revenue curve, evaluated from O to Q_0, as the total revenue, or the area under the marginal revenue curve. Mathematically, marginal revenue can be identified at point B as follows:

Since	$MR = \dfrac{dTR}{dQ}$
and	$TR = PQ$
then	$dTR = dP\,Q + P\,dQ$
and	$MR = \dfrac{dTR}{dQ} = \dfrac{dP}{dQ}Q + P$
Since	$\dfrac{dP}{dQ} = \dfrac{-P_0P}{OQ_0} = \dfrac{-AB}{OQ_0}$
then	$MR = \dfrac{-AB}{OQ_0}OQ_0 + OP_0$
and	$MR = OP_0 - AB = AO_0 - AB = BQ_0$

AR curve, one need only draw a tangent to it at the appropriate price, construct point B, and this point is the point on the marginal revenue curve for the chosen rate of output. Each point on the marginal revenue curve will have to be constructed separately. From the discussion of elasticity in Chap. 7 it appears that, in terms of line segments,

$$\epsilon = -\frac{QA}{AP} = -\frac{QQ_0}{Q_0O} = -\frac{OP_0}{P_0P}$$

But since $P_0P = AB = AQ_0 - BQ_0$, and $OP_0 = AQ_0$, by substituting for OP_0 and PP_0 in the elasticity formula,

$$\epsilon = -\frac{AQ_0}{AQ_0 - BQ_0} = \frac{-P_0}{P_0 - MR} = \frac{P_0}{MR - P_0}$$

By transformation

$$MR = P + \frac{P}{\epsilon} \quad \text{and} \quad P = MR\,\frac{\epsilon}{\epsilon + 1}$$

(Elasticity is sometimes defined so as to remove the minus sign from the formula, and if so the relations must then be amended.[1])

With due caution for those cases in which the equality $MC = MR$ is insufficient to ensure profit maximization, one can replace MR with MC and arrive at

$$P = MC\,\frac{\epsilon}{\epsilon + 1}$$

for a maximizing monopolist. The formula indicates that if a monopolist knows the elasticity of demand for his good and if he also knows the marginal cost of production, he can then determine the price he must set on his good in order to maximize profits. This may seem like a simple thing to do, but, in fact, it is extremely difficult. First, ϵ may differ at each rate of output, and, second, MC may differ at each rate of output; and if all of this information is known, then one has nearly enough information to construct TC and TR curves, from which the

---

[1] In other texts, when elasticity is defined to be positive, the derived formulas become

$$\epsilon = \frac{P}{P - MR} \qquad MR = P - \frac{P}{\epsilon} \quad \text{and} \quad P = MR\,\frac{\epsilon}{\epsilon - 1}$$

maximizing price can readily be determined. On the other hand, if managers of the firm have a reasonable estimate of marginal cost and believe that it is constant over a relevant range of output, and if they also have a reasonable estimate of the elasticity of demand at the current price, this information may indicate the direction of a price adjustment that might lead to greater profits. Of course, whether or not the formula is useful to a businessman depends on many and varied circumstances. It is important, however, in many theoretical contexts to understand how price, marginal revenue, and elasticity (and marginal cost for a maximizing firm) are uniquely related to each other.

9.5 REGULATED MONOPOLIES

This concludes the description of the maximizing behavior of unregulated monopolists, and now it is appropriate to consider briefly how regulation of a monopolist will affect his behavior. Public utilities are regulated by duly constituted public commissions. Adam Smith, the father of economics and the one who provided the original rationale for a laissez faire pricing system, wrote extensively on the question of "natural" monopolies that must be regulated in the public interest. These are industries that are subject to decreasing costs of production as the rate of output increases. In the modern economy they are producing units that provide services of electricity, gas, water, transportation, etc. In these industries, an obvious waste of resources would occur if duplicate facilities were to be provided simultaneously by more than one firm. The rationale for regulation of monopolies applies just as well, of course, to those that stem from patent rights or to monopoly in general, whatever its source, although governments have chosen to regulate directly, for the most part, only those firms that are in the "public utility" category.

If a monopolist faces TC and TR conditions as depicted in Fig. 9.9, the unregulated price is the slope of the radius vector to point a, for at this price the monopolist maximizes profits. A regulatory commission setting a price higher than this would have no effect on the industry, for the monopolist is led by maximization motives to set only a price this great, and managers would ask the commission for permission to lower the price. Such a request would surely be granted. However, the

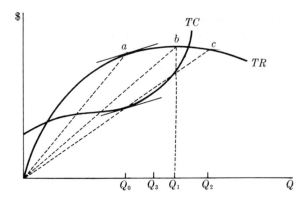

Figure 9.9

regulatory commission can set a price lower than this, as, for example, that price equal to the slope of the vector to point *b*. Living under this legal restraint, in a real sense the monopolist now faces a total revenue curve that follows the vector from the origin up to point *b*, and it kinks there to follow along the original TR curve rightward. This is because the monopolist has no power to charge any higher price. Thus, at any rate of output just below Q_1, $MC < MR$, for MR is now the slope of the regulated price vector; but at any rate of output greater than Q_1, $MC > MR$, for MR is now the slope of the TR curve. Hence, the maximum profits, under regulation, now exist at rate of output Q_1.

What if regulators become even more aggressive in their desire to eliminate monopoly profits and impose that price indicated by the slope of the vector to point *c*? Consumers will wish to purchase rate of output Q_2 each period, but the monopolist will only wish to sell Q_3, for it is here that profits are maximized under the new price constraint. This situation is obviously unstable. If the regulators insist that all consumer demand be satisfied at this price and force the monopolist to produce at Q_2 each period, the business will soon fail from losses it makes each period. If the regulators do not insist, then customers will queue for the available supplies and those privileged to be first in line may buy large amounts and sell to those at the end of the line at higher prices. The firm would have no incentive to advertise its product and might even actively discourage sales in various subtle ways. After World War II, in the United States it was accepted that someone new moving into town would have to wait 6 months to have a telephone installed in his home. Thus, on occasion, the situation depicted has existed. But, after a time the pressures for larger output by dissatisfied customers and the costs of increased output lead regulators to revise their prices upward.

In Fig. 9.10 the regulated price is such that regulators can insist that demand by consumers is satisfied, at Q_1 units per period, even though profits would be greater at some lower rate of output Q_0. At Q_1, $MC > MR$ and again the firm would wish to discourage sales by offering inferior service, even though some profits accrue to the firm each period and no threat of bankruptcy exists if consumer demand is satisfied.

In Fig. 9.11, care has been taken to ensure that the TR curve is drawn through the point on the TC curve at which average costs are a minimum. Thus, the slope of the radius vector just

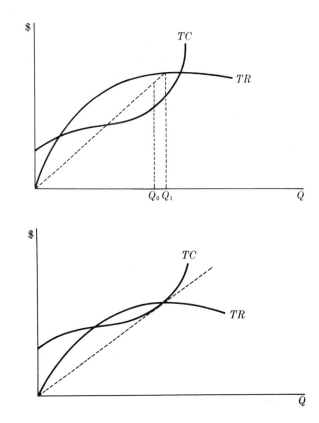

Figure 9.10

Figure 9.11

equals average cost, marginal cost, and regulated price. Here, regulators are able to simulate conditions of perfect competition by the simple expedient of setting just that price for the product that leaves profits zero, demand satisfied, and $P = MC$. Costs, of course, include all implicit and explicit costs of production. Managers are paid salaries commensurate with their responsibilities, and stockholders and bondholders receive returns on their investments that approximately equal returns on their investments of similar quality. When $P = MC$, the paretian condition for maximum welfare is satisfied (see Chap. 6) just as it is in perfect competition; and $P = $ minimum AC, which is the long-run equilibrium condition of the firm in perfect competition. The curves were drawn to show this unique case.

9.6 LUMP-SUM TAXES AND SUBSIDIES

It must be only by the remotest accident that demand and cost would be such as to bring about a TR curve that intersects the TC curve precisely at the point of minimum AC. And therefore, it is unlikely that regulating authorities can bring about conditions of equality between marginal cost and price using their price-setting powers alone. However, if we permit the regulating authority to tax the monopolist a lump sum each period as well as regulating the price charged, an optimum position can always be reached; an example is given in Fig. 9.12.

The regulating authority must now consider a variety of possible prices. Of course, for each rate of output there is some value for marginal cost that can be observed by looking at the

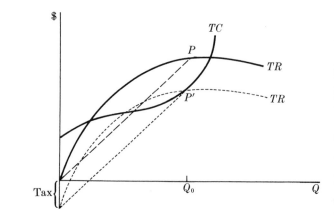

Figure 9.12

slope of the TC curve, and so for each possible price there is some rate of output such that $P = MC$. However, there is only *one* rate of output for which $P = MC$, *and* the quantity that people will purchase each period at that price just equals the output that the monopolist will produce each period. That is, there is only one point on the TR curve for which the slope of the vector to that point P equals the slope of the TC curve for that value of Q_0. The regulating authority should set this price and simultaneously impose a lump-sum tax to be paid each period just equal to the profits made by the firm each period when charging that price and producing and selling the relevant output each period.[1] The tax can be viewed as a vertical lowering of the TR curve, and the new TR curve representing the firm's revenues inclusive of subsidy for different rates of output (dotted) intersects the TC curve at the point where $MC = P$. However, at P', $MC > AC$ and therefore $P > AC$, which accounts for the firm's profit position. Only at a slightly lower rate of output would AC be minimized.

In the case of combined tax and price-setting regulations, the optimal welfare condition of $P = MC$ can be achieved and profits can be eliminated while leaving the amounts that people will buy equal to the amounts that the producer is willing to sell each period. It is a general principle that if one has two goals, then one needs at least two policy tools in order to achieve them. Thus, except in special cases, to achieve the paretian optimum welfare condition *and* ensure that the demand for output just equals its supply while eliminating profit, authority needs both power to set price and authority to levy taxes.

The counterpart case in which subsidies are paid to the producer is illustrated in Fig. 9.13. Once again think of rotating the price vector downward until a point on the TR curve is reached such that the slope of the vector (price) just equals MC for that rate of output. Then, if a lump-sum subsidy is allotted to this producer each period to make up his loss from operating at such a low price, he will move to the rate of output at which the optimum condition $P = MC$ is just met, profits and losses are nonexistent, and the quantity supplied by the firm at that price just equals the quantity that consumers will buy at that price each period. At this rate of output, $AC > MC$

[1] Some economists suggest that remaining profits could be "taxed away" by selling a license to operate the firm through competitive bids as in an auction.

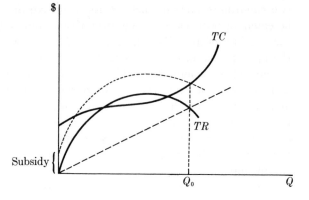

Figure 9.13

and $AC > P$, which explains the basic loss position. Losses are made up by the subsidy. The subsidy can be thought of as raising the TR curve at every point by the amount of the subsidy. In this case the new dotted TR curve just intersects the point on the TC curve where $P = MC$. The dotted curve represents the amounts that producers receive for various rates of output, while the original TR curve still represents the total amount consumers pay for different rates of output. Minimum AC occurs at a slightly higher rate of output than that for which $P = MC$.

In these cases one objective is to remove profits or losses, as the case may be. It is because public utilities supposedly exist at the pleasure of the public and are supposed to operate in the public interest that such objectives are of concern. The monopolist in these cases is *compensated* for his loss (in the case of profit one thinks of the tax as *negative compensation*) in order to arrive at the suitable result. However, if we concern ourselves with monopolies that exist because of patent rights, we may not wish to remove profits. Patents are offered so that inventors may be rewarded for their inventions by exploiting whatever market potential exists for the invention. Unfortunately, to exploit the invention the firm sets prices on the monopolized good that gives a profit to the inventor, and this price will not equal marginal cost. If, however, a governmental authority were to bargain with the holder of a patent and offer to pay him a lump-sum difference between what his profits would be if he set the price that maximized profits and what profits would be if he set a price equal to marginal cost at a point on the TR curve, then he would be indifferent as between the two conditions since his net returns inclusive of subsidies would be equal in both cases. The authority would then offer to pay the subsidy as a "bribe" in exchange for the privilege of setting the appropriate price. Thus with the subsidy production could be carried on where $P = MC$ (a welfare-maximizing position), and at the same time the patent owner would be compensated and rewarded for the value of his contribution to society. In this way a program of compensation may be applied in those cases in which we wish to reward the monopolist just as in the case of public utilities in which we wish only to accommodate the monopolist.

9.7 COMPENSATION AND THE BOX DIAGRAM

To show how consumers can be better off by paying a lump-sum tax and then being able to purchase the good at a lower price, while compensating the monopolist, requires that we shift to the box diagram as a tool of analysis. The box diagram, used to describe the paradigm of the consumers' market in Chap. 2, is useful as well in helping one to understand many of the essential ingredients of monopoly power and the theoretical justification for compensating monopolists.

In Fig. 9.14 point a represents the solution to the distribution of the available quantities of goods 1 and 2 between consumers A and B when neither A nor B have any market power. Mr.

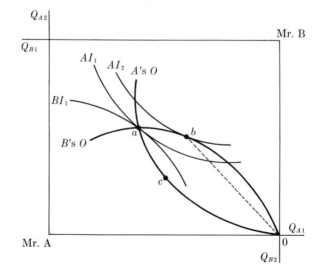

Figure 9.14

A's O is his offer curve generated by points of tangency of price lines (to Mr. A's indifference curves) as they are rotated while hinged onto the origin 0 representing the quantity of good 1 that Mr. A brings to market each period (the reader may recall this from Chap. 2). Mr. B's O curve is generated in the same fashion; point a is the point of intersection of the two curves, and AI_1 and BI_1 are, respectively, Mr. A and Mr. B's indifference curves through point a. These curves are tangent, indicating that at a $_AMRS_{1,2} = {_B}MRS_{1,2}$, which is a paretian optimum welfare condition. Furthermore, these rates of substitution equal the slope of the line from a to 0, which equals $-P_1/P_2$, all of which should be familiar to the student from Chap. 2. Point a tells us how the available amounts of goods 1 and 2 are divided between Mr. A and Mr. B in conditions of perfect competition.

Let us assume now that Mr. A is a monopolist and Mr. B has no economic power but must simply be a *price-taker* in the market. Mr. A has the ability to set any price he likes. In order for him to maximize his utility he raises the price of good 1 (the good he enters the market to sell) until the price ratio indicated by the slope of the line from b to 0 prevails. If Mr. A is a maximizing monopolist, at the price implicit in this ratio he reaches point b, the point at which Mr. A's indifference curve is just tangent to Mr. B's offer curve. AI_2 is the highest indifference curve that Mr. A can reach by setting the price of good 1, for Mr. B will also be willing to move to point b if faced with the price of good 1 set by Mr. A. Of course, point b is not a point on the contract curve. Therefore, the condition of maximum economic welfare is not met if the goods are divided between Mr. A and Mr. B according to the division implicit in point b.

In Fig. 9.15 some of the original curves are omitted to avoid clutter, while the contract curve does appear. AI_2 is the indifference curve of Mr. A tangent to B's O, and BI_2 is Mr. B's indifference curve that intersects point b, while tangent to the price vector from 0 to b. These two indifference curves form a cigar-shaped area through which the contract curve runs from b' to d. Thus, a redistribution of goods 1 and 2 represented by any point between b' and d would make *both* Mr. A and Mr. B better off than they are at point b because they would both be on higher indifference curves.

A movement to point b' can be accomplished if a lump-sum subsidy is offered to Mr. A in exchange for a lower price of

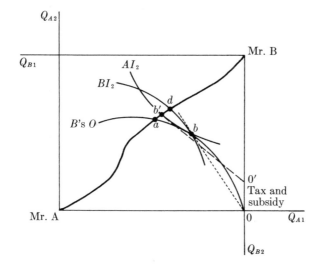

Figure 9.15

good 1. Since Mr. A is just as well off at point b' as he is at point b (he is on the same indifference curve), he should not object to this proposal. Thus, transfer a fixed amount of good 2 to Mr. A each period so that he begins his trading from point $0'$ instead of point 0. Mr. B is taxed this amount, and Mr. A is paid a subsidy of the same amount. Now, set the price of good 1 such that the ratio $-P_1/P_2$ equals the slope of the line from b' to $0'$. At this price ratio Mr. A and Mr. B will freely trade goods 1 and 2 until the final distribution of goods between them is that represented by point b'. Mr. A is as well off as before. Mr. B has suffered a tax burden, but the lower price of good 1 enables him to reach a higher indifference curve, so his welfare position has improved. Mr. A has been compensated for his monopolist's position and has been bribed to set a lower price so that the composite welfare of the community has increased.

Consider Mr. A in this example to be a monopolist domestically but a competitor if foreign imports are allowed; that is, for some reason the people of a community may wish to *protect* certain *private interests* at home by setting quotas or tariffs on imports. These restrictions on imports allow the monopolist to charge higher prices than the competitive price that would prevail under free importing. Thus, the example of bribing the monopolist with a direct lump-sum subsidy would apply to monopolists whose position is protected by import barriers just as well as to those protected by patents or some other market power device. Better use is made of the limited resources that are available than would have been the case if the monopolist's power prevailed unharnessed. Thus, for example, a program under which the government would tax the people of the community, buy up the patent rights on an invention from the inventor, and release the patent to be freely used might enable everyone in the community to be better off than they would be if the inventor were to exploit the patent by monopolistic selling practices. The political and administrative difficulties in implementing such a program are, of course, quite great. Difficulties may also arise in the case of lump-sum subsidies or taxes for regulated monopolists if these monopolists should learn that, say, the compensating tax they paid depended on their output decision. They might no longer care about minimizing costs of production if they knew higher costs would simply mean smaller taxes. In the world of political and administrative reality these optimizing goals are beyond reach. But one should recognize that the existing program for supporting inventors in their work is economically inefficient in the sense that welfare is not being maximized under it and that the search for a closer approximation to efficiency should continue.

9.8 PRICE DISCRIMINATION: THE ALL-OR-NOTHING OFFER

The box diagram can also be used to show another type of monopolistic pricing, sometimes called *perfect price discrimination* or the case of the *all-or-nothing* offer. In Fig. 9.16 point c is on Mr. B's indifference curve BI_3, which also is the curve that passes through point 0. This means that Mr. B is just as "happy" at point c as he would be if he simply kept his original periodic endowment of good 2 at point 0 for his own consumption; point c is also on the contract curve. Now if Mr. A offers to trade 10 units of good 1 for 30 units of good 2, and if he makes this offer on an all-or-nothing basis, then Mr. B is left undecided. Thus Mr. A offers only the slightest extra inducement, Mr. B then agrees to the trade, and the two exchange goods in amounts implicit, approximately, in point c. In a pertinent sense there is no price ratio in this case, for when faced with the offer Mr. B might have said, "Couldn't I purchase a smaller quantity at this rate?" But, Mr. A will permit no purchases of smaller amounts; he offers to exchange

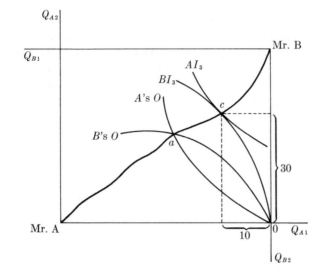

Figure 9.16

on an all-or-nothing basis only—take it or leave it! Mr. A gets to the highest indifference curve that he possibly can in carrying out any trade with Mr. B. In this Mr. A is a perfectly discriminating monopolist, and Mr. B gets essentially only the smallest benefit from trading with Mr. A. And yet welfare is maximized in the sense that a movement away from point c would cause at least one of the two parties to the exchange to be worse off.

All-or-nothing offers are rare in the real marketplace. On occasion one takes place on a *once-and-for-all* basis. Consider, for example, a highly specialized surgical operation that Mr. B desires and only Mr. A can perform; rarely does it take place repeatedly period after period. And one must remember that the quantity of good 1 and quantity of good 2 are outputs per period of time. Examples of perfect price discrimination in practice are impossible to find when remembering that the purchases by Mr. B are repeated period after period according to the substance of the diagrams. If, for example, Mr. B can substitute one period's consumption for the next period's, then he may accept the all-or-nothing offer in the first period but hold some of it over until the next period and thereby reduce his rate of consumption in each of the two periods—which Mr. A had tried to prevent him from doing when imposing the all-or-nothing offer in the first place.

9.9 BILATERAL MONOPOLY

The box diagram can also be used to help one understand bilateral monopoly, that is, the case in which both Mr. B and Mr. A were monopolists facing each other in the marketplace. Mr. A would try to set a price for good 1 such that the price line passes through point *b* (Fig. 9.14 above). Mr. B would try to set a price on good 2 such that the price line would be much more flat and might intersect point *c* on Mr. A's offer curve. (This line is not shown on the diagram.) In this case all one says is that the final bargaining position would be between these extremes, for Mr. A would pay no more for good 2 and Mr. B would pay no more for good 1 so that points *b* and *c* set the limits for the outcome of prices and quantities. The relative bargaining strength of the two monopolists, if one could evaluate it, would determine the final solution for prices and quantities. Economists have no way of determining anything other than the *limits*, or *range*, within which bargaining will take place.

An essential characteristic of all forms of price discrimination engaged in by monopolists is that markets must be separated in one way or another and kept separate. In the case of perfect discrimination involving the all-or-nothing offer, it is clear that Mr. B would prefer to buy less than the quantity offered at the implicit price ratio. If he could sell off part of his purchase in a secondary market, then he could improve his position. Thus, if Mr. A is going to practice this form of price discrimination with more than one other person, his customers must be barred from getting together, otherwise they would arrange to buy, say, one package of goods from Mr. A and split this quantity among themselves.

9.10 TWO MARKETS—MARGINAL REVENUES EQUAL

That markets must be kept separate also applies in the case of other forms of price discrimination. For example, if there are two separate markets for a good, a monopolist faces two separate demand curves (TR curves) and can set different prices in each of the two markets. Maximizing profit here necessitates the condition that $MR_I = MR_{II} = MC$, where the subscripts I and II indicate the two separate markets. Of course, the quantities sold in each market and the prices charged in each market may, and doubtless will, differ. An example might be found in the general practice of utility companies of charging lower prices to industrial users (of, say, electricity) than they charge to household users. It would seem that under this arrangement an industrial user, if permitted, would resell electricity from his own shop to householders in the neighborhood and profit by doing so. This does not happen only because these markets are legally separated.[1]

9.11 THE QUANTITY DISCOUNT AS PRICE DISCRIMINATION

There is yet another general form of price discrimination commonly found to be practiced by monopolists—the *quantity discount;* again it is especially noticeable in the case of public utilities. A householder may, for example, pay 3 cents per kilowatt hour of electricity for the first 1,000 kilowatt hours used each month, 2 cents for the next 1,000, and 1 cent for all kilowatt hours above this. In Fig. 9.17 there is illustrated an example of this sort, with prices magnified in order to show the impact of the discount pricing mechanism. (The reader will recognize the figure and the following discussion as repetitive of the discussion of discount pricing that appears at the end of Chap. 3. There the consumer was the focal point of our concern; here the emphasis is on the market power of the producer to set such patterns of prices.)

---

[1] There are, however, doubtless some differences in the cost of providing service to householders and the cost of providing it to industrial users. Insofar as these costs differ, there is some justification for some amount of difference in the price charged.

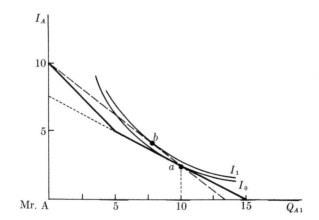

Figure 9.17

Mr. A's indifference map, drawn in the figure, differs slightly from prior maps in that there is a measure of his money income on the vertical axis. It is given to represent, for heuristic reasons, the value he places on the packages of all goods other than good 1 that Mr. A can buy with his income. To do this it is implicitly assumed that the marginal utility of money income to Mr. A is constant. This simplifying assumption allows one to speak in terms of dollar prices rather than price ratios and facilitates the provision of a numerical example. Assume that Mr. A's income each period is $10. If he must pay $1 per unit for each unit of good 1 that he buys up to 5 units, the budget constraint follows the heavy line down to the point where $5 are spent on 5 units of good 1. From here if he must pay only 50 cents per unit for all quantities purchased over 5, the budget line moves on down intersecting the horizontal axis at 15. Thus, if he spent all of his income on this good, he would be able to purchase 15 units; the budget constraint shows all the various quantities that he can buy for various amounts of expenditures on good 1, given his income and the pattern of prices he faces.

Mr. A maximizes his satisfaction, in the case illustrated, when he buys 10 units of good 1 each period and reaches point a on indifference curve I_0. The *average* price that he pays for all 10 units ($1.00 for 5 units and 50 cents for another 5 units) is 75 cents, and he spends $7.50 on good 1 each period. If he had had to pay only 75 cents per unit for each unit he bought, he would have purchased only 7 units and maximized his satisfaction by moving to point b on indifference curve I_1. Thus he could improve his position if he could be charged only what he pays on the average. However, he would buy less good 1, and the purveyor of good 1 takes in less revenue. Under this form of price discrimination, then, revenues to the monopolist increase as well as the quantity sold.[1]

If we imagine that the part of the price line representing $P_1 = 50$ cents were extended leftward along the dotted line until it intersected the vertical axis, another form of price discrimination can be shown. Assume that Mr. A was charged a hookup fee of $2.50 per period and then allowed to consume as much

---

[1] Earlier in the chapter the question was raised as to whether monopolists raise prices and restrict output. It was mentioned then that this is a difficult proposition to show; here a discriminating monopolist is shown to expand output.

as he liked at 50 cents per unit. He would again move to indifference curve I_0, spending a total of $7.50 on good 1. Examples of this sort of pricing practice are easily found. Telephone companies sometimes have monthly charges plus 5 cents per call. To see Disneyland one pays an entrance fee and then pays set charges for single displays inside. When collection costs are moderate, these pricing policies are more profitable to the firms practicing them than single prices would be. It might also be noted that Mr. A could have an indifference curve that just touched the budget constraint at two points, one where $P_1 = \$1.00$ and one where $P = 50$ cents. In this case there would exist no *unique* solution to the determination of price and quantity.

The equilibrium point on I_0 illustrated above could be a point on the contract curve if Mr. A and the monopolist were the only two persons in the economy; hence welfare could be *maximized* here. However, if the monopolist sells to two persons, Mr. A and Mr. B, and one of them ceases to purchase additional amounts before the price reverts to its lower level, then we have the condition under which two different prices are charged for the same commodity. Hence, it is not the case that Mr. A's marginal rate of substitution of good 1 for other goods will equal Mr. B's marginal rate of substitution of good 1 for other goods. If Mr. A could do so, he would sell some of his 10 units of good 1 to Mr. B at 75 cents, and be better off. Mr. B would also be better off. Once again, the markets must be segregated to effectively charge different rates. Note, however, that hookup charges amount to de facto price differentials and that they effectively bar the possibility that one person would pay a different price per unit of commodity than another.[1]

The monopolist's decision to set a particular price or set of discount prices, as described in these illustrations, depends, not only on the demand conditions as represented by consumers' indifference maps, but also upon costs of production; these costs are not shown in the figures. Suffice it to say that costs of supplying the quantity measured on the horizontal axis will differ for each quantity, and for maximization of profits $MC = MR$ as usual. Here, MR is the lowest of the discount prices. If MC approaches zero, then the hookup, or gate fee, concept plus zero charges ($MR = 0$) per unit would enable the

[1] Of course, under the hookup charges some persons will not have a telephone installed but will pay 10 cents per call from time to time.

monopolist to acquire the largest profits. Of course, to maximize profits from sales to *each* individual in the community might require charging each consumer a different hookup charge. (Refer to Sec. 2.16 for notes on maximum hookup charges.)

Since in this case in which the equation $P = MR = MC = 0$ holds, the paretian conditions for maximum welfare are met and one can see the analogy with the case of the all-or-nothing offer of the perfectly discriminating monopolist in which paretian maximizing conditions held. To buy telephone service for his home a consumer typically faces an all-or-nothing offer. If a different fee could be set for each household, the telephone company could act as a perfectly discriminating monopolist. If, however, the fee charged each household represented interest charges on the proportionate share of the capital cost of the installation of equipment, then the system of pricing is efficient in the paretian sense and also "fair." For example, assume installation costs amounted to $900. If the market interest rate is 8 percent then interest on this amount would be $72. A telephone bill of $6 per month for 12 months of the year would equal $72. Thus, charging each household $6 per month and pricing telephone calls at zero is efficient and the consumer pays full cost. A price higher than $6 under these conditions could be considered "exploitation" of some sort but in any case it should be noted that the fee-setting decision is separate from the pricing decision when by price we mean, not the monthly fee, but the price per unit of service provided. The cost of telephone service to a consumer is different from the price of a call.

In this chapter the theory of monopoly and its regulation have been the subjects of discussion. Of course, monopoly changes its face over time. In 1870 who would have thought that by 1970 trucks and airplanes would offer such heavy competition to railroads? Should railroads be regulated now? Should they be subsidized? Whatever the politician's answer to these questions, it is clear that the monopoly position once enjoyed by railroad entrepreneurs is absent today. The static analysis provided by formal theory must be applied with caution in a dynamic world.

EXERCISES

9.1 Draw TC and TR curves to illustrate the case of a monopolist who maximizes profits but who also happens to produce at minimum average cost of production. It may be best to draw the TC curve first, note the rate of output at which AC is a minimum, and then draw in a TR curve such that profits (the vertical distance that TR is above TC) are a maximum.

9.2   The TC curve in Fig. 9.1 is presumably a short-run cost curve because of the existence of fixed costs. Draw the long-run cost curve of a monopolist which faces a production function showing constant returns to scale (assume fixed factor prices); draw his TR curve too. If the monopolist can make profits, will he produce at minimum average cost? Will the price he sets be equal to, less than, or greater than average cost? Will marginal cost be greater than, equal to, or less than average cost?

9.3   Draw TC and TR curves to illustrate a monopolist minimizing his *losses* by his operation.

9.4   Draw a graph similar to that in Fig. 9.3, and then in another graph with price on the vertical axis and quantity on the horizontal axis note a selected set of pairs of prices and quantities in an attempt to show the supply curve for a monopolist. Note the segment of this curve that is a *supply* curve and the segment that is a *demand* curve as well as a *supply* curve.

9.5   Draw a figure similar to Fig. 9.8 and calculate, by means of line segments, the numerical value of the coefficient of elasticity of demand and the marginal revenue that correspond with the chosen price.

9.6   If marginal cost were constant and equal to $28 per unit, what price should a profit-maximizing monopolist set when selling this good if the elasticity of demand were constant and equal to -5?

9.7   The box diagram of Fig. 9.14 illustrates the case of Mr. A as a monopolist. Draw a similar diagram and show the price ratio when Mr. B is the monopolist and Mr. A has no market power.

9.8   The box diagram of Fig. 9.15 illustrates how a monopolist might be bribed by a lump-sum subsidy to set a lower price and leave everyone in the community on higher indifference curves. This diagram is difficult to draw. Assume that Mr. B, rather than Mr. A, is the monopolist and illustrate the case of improved welfare under lump-sum subsidies for the compensated monopolist.

9.9   Using the box diagram of Fig. 9.16 as a reference, illustrate the case of Mr. B, rather than Mr. A, as the perfectly discriminating (all-or-nothing) monopolist.

10

Other Forms
of
Market Structure

Imperfect competition is a comprehensive term; it covers four recognized subcategories of market structure: monopoly (the subject of Chap. 9), duopoly, oligopoly, and monopolistic competition. For many purposes, *duopoly*, meaning *two firms*, and *oligopoly*, meaning *a few firms*, can be used interchangeably.

10.1 RIVAL'S BEHAVIOR

The theory of the firm in perfect competition is relatively straightforward and useful. The theory of monopoly is more complicated, and prediction of monopoly prices and outputs is more difficult because a greater variety of behavior patterns are consistent with the pursuit of profits by a monopolist. But the theory of duopoly is even less satisfactory. Indeed, one should refer to *theories* of duopoly, for economists recognize several, each of which provides a different picture of the determination of price and output. A duopolist's decisions with respect to the price that he sets and the output he produces each period depend upon his rival's *reaction* or what he believes his rival's reaction will be. Unless a duopolist knows, or thinks he knows, what his rival's reaction will be, there simply exists no such thing as a *demand curve* for the output of his firm, at least not in the usual sense of the term. Thus under simple monopoly there exists no supply curve and under duopoly or oligopoly there may exist neither a demand nor a supply curve.

10.2 KINKED DEMAND

Paul Sweezy's *kinked demand curve* provides an excellent format to illustrate the importance of "a competitor's reaction" in understanding price and output under duopoly or oligopoly.[1] Figure 10.1a and b helps in understanding Sweezy's theory. In Fig. 10.1a the vertical axis measures price, or average revenue, marginal revenue, and marginal cost; in Fig. 10.1b the vertical axis measures total revenue and total cost. In both figures, the reader will note that quantity per period is measured on the horizontal axis.

Assume that the current price of an oligopolist's good is the vertical height of point a in Fig. 10.1a. According to Sweezy, if the managers of this firm raise the price of the good, competitors will *not* raise their prices too; thus, the solid line to the left of point a is the average revenue, or demand, curve. If the competitors would raise their prices too, the dotted line to the left of point a would be the average revenue curve. The solid average revenue curve falls to the right of point a because managers believe that if they lower the price of this good competitors will also lower their prices; hence, sales volume will not increase greatly. The dotted line to the right of point a indicates that a larger volume of sales could be expected if other competitors did *not* lower their prices too. Thus, one might say that, in Sweezy's view, oligopolists are pessimists. Attempts to raise prices to improve profits will *not* be followed by competitors, but attempts to lower prices to improve profits will immediately *be* followed by competitors. In either case, it turns out that profits cannot be improved by changing prices in either direction. This argument is often used to explain the "stickiness" of some prices. (Chewing gum was 5 cents per package for several decades.)

Since the average revenue curve has a "kink" in it at point

---

[1] Paul Sweezy, Demand under Conditions of Oligopoly, *J. Political Econ.*, vol. XLVII, pp. 568–573, 1939.

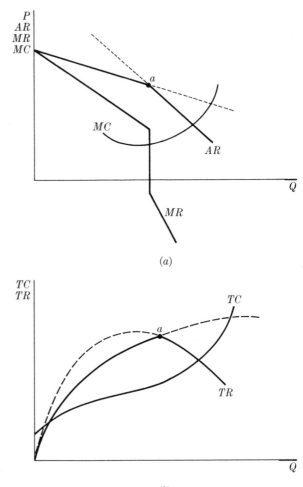

Figure 10.1

(b)

a, the marginal revenue curve assumes any one of many values
for the relevant rate of output. Thus, the maximizing condition
that marginal cost equal marginal revenue is met for many
different values of marginal cost. If wage rates increased, the
marginal cost curve would shift upward. But if the upward
shift were not too great, the oligopolist would not raise his price
in response to this increase in his costs as would a monopolist
or managers of a firm in perfect competition; nor would he
lower his price if marginal costs fell somewhat.

The total revenue curve in Fig. 10.1*b* has a kink in it at point *a*. The curve has been drawn so as to rise up to point *a* and fall for larger rates of output. Thus, marginal revenue is falling but positive in the range to the left of point *a*, and falling and negative to the right of point *a*. The dotted portions of the total revenue curve are analogous to those in Fig. 10.1*a*; they indicate what demand would be if competitors raised prices too and what demand would be if competitors failed to lower prices too.

Perhaps the fundamental weakness of Sweezy's theory is that although it explains why oligopolists' prices are sticky, it fails to explain how the oligopolist's price came to be what it is in the first place. Thus, if one wants a theory to explain *price determination* as opposed to *price rigidity*, the Sweezy theory is of little help. The theory of *kinked demand* can be used to rationalize sticky prices and also to illustrate the importance attached to the reactions of competitors to each other's price- and output-setting decisions. When these reactions are important to the participants, the market is called a duopoly or an oligopoly. *Reactions* form the distinguishing characteristics of these market structures.

10.3 SPATIAL COMPETITION

Competitors' reactions play a fundamental role in the interpretation of duopolistic behavior in establishing *location* as well as prices. The analysis of what is often called *spatial* competition stems largely from the work of Hotelling.[1] He explains why one finds several service stations congregated at one intersection; why furniture stores or banks are often grouped together in particular areas of town; why television networks tend to show the same type of program leveled at the same "median" viewer; and even why intermediate economics textbooks cover the same material for the most part.

Space, in its generic sense, refers to any criterion for measurement. Thus, points *A* and *B* form the line in Fig. 10.2 that may represent two ends of Main Street in a small town, or they may represent the low and high intelligence levels of viewers in a regional television area. Assume that two producers of

[1] Harold Hotelling, Stability in Competition, *Econ. J.*, vol. XXXIX, pp. 41–57, 1929.

Figure 10.2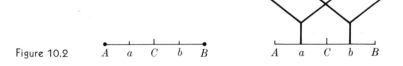

a good are located at points a and b; also assume that customers are distributed evenly along the line from A to B, and that they incur transportation costs equal to a given amount per unit of distance traveled for delivery. Thus, all customers between points A and C will buy from the supplier at a, and all those between B and C will buy from the supplier at b. The right-hand part of Fig. 10.2 helps illustrate this result. The vertical distances of the lines at points a and b may represent production costs at the originating supply points, and the sloping lines show transportation costs. Thus, the height of the line at A indicates the total cost—both supply and transport—of this good to a customer who lives at A. The customer who lives at C is indifferent in his attitude toward suppliers, but all other customers can buy the good at a lower cost if they trade with the supplier closest at hand.

Thus far, it is assumed that the suppliers just happened to be located where transportation costs will be minimized for the consumers (the quartile points along the line). However, if the supplier at point a lost his plant as the result of a fire and was faced with the choice of relocating, where would he set up business? Choosing the location just to the left of point b would give him the largest number of customers; similarly, though, relocation on the part of the supplier at point b would involve a move to the left toward point a. Thus, the two suppliers would tend to move closer to each other, and in the long run both would end up at point C. Because this position maximizes the transportation costs that must be incurred by the customers who live along the line, it is clear that the community welfare is not being maximized.

Figure 10.2, of course, can be altered to show differences in costs of production and differences in transportation costs; furthermore, the argument can be extended from location to other differences in product. Duopolistic market structure leads firms to mimic each other and provide less than the desirable amount of product differentiation from the point of view of the consuming public.

In 1838 Augustin Cournot tackled the question of duopoly price and output. His mathematical treatment was foreign to economists of his day and his work went unnoticed for many years. He assumed that there were two producers of water from mineral springs, that the water could be provided to customers at zero cost, and that each producer believes that his rival's output will remain unchanged no matter what rate of output he himself decides to set.[1]

Since $MC = 0$, then for maximum profits to exist, $MR = 0$. In Fig. 10.3a there appears a hypothetical linear demand, or *average revenue* (AR), curve for the mineral water produced by the two rivals. *Marginal revenue* (MR), shown by the dashed line, equals zero at its point of intersection with the horizontal axis. Since the demand curve is linear, output per period will be just half of the distance from the origin to the point at which the AR curve intersects the horizontal axis and price per unit of output will be just half the distance from the origin to the point at which the AR curve intersects the vertical axis. If the two producers got together, they could set price P_α and sell Q_α; they could collude and operate as a single monopolist. Then, through bilateral negotiation, they would have to arrange to divide the profits. In the past, market-sharing agree-

---

[1] If the two producers are α and β, then β believes that $\Delta Q_\alpha/\Delta Q_\beta = 0$ and α believes that $\Delta Q_\beta/\Delta Q_\alpha = 0$.

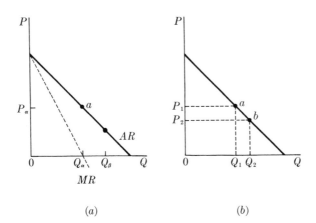

Figure 10.3   (a)   (b)

ments among rivals have constituted this sort of profit sharing. In the United States and many other countries antitrust laws prohibit such overt collusion today.

Cournot's argument did not entail collusion. Instead, he assumed that one producer set output Q_α. Then, the second producer takes this output as given and views the demand curve for his own product as that part of the AR curve from a to Q. Since this is linear, this second producer will attempt to maximize by selling in this remaining part of the market and will operate at a point halfway between a and Q and sell $Q_\beta - Q_\alpha$ each period. According to Cournot, the first producer will now assume that this rate of output by the second producer is given, and so the first producer will change his rate of output and will produce a rate of output half of the amount that is left over after subtracting the segment $Q_\alpha Q_\beta$ from OQ. The second producer, in like fashion, will now revise his original output rate and produce half of the remaining quantity; the first producer will again revise his output rate, and so forth. The convergence leads to the solution shown in Fig. 10.3b.

With one producer, maximum profit can be made by operating at point a, setting price at P_1 and output at Q_1. With two producers the price will be P_2 and the quantity produced will be Q_2, each producer selling half of the output sold. Rate of output OQ_2 is, of course, two-thirds of OQ; and OP_2 is one-third of OP. If three producers entered the market under these conditions, output OQ_3 would be three-quarters of OQ, and OP_3 would be one-quarter of OP. For n producers the rate of output would be $n/(n + 1)$ times OQ, and the price would be $1/(n + 1)$ times OP.

Bertrand criticized Cournot's model of oligopoly. While Cournot assumed that each competitor takes his rival's quantity as given, Bertrand assumed that each competitor takes his rival's price as given.[1] Thus neither competitor believes his rival will lower his price to meet a price reduction, and thus each competitor thinks he can take all of the market away from his rival by lowering his price a slight amount. Successive price cutting will stop only when price falls to equality with marginal cost. Thus in Bertrand's model the existence of two producers is suffi-

---

[1] For producers α and β, Bertrand holds that β assumes $\Delta P_\alpha / \Delta P_\beta = 0$ and that α assumes $\Delta P_\alpha / \Delta P_\beta = 0$.

cient to drive prices to the level that would hold under highly competitive conditions.

Edgeworth, in offering an amendment to the duopoly models of Cournot and Bertrand, assumed that buyers would purchase their goods equally from both suppliers when the price charged is the same. This changes each supplier's view of the demand curve he faces. It is still the case, in Edgeworth's model, that successive undercutting of price will drive price to the competitive level; however, this is not a stable price. For at this price a competitor may assume that his rival's price will not increase when he raises his own to exploit his advantage over his share of the market. The details are complicated and need not detain us here. The upshot is that, under Edgeworth's assumptions, the price is a monopoly price at first, successive undercutting drives it to the competitive level, but having reached this level it is unstable and it jumps back to the monopoly level only to start the process again. Since the price oscillates between monopoly and competitive levels, there is no single solution to the question of duopoly or oligopoly pricing according to the Edgeworth model.

Chamberlin, among others, held that either covert or overt collusion was a likely outcome and argued that under duopoly the price of the product would equal the monopoly price. Thus theories of duopoly price can be summarized as follows: Let M be monopoly price, C be competitive price, and D be duopoly price; then the prices would be, in order of development,

Cournot	Bertrand	Edgeworth			Chamberlin
M	M	M			M, D
		D	D		
D		D	D		
			D		
C	C, D	C	D		C

From this example, it is easy to see why the state of oligopoly theory is unsatisfactory. When the book *The Theory of Games and Economic Behavior* by von Neumann and Morgenstern appeared, it was thought that a framework for solving the oligopoly problem had been found. However, the theory of games, although rigorous, becomes extremely complex when one goes beyond the most simple model; theory rapidly becomes as complex as the real world. Thus, the theory of oligopoly remains in an unsatisfactory state to date.

10.5 ISOPROFIT CURVES AND REACTION CURVES

A number of very interesting insights into the oligopoly process can be obtained by formalizing the reaction one expects from competitors, as in the kinked-demand and the Cournot and Bertrand cases. To draw out these insights, isoprofit curves and reaction curves provide an excellent format.[1]

In Fig. 10.4, the output of firm α is measured on the horizontal axis and the output of firm β is measured on the vertical axis. Both firms produce the same good. The isoprofit curves that appear as hills above the horizontal axis are those of firm α, while the curves that appear as hills extending rightward from the vertical axis are those of firm β (only two are shown here). Each curve carries with it a label indicating the profit of the firm, the same at every point on the curve. Let π_α and π_β represent the profits of α and β, respectively. Thus, if α pro-

[1] For greater detail in descriptions of the theory of duopoly see: H. Gregg Lewis, Some Observations on Duopoly Theory, *Am. Econ. Rev.*, vol. XXXVIII, pp. 1–8, May 1948; William Fellner, "Competition among the Few," Alfred A. Knopf, New York, 1949; Edward J. Chamberlin, "The Theory of Monopolistic Competition," 6th ed., Harvard University Press, Cambridge, 1948; and W. J. Baumol, "Business Behavior, Value and Growth," The Macmillan Company, New York, 1959.

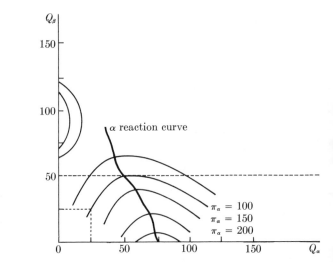

Figure 10.4

duces **25** units each period while β produces **25**, α's profits will be **100**; they will also be **100** if α produces **112.5** while β produces **25** or if both α and β produce **50**. In this way one reads the isoprofit maps of both firms. The profit that one firm makes depends upon the quantity produced by his rival.

Under Cournot's theory each duopolist assumes that the quantity that his rival produces is constant and adjusts his own output in suitable fashion to maximize his own profits. Thus a horizontal line at $Q_\beta = 50$ indicates β's output per period. To maximize profits α will react by setting output where his isoprofit curve is just tangent to the horizontal line, that is, where $Q = 50$. For each level of Q_β, firm α will react appropriately, and in this way one can construct a *reaction curve* for α. Similarly, one can construct a *reaction curve* for β. The point of intersection of the two reaction curves determines the equilibrium rate of output for each of the two firms. These reaction curves and a few of the isoprofit curves appear in Fig. 10.5, where point a represents equilibrium.

It is also worthwhile to examine the characteristics of point b, the point at which β's reaction curve is just tangent to α's highest isoprofit curve. If the managers of α *knew* β's reaction curve, they could set a rate of output Q_0 and simply let β "react"; this is called *quantity leadership*, for here β reacts the best

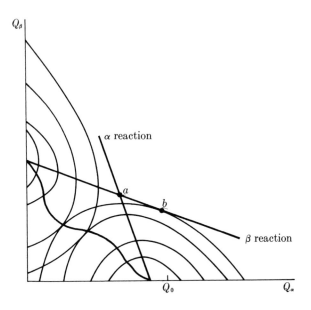

Figure 10.5

it can to the quantity set by α and α gains some advantage. In this case, α has no reaction curve, for it "leads" β and does not "react" to β's output policy. The interested reader can examine the references cited in the preceding footnotes for descriptions of similar models showing price-reaction curves and price leadership rather than quantity-reaction curves and quantity leadership. (Also see Exercise 10.2 on page 253 at the end of this chapter.)

The isoprofit map generates another curve, however, the curve that connects points of tangency of the two firms' isoprofit curves, similar to the contract curve, called here the *no-gain* curve; this is the wavy curve in Fig. 10.5. If the duopolists collude, they will set rates of output so as to end up on the no-gain curve. Which point they select depends upon their relative bargaining power. Through point a will pass one of α's isoprofit curves and one of β's. These will form a cigar-shaped area toward the origin (not shown), through which the contract curve will pass. These two isoprofit curves will set the limits to the advantage to be gained by moving away from point a toward the no-gain curve; neither of them can better his position except at the expense of the other and hence any point on the no-gain curve is optimal for the two duopolists in the paretian sense. (It is, of course, not optimal for the community at large for marginal cost will not equal price.)

It is interesting to note that in the case of bilateral monopoly and in this case of collusion of duopolists economists must revert to say that the final position depends upon *relative bargaining power*. This indicates well the unsatisfactory state of the art, for there is no theory to explain the determination of relative bargaining power. As noted earlier, modest improvements of understanding have been made with *game theory*, but this promising method of attack on the problem has yet to yield bountiful fruit. Most games are far too complex to handle formally even though the mathematical tools for doing so exist.

10.6 MONOPOLISTIC COMPETITION

In an attempt to make the theory of imperfect competition more realistic, Edward Chamberlin described the world of *monopolistic competition*.[1] He felt that most real-world business firms oper-

---

[1] Chamberlin, *op. cit.*

ated in the vague area between monopoly (a single firm with complete market power) and perfect competition (many firms, each without market power). He noted the problems of duopoly and oligopoly and the question of "recognized dependence" on each other's price and output behavior. Then he set about describing the behavior of firms that existed in an industry so highly competitive that no firm recognized in any detail any significant mutual dependence on the price or output behavior of other firms which also have a *monopoly* over the *particular* product that they produce. He called these firms producers of *differentiated products*—differentiated in the minds of the consumer by trademarks or other superficial characteristics but fundamentally the same as the products of many other firms. Products such as this come readily to mind: aspirin, cigarettes, and marmalade. Often differences in quality are associated with brand-name merchandise. To a large extent quality differences fully account for differences in price. Nevertheless, trademarks and other distinguishing characteristics provide producers with a monopoly over their own differentiated product, and managers of firms producing these products can set prices and outputs. Thus, the demand curve faced by a single firm is downward-sloping but represents only part of the overall demand for the product.

It is clear that semantic questions arise in this context: What is the product of an *industry,* and is it the same as the product of a *firm* in the industry? We speak of soup, beer, and marmalade; also, of Campbell's Soup, Guinness Stout, and Chivers Marmalade. The various firms that produce marmalade take little note of most of their competitors' activities. Their day-to-day activities are focused on such internal operational problems as minimizing costs and organizing work schedules. The marmalade business is easy to enter, and there are many firms producing this product. The demand curve for the industry's product is downward-sloping, but the firm with an established trademark also faces a downward-sloping demand curve for its product. Chamberlin believed, however, that free entry drove out all profits.

Thus, under equilibrium conditions, the individual marmalade producer faces a profit position like that shown in Fig. 10.6, where average and marginal curves for costs and revenues are shown. Free entry drives out profits so that the firm's average revenue curve (if it is located to the right), will be pushed left-

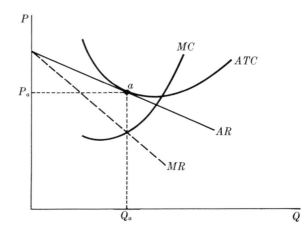

Figure 10.6

ward until it touches point a on the average cost curve. The firm will make no profits by producing Q_a rate of output and setting price equal to P_a. Since no profits are being made, there will be no incentive for other firms to enter. But unlike the case of perfect competition, the firm is *not* led to produce at the lowest average cost. This accounts for what seems to be always prevalent excess capacity on the part of most firms. Indeed, from the graph it is clear that an increase in demand bringing about a rightward shift in the AR curve would lead to *lower* average costs per unit of output and temporary profits even if prices hardly change. Thus firms in monopolistically competitive markets seem usually capable of expanding operations and lowering costs while doing so.

To summarize briefly, one might say that monopolistic competition is a market structure in which a firm has a monopoly but in which the industry is so highly competitive and entry is so free and easy that monopoly profits are driven out. Thus, maximizing price and maximizing output differ from those which would obtain under perfect competition, but there is no long-run equilibrium price and output at which monopoly profits continue to exist.

The theory of monopolistic competition is intuitively pleasing as an explanation of many everyday marketplace events, but as a theory that is useful in making predictions it lacks the same degree of strength that the models of monopoly and perfect competition have. It is a world where anything can happen—it admits both monopolistic and competitive firm behavior and is therefore very complex. However, no one will deny that the two market-structure extremes provide little solace for those concerned with business operations and that the middle ground between those extremes is the most interesting. The theory in this middle ground is least adequate.

10.7 REVENUE MAXIMIZATION

William J. Baumol offers the student of oligopoly theory the *sales-maximization hypothesis.*[1] A better term is *revenue maximization,* for the word "sales" can be interpreted either as *number of items* or as *dollars value of items* sold, and Baumol's reference is to the latter. Baumol notes that businessmen, when asked how their business went last year, most often respond with a statement such as "Our sales were up to three million dollars." Profits could have fallen; but if true, this is passed off lightly as unimportant.

It is obvious that by increasing one's losses one could expand sales. Therefore, Baumol postulates that managers of oligopolistic firms may maximize sales revenues after they have realized a certain minimum profit; that is, they *maximize sales subject to a minimum profits constraint.* To interpret this statement refer to Fig. 10.7, which contains the familiar total cost and total revenue

[1] Baumol, *op. cit.* Also see Milton Z. Kafolgis, Output of the Restrained Firm, *Am. Econ. Rev.,* vol. LIX, pp. 583–589 and bibliography, September 1969.

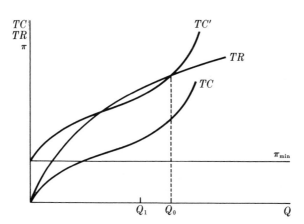

Figure 10.7

curves. The minimum profit, that profit required to satisty stockholders, is labeled π_{min}. By adding π_{min} to the TC curve, generate TC'. Where TC' intersects the TR curve, find the rate of output Q_0, which is the rate that the oligopolist will set if he maximizes sales revenues subject to a profit constraint π_{min}. The price charged by this oligopolist would be represented by the slope of a vector from the origin to the point of intersection of TC' and TR (not shown).

The profit-maximizing firm, facing identical cost and revenue curves, would produce at Q_1. Thus, the sales maximizer is likely to produce a larger output than would be produced by a monopolist. Furthermore, note that at rate of output Q_0 marginal cost is greater than marginal revenue (and also may be equal to, less than, or greater than price). This indicates that sales maximizers wish to increase the dollar volume of their operations so much that they will add to their sales even when it costs more than a dollar to produce another dollar of sales revenues, and perhaps the price of the product is less than what it costs to produce the last units of the product sold each period. All this, of course, is just another way of saying that profits are not being maximized. Operating at Q_0 the firm makes no profits above π_{min}.

As drawn, the slope of the TR curve is positively sloped at the point at which it crosses the TC' curves. If the TR curve peaked somewhere to the left of this point and then fell to cross TC', the point of maximum TR would be at the highest point on the TR curve and this would indicate the rate of output and price if sales were maximized. The firm then would realize profits in excess of π_{min}. According to Baumol, the firm in this position would use these *excess profits* for additional advertising and promotional expenses in an effort to push the TR curve further upward. Thus, sales-maximizing firms would continue to spend on advertising as long as the addition to sales revenues from another dollar spent on production costs $\Delta TR/\Delta TC$ just equals the addition to revenue from an addition to advertising costs $\Delta TR/\Delta AdvC$.

Baumol offers his theory of oligopoly more as an example of maximization than as a serious effort to explain oligopolistic behavior; that is, he shows that maximization principles can be applied in a manner that differs from profit maximization, but in an interesting and relevant way, especially when the pure cases of perfect competition and monopoly are not relevant for the issue at hand. He also draws implications for economic growth from this theory of firm behavior.

Milton Kafolgis suggests another alternative to profit maximization—output maximization.[1] A firm's managers may prefer to expand the physical scale of operation to a maximum, given that some minimum level of profits is maintained. If this is the case, funds will not be spent on advertising but will be used to increase production. Thus the output maximizer will produce a larger physical volume of output but a smaller dollar value of sales than the sales maximizer. According to Kafolgis:

> The performance of firms frequently is measured directly in terms of physical output with revenue occupying a secondary position. This is particularly the case with respect to public service enter-prises where measures of output like kilowatt hours, or number of customers served, may dominate revenue or dollar sales as yardsticks of performance. Thus, output or quantity maximization merits consideration as a distinct and separate hypothesis (from revenue maximization) which enhances the possibility of sales at prices below marginal cost.

The implications to be drawn from assumptions of revenue maximization and from output maximization are difficult to compare with one another. Whether advertising costs expenditures are the same, whether the TC curves are the same, and whether the TR curve is elastic or inelastic all affect the comparisons. Furthermore, O. Williamson has presented a model in which managers have preferences for incurring expenses for staff and emoluments, and H. Averch and L. Johnson note different results if the firm operates under regulatory control.[2] Finally, R. J. Monsen and A. Downs suggest that managers may behave so as to maximize their own long-term income streams rather than profits of the firm.[3] R. J. Monsen, J. S. Chiu, and D. E. Cooley have provided some empirical evidence in support of this theory.[4]

---

[1] Kafolgis, *op. cit.*

[2] O. E. Williamson, "The Economics of Discretionary Behavior: Managerial Objectives in a Theory of the Firm," Prentice-Hall, Englewood Cliffs, N.J., 1965; H. Averch and L. Johnson, Behavior of the Firm under Regulatory Constraint, *Am. Econ. Rev.*, vol. LII, pp. 1052–1069, December 1962.

[3] R. Joseph Monsen and Anthony Downs, A Theory of the Large Managerial Firm, *J. Political Econ.*, vol. 73, pp. 221–236, June 1965.

[4] R. J. Monsen, J. S. Chiu, and D. E. Cooley, The Effect of Separation of Ownership and Control on the Performance of the Large Firm, *Quart. J. Econ.*, vol. LXXXII, pp. 435–451, August 1969.

10.8 PROFITS AND LEISURE TRADE-OFF

Another view of the firm's behavior in response to managerial preferences is offered by Tibor Scitovsky.[1] He was concerned with managerial effort and the distaste that managers have for work. Thus, in Fig. 10.8 note that profits are measured on the vertical axis along with revenues and costs. The TC and TR curves are omitted and only the π curve representing profits $(TR - TC)$ appears. The rate of output is measured on the horizontal axis, as usual; but, assume as well that output and managerial effort are proportional, so that the horizontal axis can also represent managerial effort. If the firm's manager-owner has preferences such that he is willing to trade off money income (profit) for effort (output), then one may draw a set of indifference curves with the usually assumed shape. Three such curves appear in the diagram. It is clear that to maximize his satisfaction this entrepreneur will produce output Q_0 and will sell it at whatever price would be appropriate for the TR curve (not shown) that he faces. Because of the shapes of the profit function and the indifference curves, the chosen rate of output will be less than that predicted by profit-maximization behavior $Q_{\pi,\max}$.

[1] T. Scitovsky, A Note on Profit Maximization and Its Implications, *Rev. Econ. Stud.*, vol. XI, pp. 57–60, 1943; reprinted in American Economic Association, ed., "Readings in Price Theory," Richard D. Irwin, Inc., Homewood, Ill., 1953.

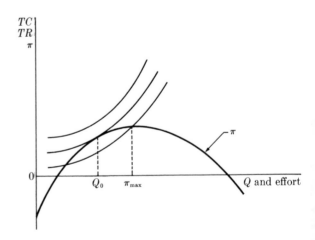

Figure 10.8

David J. Smyth has noted that the Scitovsky model can be applied to Baumol's revenue maximization model so that a revenue-maximizing, rather than a profit-maximizing, manager may trade off effort against revenues (rather than profits).[1] This also leads to lower rates of output than would obtain under simple revenue maximization. Several books could be devoted to any comprehensive discussion of imperfect competition. This brief treatment is only meant to illustrate some of the issues economists have focused upon. It is clear that, under the variety of theories, nearly any price and output situation is possible, and that the theory of imperfect competition is in a very unsatisfactory state.

10.9 MONOPSONY

Thus far we have observed the market from the point of view of a monopolistic or oligopolistic seller. However, we can look, as it were, to the other side of the market and presume that a firm might be a monopolistic or oligopolistic *buyer*. Market power of this sort is called *monopsony*, or *oligopsony*. For example, monopsony exists when the sole buyer of labor services in a community is a local firm. This firm may be able to set the price of labor (wage rate) at a lower level than would exist under conditions of perfect competition in the labor market. One might imagine a coal-mining (company) town in 1900 where local laborers were not mobile and could not seek higher, more competitive, wages elsewhere.

In Fig. 10.9 the TC curve is drawn out of the origin in a manner designed to show increasing AC and MC throughout. Assume that labor is the *only* factor of production used. Then, the TC curve represents the supply curve of labor facing the firm. The profit-maximizing rate of output is Q_a. The slope of the vector from the origin to point a represents the average cost of production *and* since labor is the only factor, this slope also represents the *wage rate*. The slope of the vector from the origin to point a' represents average revenue, or price. Slopes of the respective cost and revenue curves are equal at a and a', and the firm makes maximum profit by producing Q_a.

[1] D. J. Smyth, Sales Maximization and Managerial Effort: Note, *Am. Econ. Rev.*, vol. LIX, pp. 633–634, September 1969.

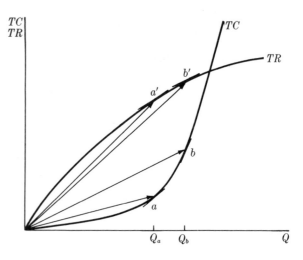

Figure 10.9

10.10 MINIMUM WAGE LAWS

Now assume that regulatory authorities establish a minimum wage, represented by the slope of the vector to point b. The slope of this vector is arbitrarily drawn so that it just equals the slope of the TR curve at b'. Thus under this constraint the firm will maximize profits by *lowering price*, hiring *more* labor, and producing a higher rate of output, Q_b. If the regulatory authority set a wage higher than that represented by the vector to b, the firm would produce *less* than Q_b in maximizing profits. This is because the TR curve gets steeper to the *left* of point b', and equality of the minimum wage rate with MR would lie to the left as well. Thus, a regulatory authority could set minimum wages in a fashion to induce this maximizing firm to produce any amount between Q_a and Q_b.

In Fig. 10.10 the same information about minimum wages appears, except that the presentation is now in terms of AC, AR, MC, and MR curves. The profit-maximizing firm sets the rate of output where MC and MR curves intersect. It produces Q_a and sells at price P_a. The wage rate is W_a. At minimum wage, W_b, output would be Q_b and price P_b. Again, rate of output Q_b represents the maximum that regulatory authorities could induce this firm to produce. Thus, as the minimum wage moves up from W_a to W_b, the equilibrium position is represented by points along the average cost curve. But as W moves higher than W_b the equilibrium position is represented by points moving up the MR curve leftward. Since the AC curve represents the supply

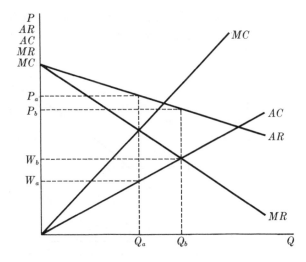

Figure 10.10

curve of labor, when the wage rate is set above W_b the amount of labor hired at the minimum wage will be less than the amount offered in the market for sale. Thus *unemployment* will result if the minimum wage is set too high.

The analogy between minimum wages and maximum prices (utility rates, for example) is quite strong. With a lower maximum price a monopolist can be induced to sell more, not less. With a higher minimum wage a monopsonist can be induced to hire more labor, not less. But there are limits: A *too low* price leads the firm to reduce output, and demand is unsatisfied; a *too high* minimum wage leads the monopsonistic firm to reduce employment, and workers will want to work but will not be hired. Is the labor force immobile? Is it the captive of a single employer? Minimum wage laws only make good economic sense if the answer to both these questions is yes.

EXERCISES

10.1 Draw a figure similar to Fig. 10.5 and assume that the managers of firm β know α's reaction curve. What rate of output will firm β produce? What rate will firm α produce? What profits will each firm receive?

10.2 Assume that the products of two duopolists are differentiated sufficiently so that each can set a different *price*. Let the price set by firm α, P_α, be measured on the horizontal axis, and the price set by firm β, P_β, be measured on the vertical axis. Draw isoprofit curves for firm β. These price-based curves will be of *reverse* shape from those of isoprofit curves for quantities. Draw β's reaction curve. It is made of points at which the isoprofit curves are vertical. This reaction curve should also be upward-sloping, not downward-sloping as in the case of the quantity-based diagrams. Now proceed to illustrate the case of price leadership under the presumption that firm β "knows" firm α's price-reaction curve.

10.3 If a firm must raise the wage rate it must pay for a factor of production in order to hire more of the factor, this firm is a monopsonist to some degree. Draw a TC curve out of the origin and upward-sloping throughout so that MC is increasing everywhere. Draw a TR curve typical of a monopolist. Show the profit-maximizing rate of output.

If labor is the only factor of production, then the TC curve represents the supply curve of labor, and AC is the wage rate. Assume the government imposes a higher wage rate than that being paid by this maximizing monopsonist. Under this constraint will output increase? Will employment increase? Will profits be eliminated? Illustrate your answers with reference to the diagram. How would your answers change, if they would, if the firm faced a straight-line TR curve as it would if it existed in a perfectly competitive market for its output? (Allow a profit potential to exist; that is, let the TR curve lie above the TC curve for some range of output.)

How would your answers change if, under the original TR curve, the firm faced a straight-line TC curve? Does monopsony exist under this condition?

10.4 Draw a TC curve showing constant average total costs over a considerable range of rates of output. Now draw a monopolist's TR curve so that it peaks and then falls to intersect the TC curve at a point where ATC is constant. Assume the TC curve includes any minimum profits constraint under which the firm operates. Show the point at which the firm will operate if its managers are *output maximizers*. Is the firm efficient in the sense of paretian optimality? At what point would the *revenue maximizer* operate? What is the relation between price and marginal cost? Show that both output and revenue maximization behavior toward price and output would be identical if ATC is constant and if TR shows demand to be elastic when it crosses the TC curve.

10.5 Draw TC and TR curves and show how introducing a preferential trade-off between revenue (not profit) and effort on the part of the firm's management will distort the output level of a pure sales-revenue maximizer.

11

Selected Topics in Price Theory

This chapter follows no particular order of development. It contains brief discussions of a set of more or less unrelated topics, each of which could have been introduced earlier in the text only by unduly disturbing the orderly presentation of more basic concepts. The selection of topics reflects the author's special interests. Material under each subheading can be read as a separate entity.

11.1 MANAGERIAL CONTROL OF THE FIRM

In 1932 Berle and Means published a book devoted to an analysis of the separation of ownership from control of the modern corporation.[1] When a corporation issues millions of shares of stock to thousands of different stockholders, what does it mean to say that stockholders are the owners of the firm? It is clear that managers control the firm. It is also possible, of course, that stockholders will become sufficiently upset to combine in

[1] A. A. Berle and G. C. Means, "The Modern Corporation and Private Property," rev. ed., Harcourt, Brace, Jovanovich, New York, 1968.

a proxy battle and replace the existing management. But this happens rarely, and is the *exception* that may prove the rule. Does the threat of stockholder dissatisfaction hover over managers so that they manage in the owners' interest? Or do managers feel immune from stockholders' threats? Unfortunately, there is no clear answer to these questions. Edward Mason has observed that ". . . about everyone now agrees that in the large corporation, the owner is, in general, a passive recipient; that typically control is in the hands of management; and that management normally selects its own replacement."[1]

Management control of productive activity also exists in the case of government enterprise and in the case of many nonprofit enterprises. Government enterprise can feel the sting of public dissatisfaction when people go to the polls. But do government enterprises usually operate to serve the public interest? Should the Tennessee Valley Authority make the largest possible profits and turn these over to the government to be used to reduce the tax burden of the citizens around the country? Nonprofit enterprise must specifically declare that management will *not* promote the "owners'" interests. What guiding rules can management of such enterprise use if profit maximization is ruled out? Where is the incentive to minimize costs and achieve productive efficiency?

In *University Economics*, Professors Alchian and Allen have devoted an entire chapter to the subject of "Allocation without Private-Property Rights."[2] In one example Alchian and Allen ask and answer their own question: If the manager of a nonprofit institution must set a price, what price will he set? Their answer is ". . . at the price that maximizes the decider's utility."[3] Of course, the pricing decision as a general rule is inseparable from the output decision. Given the demand situation, a decision to lower a price and expand the rate of output are two sides of the same coin.[4] Each of us, whatever we decide

---

[1] Edward Mason, "The Corporation in Modern Society," p. 4, Harvard University Press, Cambridge, Mass., 1960.

[2] Armen A. Alchian and William R. Allen, "University Economics," 2d ed., chap. 9, pp. 129–148, Wadsworth Publishing Company, Belmont, Calif., 1967.

[3] *Ibid.*, p. 43.

[4] Unless, of course, the organization in question has the power to prohibit resale of the service or commodity being supplied and can act as a discriminating monopolist.

to do in everyday life, presumably maximizes our own *utility* or *satisfaction* within the realm of whatever constrains our behavior. Thus, to make their explanations testable economists have asserted that businessmen and laborers maximize their own profits, or wages, or rents as the case may be, and we call these returns money income. If we replace *utility* with *money income,* then the question posed by Alchian and Allen can be answered ". . . at the price that maximizes the decider's income stream." This alteration preserves the spirit of their presentation, and the answer is now in a form appropriate to the following development of one possible neoclassical description of the answer. Monsen and Downs have agreed that manager-controlled firms are operated by managers so as to maximize the manager's own lifetime income stream.[1] The same could be said of government enterprise.

Now return briefly to the explanation of the determination of wage rates provided by neoclassical economic theory. Economists contend that in a profit-motivated economy a worker will be paid the "value of his marginal productivity." Competition in the labor market for available jobs will ensure this result. The *value* of the laborer's *marginal productivity* (*VMP*) is made up of two components: the price that the good produced by the firm will fetch in the marketplace P and the amount of this good that is produced above and beyond the amount that would have been produced if the laborer had not been hired MP. Thus, $VMP = P(MP)$. A numerical example may be helpful. Assume that the firm produces 100 units of output each week without the laborer, but when he is added to the working force, the firm's output increases to 115 units each week. Then, the 15 extra units of output each week are attributed to the laborer's effort and this extra 15 units is called his *marginal productivity.* If the going price of each unit of output is $2, then $VMP = \$2(15) = \$30$ per week, the laborer's weekly wage. This $30 wage payment is *precisely equal* to the value of the laborer's contribution to total output of the firm. In the case of monopoly, of course, marginal revenue, MR, replaces price in the equation so that $VMP = MR(MP)$.

In most production situations economists believe that the technology of production is such that the larger the amount of other

[1] R. J. Monsen, Jr. and Anthony Downs, A Theory of Large Managerial Firms, *J. Political Econ.*, vol. 73, pp. 221–236, June 1965.

factors with which the laborer works, the larger will be the laborer's own (marginal) productivity. If a worker has more tools at his disposal, the larger will be the value of his own production, and hence, the larger will be the wage that he can command for himself. Of course, it is conceivable that managers could burden the laborer with so many tools that they would interfere with his productivity, rather than enhance it. But, *within some range* of operations each laborer could achieve greater productivity with more tools at his disposal.

In the analysis above, substitute "manager" for "laborer," and one can see that *a manager can increase his own productivity the more subordinates he has working for him.* The larger the plant he manages, and the larger the operations he oversees, the greater his (marginal) productivity. Hence, if he received a salary equal to his own marginal productivity, his own salary will be higher if he can "build his empire" in the organization. The value of his marginal product is also increased if, through advertising or other promotional activities, he can increase the price of the product his organization produces.[1] Under competitive enterprise the owners of a firm would readily fire a manager who hired excessive amounts of other factors to work with him. The profits of a firm would fall under these conditions. Therefore, to argue the prevalence of wasted resources in such cases one must also note the absence of competition, or the absence of owner-control.

The following assumptions are made: (1) A manager seeks to maximize his lifetime income. (2) The criterion by which a manager is judged is his *apparent* ability to maximize production from a given input of resources. For the giant private corporation this is partially quantifiable with measures such as profit and growth. For government and nonprofit organizations maximizing production (minimizing costs of production) is less amenable to precise computation. The value of a manager is, in part, due to his ability to achieve output goals while preserving tranquility within the organization. (3) Owners and taxpayers are forced by the nature of the management function to rely on hired managers to run giant organizations. The flow of information about the system from within the organization

---

[1] See O. E. Williamson, "The Economics of Discretionary Behavior: Managerial Objectives in a Theory of the Firm," Prentice-Hall, Englewood Cliffs, N.J., 1965. Williamson also feels that managers hire *excessive* staff, but in a slightly different context from that suggested here.

is compiled and analyzed for management. Only the most general information is passed on to the owner or taxpayer. Information must pass through the management to reach the owner. (4) The organization operates in (or creates) markets which often tend to be concentrated or monopolistic rather than competitive. (5) Management has control over all subordinates and has the power to manage inputs to satisfy the goals of top management, including the power to restrict entry by subordinates into the management elite.

Let P_M be the wage or salary of management, and let management, M, be one of several factors of production. If the production function is Cobb–Douglas in form, then $Q = aM^\alpha X^\beta Y^\gamma$. Assume $\alpha + \beta + \gamma = 1$. The reader will recall from Chap. 3 that if M increases when X and Y are fixed, the marginal productivity of M will decrease; also, if M is fixed, then the marginal productivity of M is increased as X and Y are increased.

$$MP_M = \frac{\Delta Q}{\Delta M} = \alpha(aM^{\alpha-1}X^\beta Y^\gamma) = \alpha \frac{Q}{M}$$

Thus, if M is fixed, MP_M is proportional to Q and α is the proportion in question. Figure 11.1 contains this curve, labeled MP_M. Since it is assumed that the firm has some monopoly power, MR falls as output increases. The MR curve can also be found in Fig. 11.1. Thus both MR and MP are functions of output.[1] The figure indicates that P_M is a maximum when $Q = 5$, and the rate of output decided upon by the manager will be 5 because here the value of his productivity is largest and he can justify for himself the largest wage.

It is generally agreed that monopolists tend to restrict output. Here, the monopolist manager would not restrict output by as much as the monopolist owner would, but the monopolist manager does not utilize the optimum factor combination in the production process. It is desirable, therefore, that economists should examine the implication for economic efficiency of the independent management of these large sectors of productive

---

[1] In the figure assume that the marginal revenue function is $MR = 10 - Q$. Assume that the marginal productivity function is $MP = \frac{1}{2}Q$. Then if the manager's wage is based on marginal revenue productivity

$$P_M = \frac{1}{2}Q(10 - Q) = 5Q - \frac{1}{2}Q^2$$

set $dP_M/dQ = 5 - Q = 0$ to find the maximum P_M. Here it occurs when $Q = 5$, and at this rate of output $P_M = MR(MP) = 5(2.5) = 12.5$.

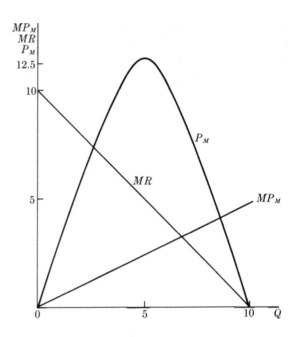

Figure 11.1

activity that is comprised of nonprofit organizations, government, and many large corporations. Perhaps the most astute observer to date has been C. Northcote Parkinson. The "laws" he has offered, partly in jest, have serious undertones that refuse to be dismissed lightly.[1] Parkinson's law is: "Work expands so as to fill the time available for its completion. . . . Granted that work (and especially paper work) is thus elastic in its demands on time, it is manifest that there need be little or no relationship between the work to be done and the size of the staff to which it may be assigned." According to Parkinson, ". . . we may distinguish two motive forces . . . , thus (1) 'an office wants to multiply subordinates, not rivals' and (2) 'officials make work for each other.' "[2] Thus, the staff grows, irrespective of the amount of work to be done, if any.

Laurence J. Peter and Raymond Hull have followed in Parkinsonian footsteps in enunciating *the Peter principle*, which is that, under our present system in business, professions, and

---

[1] C. Northcote Parkinson, "Parkinson's Law and Other Studies in Administration," chap. 4, p. 33, Houghton Mifflin Company, Boston, Mass., 1957.

[2] *Ibid.*, p. 43.

politics, "for each individual, for you, or me, the final promotion is from a level of competence to a level of incompetence." A corollary is: "In time every post tends to be occupied by an employee who is incompetent to carry out his duties."[1] Thus, the administrator who hires excessive staff à la Parkinson is definitionally incompetent à la Peter and Hull.

Given the assumptions, in attempting to maximize his own income a manager will be well aware of the general performance required of him. Managers will realize that for any given expenditure they must appear to create the maximum consumer or taxpayer satisfaction through goods and services rendered while avoiding serious internal conflict within the organization. Two conflicting alternatives are presented to the manager. If the organization operates in monopolistic markets the manager can increase the market price of the product or service in which he deals by restricting output below the competitive efficiency norm. Simultaneously, the manager will attempt to increase his apparent productivity or value to the organization. Given a fixed managerial input his marginal productivity can be increased by increasing the rate of input of complementary factors of production. Thus in terms of inefficiency the manager will overspend in terms of secretaries, consultants, assistants, and computers. Such action by managers will tend to increase output of the organization. A trade-off exists between attempts to increase product price and attempts to increase managerial productivity. A manager will try to maximize his income by manipulating the price of the product and his apparent productivity since the apparent incremental value created by a manager is defined as the amount he adds to output times the value of the output. Although neither management nor taxpayers are likely to recognize this procedure explicitly, in pursuit of his own self-interest a manager will tend to maximize the value of his own marginal product (VMP). Such action generally will not cause internal conflict within the organization since complementary factor inputs (to management) will be hired in excessive amounts and thus are likely to be paid in excess of their real worth to the organization (their VMP). DeAlessi suggests, for example, that this money income ". . . maximization hypothesis implies that presidents of tax-supported universities

---

[1] Laurence J. Peter and Raymond Hull, "The Peter Principle: Why Things Always Go Wrong," William Morrow & Company, New York, 1969.

usually allocate relatively more of their resources to building and equipment and relatively less to faculty than presidents of private institutions (buildings and equipment are more readily observed and understood by legislatures and, ultimately, by taxpayers)."[1]

When productive enterprise is carried on without the control and supervision of directly interested private parties, enterprise managers tend to serve their own best interest by mismanagement of the enterprise's resources. This is because the profit motive, the guiding "invisible hand" of Adam Smith's economy, is now under the control of one of the participants in the production process, and not in the hands of a profit-seeking overseer. The *owner* of Adam Smith's world is not a participant in the production process, but modern-day managers or bureaucrats are participants, and they can usurp sufficient control from the nominal boards of directors or political committees to alter the production process to suit their own goals. And, insofar as their goals are similar to those of the rest of a profit-seeking society, namely, to maximize their own money incomes, their control leads them to distort the production process in the manner described so articulately by Parkinson. In doing this they become incompetent in the manner described by Peter and Hull.

How can society eradicate inefficient management of this sort? If this neoclassical economic explanation is correct, then it suggests certain broad policies. For example, boards of directors of nonprofit institutions might be paid a salary for their efforts based upon the achievements of the goals of the institution at minimum cost, in some fashion similar to the way a bonus system is based on a private firm's profits. The boards of directors, as overseer, would then have more of an incentive to see that management did not permit the enterprise to engage in wasteful activities. With respect to the public sector, the administrative problems become more difficult. How can a mayor or city manager be paid bonuses out of taxpayers' savings that he could generate? Until our political system enables us to reward managers of public enterprises on the basis of objective criteria for efficient performance, the inefficiencies of bureaucratic enterprise will prevail. Until then, many governmental produc-

[1] Louis DeAlessi, Implications of Property Rights for Government Investment Choices, *Am. Econ. Rev.*, vol. LIX, pp. 13–24, March 1969 (quotation is from p. 18).

tive activities that could be undertaken by competitive private enterprise might be turned over to the private sector.[1]

11.2 INFERIOR FACTORS OF PRODUCTION

Chapter 2 contains an analysis of inferior consumption goods. The reader will recall that a good is *inferior* if Mr. A consumes less of it as his income increases. In Fig. 2.11 good 2 is an inferior good; in Fig. 2.12 good 2 is a *Giffen* good. (The reader may wish to glance at these figures briefly before continuing with this discussion.)

A good is a Giffen good if Mr. A consumes less of it, not only when Mr. A's income increases, but also when the price of the good falls. A Giffen good is an inferior good, a *very* inferior good—so inferior that a price reduction has such a strong positive income effect that Mr. A will purchase *less* of the good even if its price falls. This means that the demand curve for the good has a range for which the slope of the curve is positive rather than negative. Thus, a Giffen good is a curiosity among economists because it is a logically consistent exception to the law of demand, which holds that demand curves are negatively sloped.

The question raised in this section is "Do inferior factors of production exist in the same sense that inferior consumers' goods exist?" If so, can the demand curve for a factor of production be sloped in a positive direction if the inferiority is strong enough as it is in the analogous case of the Giffen good? It is certainly reasonable to believe that the production function for a firm may have characteristics such that, as the firm's budget expands and its rate of output expands, less of a given factor is employed by the firm. That is, if we assume that factors of production X and Y appear on the axes and rates of output are indicated by a map of isoproduct curves in the usual fashion, it is reasonable to suppose that an expansion path made up of points of tangency of budget constraints and isoproduct curves may bend back toward one of the axes indicating that the factor measured on the other axis is inferior. (See, for example, Fig. 11.2. For the time being ignore the dotted lines.) Here, an expansion

---

[1] The author and John R. McKean have worked jointly on this subject. See our paper: A Neo-Classical Foundation for a Theory of Manager-Controlled Firms, *R. Econ. Louvain*, pp. 3–13, February 1969.

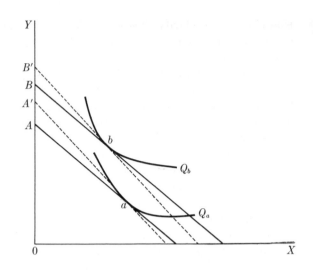

Figure 11.2

path drawn from the origin through point a and then point b would bend back toward the Y axis and indicate that X is an inferior factor of production inasmuch as there exists a range for which less X is used as output expands. If X were labor and Y were capital, technology and efficient production may require that production becomes more and more capital intensive as output expands and that this capital intensiveness may be so strong that enlarged output requires *less* labor. (One must remember that we are thinking of existing technology and not about the introduction of new, laborsaving technology which would change the isoproduct map itself. Here, the map is assumed to be fixed.)

Thus, the answer to the question of whether inferior factors can exist is surely affirmative. Homogeneous production functions, of course, have linear expansion paths, and therefore no inferiority could exist if production functions were homogeneous. But there is little in theory that tells us that a *firm* is likely to have a homogeneous production function (although if industry expands by replication of firms, the *industry production function* may be reasonably approximated by homogeneous functions).

But can factors of production be Giffen factors and have demand curves that are positively sloped in defiance of the law of demand? Here, the answer is not analogous to that given in the theory of consumer choice; for the case of *unconstrained* profit-maximizing firms the answer is no. The following discussion is meant to clarify this point. When the price of a normal, or noninferior, factor of production rises, marginal cost of production also rises. A profit-maximizing firm facing a given demand function will, if the MC curve rises, produce a smaller amount of output each period. Thus, if the price of the factor rises, the firm's rate of output falls (see Fig. 11.3). If, on the other hand, the factor in question is inferior, when the price of the factor increases the marginal cost of production does not increase; rather it falls (a proposition to be clarified below). If marginal cost falls, then output will also increase. Some authors define an inferior factor as one for which change in price leads to change in equilibrium rate of output in the *same* direction.

In Fig. 11.3 the MC and MR curves are given for a firm in perfect competition. This firm is making short-run profits.[1] Let MC represent the marginal-cost curve for the firm originally and let an increase in the price of a normal factor shift the MC curve upward. Equilibrium output is contracted from Q_a to Q_b. Beginning with MC' and allowing the price of an inferior factor to increase, it can be shown that MC will decrease to, say, MC, and equilibrium output will expand.

From Fig. 11.2 it is clear that as output expands *less* of an *inferior* factor is employed. Therefore, as the price of an inferior factor increases, marginal cost of production decreases, output of a maximizing firm increases, and less of the inferior factor is utilized. Hence, an increase in the price of an inferior

[1] This assumption is not shown in the graph but is made merely to avoid concern over the firm's profit position at this point.

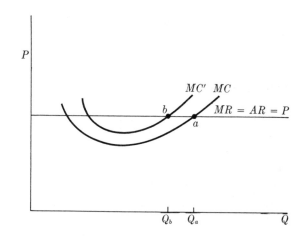

Figure 11.3

factor leads to *reduction* in the amount of it demanded by a firm, so that the demand curve is negatively sloped for inferior as well as normal factors in accord with the law of demand.

This analysis rests on the proposition that an increase in the price of an inferior factor will lead to a decline in the marginal cost of production. To illustrate let us return to Fig. 11.2; remember that the budget line from A through a is drawn for fixed prices of X and Y and a given total expenditure.[1] Let this total expenditure be called C for *cost*. Then, $C = P_X X + P_Y Y$, or $Y = C/P_Y - (P_X/P_Y)X$, which is the equation for the budget line with an intercept C/P_Y and a slope of $-P_X/P_Y$. For simplicity let $P_Y = 1$ so that the intercept C/P_Y is just C, and the distance in the diagram from O to A now equals C, or the total cost or expenditure to produce output Q_a. This procedure in general allows us to examine total cost and marginal cost by observing intercepts along the vertical axis in discrete (not continuous) form. Note that the total cost of producing Q_a is the distance OA and that the total cost of producing Q_b is OB. Thus the marginal cost of increasing the rate of output from Q_a to Q_b is measured by the distance AB.

Now let the price of factor X increase; factor X, of course, is the inferior factor. The budget lines become steeper and are illustrated by the dashed lines in the diagram. (Ignore any substitution effects from the change in the price of X because the convex isoquant clearly implies that the substitution effect is negative; that is, if the price of X increases, less X will be employed to produce a given rate of output and what we want to show is this consistency with the law of demand even if the factor is inferior. Thus, the substitution effect supports the argument—the question is, how does the income effect work?) The dashed lines intercept the vertical axes at A' and B'. Thus, under the new higher price of X, to produce Q_a requires total cost measured by the distance OA' and for Q_b the distance OB' so that a discrete estimate of marginal cost is now $A'B'$.

Clearly, if point b lies to the left of point a, then $A'B' < AB$; that is, marginal cost under the new higher price of the inferior factor is less than it was at the lower price. From this proposition it follows that if P_X increases, MC falls and equilibrium output will increase. Since the factor is inferior, *less* of it is used as output increases. Therefore, as the price of an inferior

[1] The author is indebted to Thomas E. Borcherding for providing this simplified graphic (nonmathematical) exposition.

factor increases, less is demanded by the firm and the demand curve for the factor is downward-sloping in a manner consistent with the law of demand. The substitution effect *also* suggests that less is demanded when the factor price rises, and so the substitution effect *reinforces* the effect of the change in equilibrium output on the demand for the inferior factor. Thus, there is no Giffen factor in production theory analogous to the Giffen good in the theory of consumer choice.[1]

In consumer choice theory, a Giffen effect leading to a positively sloped demand curve arises when the good is so inferior that the positive income effect outweighs the negative substitution effect of an increase in the price of the good and more of the good is consumed although the real level of satisfaction achieved by the consumer is lower. But it is assumed in consumer choice theory that the individual spends all of his income both *before* and *after* the change in the price of the inferior good. If producers were to spend the *same* budget on factors of production and produce whatever maximum quantity of the good they could within their budget, then producers' response to an inferior factor would be the same as consumers' response to an inferior good. But maximizing producers can vary their budget to maximize profits, not output, and the profit-maximizing rate of output varies directly with changes in factor prices. If the factor is inferior, increase in price leads to *decrease* in marginal cost, increase in rate of output, reduction in amount of the inferior factor employed, and reduction in profits below the level prior to the factor-price increase. Total costs increase and profits fall, but output increases too.[2]

---

[1] Several recent articles deal with the subject of inferior factors of production: see especially D. V. T. Bear, Inferior Inputs and the Theory of the Firm, *J. Political Econ.*, vol. LXXIII, pp. 287–289, June 1965; C. E. Ferguson, "Inferior Factors" and the Theories of Production and Input Demand, *Economica*, vol. XXXV, pp. 140–150, May 1968; and a "Comment" by L. R. Bassett and T. E. Borcherding, *Economica*, vol. XXXVI, pp. 321–322, August 1969. Bassett and Borcherding also have written a paper, The Firm, the Industry and the Long-run Demand for Factors of Production, *Can. J. Econ.*, vol. XXXVI, pp. 140–144, February 1970, dealing with an extension of the subject. See also W. J. Stober, Cost Constraints and Factor Inferiority, *Western Econ. J.*, vol. VII, pp. 379–384, December 1969, and other references cited in these articles.

[2] Stober, *ibid.*, examines the case of inferior factors under cost (budget) constraints and finds a paradox that under certain conditions *both* increases and decreases ". . . in the price of an inferior factor may lead to an increase in its employment" (p. 384).

If a firm is operating under perfect competition in long-run equilibrium, it is making zero profit. Then, if the price of any factor increases, output will increase but the firm will be making a short-run loss. Increased output by all firms in the industry facing these same factor prices will lead to a reduction in the price of the product if the product is a superior good. Thus, some firms must leave the industry although the firms that remain produce a larger rate of output. As the firms leave the industry, again less of the inferior factor is demanded and again as its price rises the amount of an inferior factor purchased declines, consistent with the law of demand.[1] In the analysis to this point it was assumed that the price of the product would be unchanged in the face of a change in the price of a factor; but now it is recognized that changes in factor prices will affect product prices. In this analysis general equilibrium considerations are being introduced. As any problem of this sort is examined more and more deeply, it becomes more and more necessary to bring into account those factors noted to be relevant in general equilibrium analysis.

One problem with production theory, however, may be even more intransigent. Production functions may be written $Q = f(x_1, x_2, \ldots, x_n)$ for factors of production $i = 1, 2, \ldots, n$. Some of these factors may assume the value of zero for a given scale of operations, while for a greatly enlarged scale of operations these factors may be positive and others become zero.[2] Technology seems to be quite specific. For a small rate of output of electricity, a small gasoline generator may suffice and be most efficient; but for large-scale output, oil fuel may operate steam generators for maximum efficiency. If this is so, then gasoline engines are inferior factors of production and expansion paths tend to be discontinuous at the point at which it is found that an enlarged output, if produced efficiently, requires a shift in production technique using a different set of factors than used previously.[3] As one disaggregates factors of production away from the general categories of capital and labor to the specific and distinguishable categories—such as gasoline

---

[1] Bassett and Borcherding, *op. cit.*, have explored this subject in their paper (Firm, Industry, and Long-run Demand).

[2] Walter Y. Oi has dealt with this question of corner solutions in the context of consumer theory in his paper Threshold Prices in the Theory of Consumer Demand (unpublished).

[3] See the author's paper, "Inferior" Factors of Production, *Quart. J. Econ.*, vol. LXXVI, pp. 86–97, August 1962.

engines and electric motors or skilled and unskilled labor—the problem of predicting the effect of a change in the price of a single factor becomes more difficult. Of course, this problem of the complexity of disaggregation arises in consumer choice theory and the theory of the firm as well in production theory.

11.3 PROGRESS FUNCTIONS AND LEARNING CURVES

In the theory of the firm output flows are quantities per period of time—per week, per month, per year, etc. Employment of factors of production is also measured by the flow of services such as labor hours per week or per month or the services of land or capital for a given period of time. This frame of reference appears to many businessmen to be unsuitable for their needs. For example, a printer thinks primarily in terms of *production runs*. The average unit cost of producing 100 books is much larger than the average unit cost of producing 10,000 books. The economist's typical frame of reference might lead him to say that production runs of 100 units each could be classified as a given product, while those of 10,000 would be a different product. Then consider the cost and demand functions relating an output of, say, 50 runs per month to the price of a run. This approach would allow output and factors to be measured by flows in a manner consistent with abstract economic theory.

However, some of the most interesting questions that businessmen can ask have to do with economies achievable under the longer production run. Business schools offer courses in production theory in which this subject is treated in a practical way, but economic theory also has something to say about progress functions or *learning curves*, as they are sometimes called.[1]

A progress function may be expressed as follows:

$$\frac{L}{V} = aV^{-b} \qquad (1)$$

or
$$L = aV^{1-b} \qquad (2)$$

where L is the total labor input required to produce a total volume (or batch size) of output V. The ratio L/V is the average labor input per unit of output. Equation (1) indicates how the average labor requirements diminish as the batch size in-

[1] The following material is drawn from Walter Y. Oi's excellent paper, The Neoclassical Foundations of Progress Functions, *Econ. J.*, vol. LXXVII, pp. 579–594, September 1967. (See his bibliography for further references.)

creases. The parameter a represents the man-hours needed for a unit of output (when $V = 1$), and the parameter b is the rate of progress, or the *rate* at which average labor requirements diminish as batch size increases. Equation (1), of course, is linear in logarithms, and b is the slope of the logarithmic fit indicating a constant rate of decline in labor requirements, or what might be called the *improvement in average labor productivity*.

Each factor of production presumably has its own progress function, and in each industry the progress functions differ. The airplane frame industry is one for which progress functions seem to be extremely relevant. T. P. Wright, who is credited with the original discovery of such a function, studied the cost of airframes.[1] It has been estimated that doubling the volume of airframes in a production run will reduce the average labor requirement by about 25 percent. Doubling the volume of electrical appliances will reduce average labor requirements by about 8 percent.[2]

It has been suggested that the parameter b in Eq. (1) will diminish as V increases. That is, when the total volume of a production run approaches infinity the value of b approaches zero, indicating no further reductions in labor requirements are possible. In this analysis V is the volume of the production run. Earlier, Q has been used to designate output per period and perhaps should have been written Q/t, where t stands for the unit of time such as week or month. However, we have left off the t and allowed it to be understood. Now, explicit account must be taken of it. Also, we have $V = Q/t$ only when the time period t is long enough to encompass the full production run. The estimated volume of Boeing 747 jet aircraft is in the neighborhood of 260 planes; that is, $V = 260$. At first the rate of output per month was two planes. Later it became four planes. Let i stand for months $1, 2, \ldots , n$. Then Q_i is the rate of output in the ith month. Let us assume that for the first year, monthly output is zero; that is, $Q_i = 0$ for $i = 1, \ldots , 12$; then $Q_{13} = 2$ and $Q_{24} = 4$, and so forth. In this way, output flows can be dated. This same sort of dating can be applied to input flows. Thus, L_i may refer to labor input during the ith month, K_i may refer to capital input during the ith month, and so forth.

[1] T. P. Wright, Factors Affecting the Cost of Airframes, *J. Aero. Sci.*, vol. 3, pp. 122–128, February 1936.
[2] See references in Oi, *op. cit.*

Having dated output and input flows, it is now possible to construct a production function with dates: $Q_i = f(L_i, K_i)$, or, transferring all elements to the left side of the equation and noting a time horizon of n periods,

$$\phi(Q_1, Q_2, \ldots, Q_n; L_1, L_2, \ldots, L_n; K_1, K_2, \ldots, K_n) = 0$$

Managers of this firm view a time horizon of n periods. All arguments in the function are flows per period of time. The maximizing managers must choose a set of Q's, L's, and K's that will maximize profits.[1]

If all output is to be produced in a single period, the function becomes $Q_1 = f(L_1, K_1)$, or $\phi(Q_1, L_1, K_1) = 0$. Assuming prices of factors P_L and P_K do not change over the production period, a familiar maximizing principle is that the marginal productivity of labor is to the price of labor *as the marginal productivity of capital is to the price of capital:*

$$\frac{\Delta Q_1 / \Delta L_1}{P_L} = \frac{\Delta Q_1 / \Delta K_1}{P_K}$$

In terms of the marginal rates of substitution this can be written

$$\frac{\Delta K_1}{\Delta L_1} = \frac{-P_L}{P_K}$$

If production is to be carried out over two periods, the function becomes

$$\phi(Q_1, Q_2; L_1, L_2; K_1, K_2) = 0$$

and for maximization we now need

$$\frac{\Delta K_1}{\Delta L_1} = \frac{\Delta K_2}{\Delta L_2} = \frac{\Delta K_2}{\Delta L_1} = \frac{\Delta K_1}{\Delta L_2} = \frac{-P_L}{P_K}$$

$$\frac{\Delta L_1}{\Delta L_2} = \frac{-P_{L_2}}{P_{L_1}} \qquad \begin{matrix} (= -1 \text{ since } P_L \text{ is} \\ \text{assumed constant}) \end{matrix}$$

$$\frac{\Delta K_1}{\Delta K_2} = \frac{-P_{K_2}}{P_{K_1}} \qquad \begin{matrix} (= -1 \text{ since } P_K \text{ is} \\ \text{assumed constant}) \end{matrix}$$

Thus the possibility of intertemporal factor substitution is introduced. Labor this month can be substituted for capital this month or for capital next month; also, labor this month can

---

[1] Rather than maximization of profits in an absolute sense, it is quite consistent to refer to the maximization of the present value of the firm's expected net receipts over the time horizon.

be substituted for labor next month. Obviously, future inputs cannot be substituted for present inputs, but present inputs can be substituted for future inputs. Thus, a firm planning a production run can adopt roundabout methods of production that allow present inputs to be substituted for future inputs. The longer the time period over which the production run is to take place, the greater the possibility for such substitution and the lower the labor and capital requirements per unit of output.

Professor Oi lists two theorems derived from the above analysis: (1) "The cost of producing any given flow of output can be reduced by postponing the period in which delivery is to be made," and (2) "the cost of an integrated output programme in which the plan is to produce output flows in several consecutive periods will be lower than the combined cost of unrelated output programmes that yield the same vector of dated output flows [that is, set of dated variables]."[1]

The progress function has been empirically verified and often it has been attributed to "learning" on the part of factors of production. It is as though a laborer acquires greater skill as the batch is produced. Other economists suggest that technical progress occurs during the production run. Both learning and technical progress are treated as if they are exogenous forces; hence, they are left unexplained. In the Oi model, however, by allowing for intertemporal factor substitution, the neoclassical frame of reference can accommodate the empirical findings without recourse to the ephemeral concepts of learning or technical change.[2]

11.4 SECOND-PARTY PREFERENCES[3]

In all of the theory of consumers' choice presented above an implicit assumption prevailed: that individual preference functions are independent of each other. That is, Mr. A's utility derived from his consumption of goods 1, 2, . . . , N, is inde-

---

[1] Oi, *op. cit.*, pp. 583 and 585.

[2] Professor Oi summarizes the model offered by Professor Alchian and indicates the consistencies in the elements of the two models. Alchian describes a firm's cost function with four dimensions: output flow per time period, total volume of output, the initial delivery date, and the period of production. The interested reader should pursue the references cited in Oi's paper.

[3] For a more extensive discussion of this subject, see the author's paper, Avarice, Altruism, and Second Party Preferences, *Quart. J. Econ.*, vol. LXXXVI, pp. 1–18, February 1972.

pendent of the levels of consumption of these goods by Mr. B. In a two-person world the preference functions would be written

$$U_A = f(Q_{A,1}, Q_{A,2}, Q_{A,3}, \ldots, Q_{A,N})$$
$$U_B = g(Q_{B,1}, Q_{B,2}, Q_{B,3}, \ldots, Q_{B,N})$$

Relaxing the assumption of independent preference functions and allowing Mr. A's utility to depend, not only upon his own rate of consumption of the several goods, but also upon their rate of consumption by Mr. B, one may write

$$U_A = h(Q_{A,1}, \ldots, Q_{A,N}; Q_{B,1}, \ldots, Q_{B,N})$$
and $$U_B = j(Q_{B,1}, \ldots, Q_{B,N}; Q_{A,1}, \ldots, Q_{A,N})$$

To simplify, assume a world with a single good, good 1, and examine Mr. A's preference function $U_A = f(Q_{A,1}; Q_{B,1})$. This function should generate an indifference map something like that appearing in Fig. 11.4. Indifference curves U_0, U_1, and U_2 denote successively higher levels of satisfaction for Mr. A. At point a, Mr. A has relatively large amounts of good 1 to consume and would be on a higher indifference curve if Mr. B had more to consume—as at point b. However, if Mr. B has a larger amount to consume as he does at, let us say, point c, then Mr. A is less satisfied than he would be at point b, and only just as satisfied as he would be at point a. Any movement to the right means that Mr. A has more to consume for a given level of B's consumption. It also means Mr. A is on a higher indifference curve—that more is to be preferred to less. If the curves

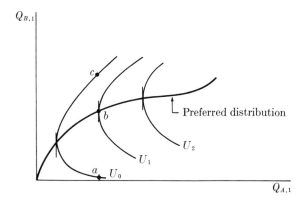

Figure 11.4

were drawn sufficiently far to the right, presumably they would turn upward, indicating satiation of desire by Mr. A.

A point at which an indifference curve is vertical, such as point b, indicates that if Mr. B has either more of or less of good 1, Mr. A would be worse off than he is at point b. Thus, a line connecting all points at which Mr. A's indifference curves are vertical can be called a *line of preferred distribution*. If this line had a slope of $+1$ out of the origin it would mean that Mr. A is a strict egalitarian—preferring that good 1 be *equally* distributed between himself and Mr. B. Any given indifference curve has a positive slope above the line of preferred distribution. But this positive slope is unlikely ever to be less than 1. A slope equal to 1 would mean that Mr. A is no happier even if both he and Mr. B receive equal increases in their rates of consumption of good 1—an unlikely outcome.

Assume there is a limited amount of good 1 available to be distributed between Mr. A and Mr. B. Figure 11.5 indicates this by the *distribution possibility line* which allows 20 units of good 1 to be distributed either to Mr. A, or to Mr. B, or to be divided between them. Point d is the point of tangency of this distribution possibility line with the highest indifference curve obtainable by Mr. A. If Mr. A were given the opportunity of deciding how this limited supply of 20 units of good 1 were to be allocated, he would choose that allocation represented by point d. Mr. A would be on a higher indifference curve if only Mr. B had more to consume, say, the amount indicated by point e. But point e is not an element of the

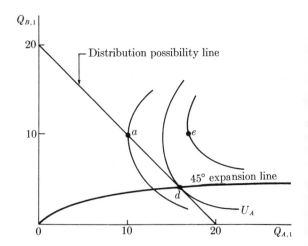

Figure 11.5

feasible set. Point *a* is a point on the preferred distribution line for Mr. A, and it shows he prefers an equal amount for Mr. B; but if given authority he will move away from point *a* to point *d* because the increase in satisfaction he obtains from his higher rate of consumption of good 1 more than offsets the loss in satisfaction he suffers from the observation that Mr. B consumes less. Since the slope of the distribution possibility line is —1, the angle with the axis is 45° from the horizontal. The curve of such points of tangency as point *d* under a variety of total amounts of good 1 can be called a *45° expansion line.*

Suppose, now, that we superimpose Mr. B's preference map upon the same graph upon which Mr. A's map appears, as in Fig. 11.6. Point *a* is on Mr. A's 45° expansion line, and point *b* is on Mr. B's 45° expansion line. Any point down and to the right of point *a* along the distribution possibility curve would not obtain because Mr. A would engage in charity and donate some of good 1 to Mr. B. Similarly, any point upward and left of point *b* would not represent a realistic allocation of good 1 because Mr. B would happily donate some of good 1 to Mr. A. In both cases the receiver of the good would willingly accept it. Thus, actual allocation takes place in the range between points *a* and *b*. This range of points is paretian optimal because any movement from one to another leaves one of the two parties better off and the other worse off. Also, within this range the individuals both appear to be avaricious; outside the range one or the other of the individuals is charitable or altruistic. Whether one individual appears to be avaricious or altruistic

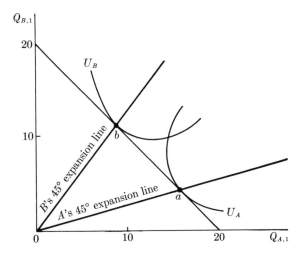

Figure 11.6

depends upon which point on the distribution possibility curve is chosen for examination. Given a set of convex indifference curves, all individuals are *both* avaricious and altruistic at the same time; different distributions of the available goods will bring out these different attitudes.

If Mr. A's indifference curves were to shift generally upward, his own pleasure would be enhanced by the observation that Mr. B had more to consume generally. Such a shift would occur if Mr. A had a change in attitude, that is, if he became more altruistic in response to St. Francis's admonition "For it is in giving that we receive." Increased altruism on the part of both parties *could* lead to a superimposition of 45° expansion lines. This would indicate a *maximum maximorum* of welfare in the sense that any other distribution of the good among the parties would leave *both* parties worse off. It is clear that such a result could only occur by chance, and yet it often exists in families in which the welfare of each is paramount.

By allowing the utility functions of individuals to include in their domain not only the amounts of goods that each individual consumes himself but also the amounts consumed by others, a variety of policy questions arise. Consider, for example, the propensity of political groups to approve tax transfers in favor of housing, food, education, and medical services for the poor, but at the same time taxing the consumption of cigarettes, alcohol, and luxuries. Excise taxes and *ad valorem* subsidies were shown in earlier chapters to be inefficient from the point of view of the individual being taxed or subsidized. However, the individual being taxed to provide subsidies *prefers* that his tax monies be devoted, not to the *general* welfare of the poor, but only to the welfare to be received from shelter, food, learning, and medicine. Taxpayers clearly have preference functions that include the quantities consumed by second parties.[1]

11.5 SOCIAL COSTS AND BENEFITS; COMMON PROPERTY AND EXTERNALITIES

Some products and services are not exchanged in the marketplace. An orange grove provides blossoms for bees from a

[1] For earlier examinations of this subject, see S. Valavanis, The Resolution of Conflict When Utilities Interact, *J. Conflict Resol.*, vol. 2, no. 2, pp. 156–169, 1958; L. E. Preston, Utility Interactions in a Two-person World, *J. Conflict Resol.*, vol. 4, pp. 354–365, December 1961; and K. H. Borch, "The Economics of Uncertainty," Princeton University Press, Princeton, N.J., 1968 (especially pp. 119–127.)

nearby farm, but the owner of the orange grove does not charge the beekeeper for feeding his bees. Thus, the orange-grove owner not only produces oranges but also provides a *social benefit* by assisting in the production of orange blossom honey. Assume, now, that a local real estate dealer believes the orange grove would be a good location for residential construction. Assume further that the owner of the grove finds the offer made by the real estate developer only just sufficiently attractive to induce him to give up the orange grove. Thus, the land use is changed in favor of residential construction. Resources are reallocated and bid away from the production of oranges and also away from the production of orange blossom honey. If the owner of the orange grove had received some compensation for the services he provided to the beekeeper, he might not have been willing to sell the land. Thus, because *all* benefits are not measured in the marketplace, it is possible that resources will be misallocated from their social optimum use.

The classic example of a social cost as opposed to a social benefit is the smoke from a factory that creates a nuisance in the neighborhood. Just as orange blossom honey is produced jointly with oranges, smoke is jointly produced along with paper, say, from the factory. If local citizens could charge the paper maker for the social cost the factory imposed upon them, the factory might not be profitable. Thus, resources may remain in production of paper when, in fact, if *all* costs (both private and social) were incurred by the factory owners, the costs would be so large that production would be unwarranted. Again, social costs may lead to misallocation of some resources at the margin.

Costs and benefits like those described are external to the producing unit, and are, therefore, referred to as *externalities*. It is important to note that these externalities arise because of the high cost of ownership of certain property. The one who owns orange blossoms cannot (except, possibly, at exceptional cost) prevent bees from coming to his trees and helping themselves to the pollen. Indeed, bees sometimes help pollinate fruit trees, and there is no incentive for the owner of the grove to prevent the beneficial joint product from being produced.[1] The factory owner has no incentive to keep the air clean, and his neighbor has no means of "owning," in any effective way, the

[1] If bees provide a service to the owner of the orange grove, and if orange blossoms provide a service to the beekeeper, then this example of external social benefit would have to focus on the *net* benefit received by the two parties.

air surrounding him. The principal point is that there are certain costs incurred in the very process of owning property. Once established, ownership may be easy to maintain; but the establishment and especially the transfer of ownership may be costly.

If transfer costs did not exist, perfect competition would lead to efficient allocation of resources. This is known as the *Coase theorem*.[1] If the air above one's property could be owned in any meaningful sense, then the factory's neighbor could sell a right to pollute the air above his house to the factory owner. Air would be a scarce resource which would have to be purchased as part of the process of producing paper. If all the costs of producing paper, including the cost of purchasing the necessary amount of air for pollution, could be internalized and recorded as the overall cost of factory operations, then the factory would continue to operate if it were profitable to do so and it would cease operations in the long run if it were not profitable. Efficiency in production would be obtained. The same analysis applies to the question of the pollution of lakes and streams.

For purposes of illustration assume that villagers obtain their water supply from a stream. Land adjacent to the headwaters of the stream belongs to a farmer. The farmer's activities begin to pollute the stream. What alternatives are available? The villagers may decide to tax themselves and purchase the land from the farmer and restrict any activities in the watershed area that would pollute the stream. In this case those subjected to the external costs would suffer the burden of preventing those costs from arising. Alternatively, the villagers might pass an ordinance against polluting the stream. In this case the farmer would be prevented from utilizing his land in the most profitable way. Thus his land would be less valuable to him and the burden of preventing the pollution of the stream would rest on him. When pollution becomes a problem, therefore, the alternatives to society are clear: Either tax yourself to pay for cleaning up the stream, or tax the polluter to pay for cleaning up the stream. Taxing the polluter to clean up the stream may mean that he will cease production and the commodity that he would have produced will be reduced in supply. Thus, consumers of this commodity will bear the burden along with the farmer who would have produced it. However the stream is cleaned up,

[1] R. H. Coase, The Problem of Social Cost, *J. Law Econ.*, vol. III, pp. 1–44, October 1960; also G. A. Mumey, The "Coase Theorem": A Reexamination, *Quart. J. Econ.*, vol. LXXXV, pp. 718–723, November 1971.

it is clear that real costs are borne by the society. The question is: Who in society shall bear the costs? The villagers or the farmer and his customers? The problem is essentially a problem of the distribution of the burden among different individuals in the society. In this example the villagers and the farmer, in essence, negotiate over the burden and who shall bear it. The villagers could threaten to pass an antipollution ordinance and then offer the farmer a low price for his land. This could be considered a form of blackmail or a form of bilateral negotiation in which the villagers hold the power position.

A few paragraphs above it was pointed out that external social benefits and external social costs (bees and smoke) could lead to misallocation of resources because of a failure to internalize all benefits and costs of production. But in the example of the stream it was argued that the essential problem was deciding who should bear the burden (or reap the benefits) of externalities. Thus, is the problem of externalities one of distribution of burden or is it one of misallocation of resources?

The answer is that it is possible for both problems to arise. If transfer costs were zero, then the orange producer and beekeeper would negotiate an efficient solution. On the other hand, if transfer costs were high and if both oranges and honey were produced under perfect competition so that the market price of oranges and honey would not change just because any one microscopically small producer decided to cease production, then *either* the beekeeper *or* the orange grower would reap the benefits of production. With positive transfer costs and perfect competition the question is not so much one of misallocation of resources as it is one of distribution or equity. Our example of the stream is one in which the transfer costs were internalized through the political process of taxation and/or legal constraints on behavior. It is, therefore, appropriate to suggest that problems of pollution are more significantly related to problems of equity and distribution than they are to problems of resource misallocation.

Resources such as clean air and clean water in streams are often referred to as *common property* resources, as distinct from *private property* resources. Private property resources are relatively easy to own; transfer costs are relatively small. Common property resources are difficult, if not impossible, to own. Fish in the sea could be trapped and tagged and released to feed, but how could the owner then enforce his right to the catch made by another? Furthermore, since no one owns the sea in which the fish feed, why should not *any* fisherman have the right to keep whatever catch he makes?

Public goods are not to be confused with *common property*. A public good is defined by authors in the field of public finance as a good with the following characteristic: The consumption of a public good by one consumer does not prevent the same good from being consumed by another consumer. Many services offered by government are public goods; for example, all consumers share in the protection afforded by police services. Consumption of protection by one consumer does not diminish its consumption by another consumer. Roadways and bridges, if not jammed by traffic, are also public goods: One consumer's use of a roadway does not prevent another consumer from receiving the services of the same roadway. Radio and TV programs are sent over the airwaves: Anyone with a set may receive a program without diminishing the ability of another to receive it. Public goods, if not provided by government agencies, are almost always heavily regulated by them.

A matrix (Table 11.1) showing in a rough way the possible classification of ownership is suggestive.[1] The lines of demarcation are *not* meant to be rigid. Private individuals own cows, houses, the wheat they produce, and so forth; here ownership is relatively easy to maintain and transfer costs are low. The private-enterprise market economy serves well in regulating the allocation of these kinds of resources. Oil and gas are listed as privately owned common properties. If an oil well is drilled,

[1] The author is indebted to Barney Dowdle for suggesting this framework for analysis.

TABLE 11.1   THE CLASSIFICATION OF PROPERTY RIGHTS

	Owned	Common	
Private	Cows	Oil	
	Houses	Gas	Government
	Wheat	Underground	regulated
	Forests	water	
Government	Buildings	Wildlife	
(*belonging*	Roadways	Streams	
to the	and bridges	Air	
public)	Forests	Beauty	

the oil coming from the well may be from a pool that extends not only under the well owner's land but also under his neighbor's land. For this reason governments have passed regulations requiring that owners of land adjacent to land on which the well sits receive a *pro rata* share of the proceeds from the sale of oil. Coal, on the other hand, is mined under a particular owner's land, and the owner can be identified with little cost.

It is interesting to note in this context that historically forest lands were considered to be common property resources, and they are still so considered in many places. In medieval times the local aristocrat reserved hunting rights in the forests but the forests were, in essence, wilderness areas belonging to no one. Even though a king said he owned the forest, he could not control ownership effectively because transfer costs were too high to prevent extensive poaching. As society has developed, however, modern methods of communication now permit forests to be owned in the same way that farmers own their wheat fields. Trees can be grown, harvested, and sold for profit just as wheat can be; the growing "season" is much longer, of course. But as long as there is a demand for lumber and wood products, private owners of forest timber land will continue to produce trees just as farmers will continue to produce grain. Forests were once considered common property because transfer costs were too high. With modern communication and mobility, there is no longer any reason to continue extensive regulation of forest lands. Of course, we have zoning regulations that limit the discretion that private homeowners have over use of their houses. In the same way and for similar purposes, private forest owners may be regulated. But, essentially, forests now fall in the categories of private and government ownership, not in the category of common property. Thus, we see how improved technology in the area of transfer costs can lead to certain common properties passing out of this class. Also, where the exploitation of common properties (such as gas and oil) still defies complete private ownership, government has devised means for regulation. Such government regulation is necessary because the marketplace does not operate to allocate these resources efficiently.

Government, of course, not only regulates the exploitation of certain common property resources and supplies certain public goods, it also owns office buildings, roadways, and even some productive resources such as forest lands. The government once sold its prairie land to homesteaders. An argument could be made that it should sell its forest land as well. If it is not going to turn the forest lands over to private ownership then, presumably, it should engage in forestry operations in a manner designed to add to the revenues of government so that taxes can be lowered in the public interest. Such a procedure could lead to efficient allocation of resources.

Finally, there is a class of common property goods that includes wildlife, streams and lakes, air, beauty, and so forth. These goods, not being owned, are subject to pollution, and they are of great concern to environmentalists. Note that public property (such as roads and public parks) is the litterbug's paradise and that common property is subject to even greater problems of pollution. Thus, the further an item is removed from private ownership, the greater the environmental problem. The Moscow subway is not littered with gum wrappers, but U.S. citizens do not have respect for government-owned property. It is difficult to see how having the government own even more property would solve the pollution problem.

With respect to streams and air, either the government can tax the polluters or they can tax people and devote the revenues to cleaning up after the polluters or buying them out. Which way the public goes on this issue is principally a matter of deciding who shall suffer the cleanup burden. In the example of the water supply described above, the villagers could either buy out the polluter, tax him, or pay to process and clean the water before it is used. Legal procedures have been developed in the case of oil and gas common properties to ensure that they are utilized in the public interest. Similar legal procedures must be developed to ensure effective utilization of our other common properties such as air and water. In this area of concern the market system must be supplemented by other measures.

Note, however, that even here the market system has an important role to play. The rational way to decide whether cleaning up the air or water is "worth it" is to consider the costs and benefits involved, and these can only be measured in money terms by the values determined in the marketplace. That part of the economy in which the pricing system freely operates provides the regulator with an index or a measure of value which can be helpful in determining the desirability of a program of control. The measure may be imperfect; but if all prices and quantities were controlled, one would have no index worthy of the name.

Adam Smith was a student of philosophy, but he was also the father of economics as a discipline separate from those of political economy and law. His followers in the classical tradition include such famous men as Thomas Malthus, David Ricardo, James Mill, John Stuart Mill, and even Karl Marx. These men all emphasized costs of production in their attempts to explain the exchange value of commodities. Adam Smith noted a paradox: some items such as diamonds have great value in exchange but little value in use, while other items such as water have great value in use but little value in exchange. He attempted to resolve this paradox by noting the relative scarcity of the two items—water is plentiful while diamonds are scarce. Water may be obtained with little effort but rare gems are found only with great effort. Thus, he held that relative value in exchange is related to the labor effort necessary to acquire the various commodities.[1]

Adam Smith's followers extended his analysis to include consideration of the cost of land, capital, and other factors along with those related to labor. Karl Marx insisted that all value was produced by labor and therefore concluded that labor should receive all the fruits of production. Relative costs of production are today still held to be the determinants of relative exchange values by those who use input-output analysis in which it is assumed that fixed coefficients of production obtain. But the idea of *value in use* as opposed to *value in exchange* would not be dismissed so easily. In the 1870s there arose a *marginal utility school* of economists. The stage was set for the *neoclassical revolution.*[2] This text, like most current books in price theory (or microeconomics) consists of an exposition of neoclassical economics. In spite of the *keynesian revolution* which launched the subject of macroeconomics into prominence, the essence of neoclassical theory was not overthrown. The keynesian revolution added another dimension to the study of economics, but it did not destroy the basic framework of neoclassical thought.

---

[1] Adam Smith used the example of the effort required to trap a beaver as compared with that required to kill a deer: "Wealth of Nations," p. 47, The Modern Library, New York, 1937.

[2] For an excellent in-depth study of the early days of the neoclassical revolution see: Richard S. Howey, "The Rise of the Marginal Utility School, 1870–1889," University of Kansas Press, Lawrence, Kan., 1960.

The leaders of the neoclassical revolution worked separately but arrived at the same destination. They were William Stanley Jevons (English), Leon Walras (French), and Karl Menger (Austrian).[1] It remained for Alfred Marshall to incorporate both the classical emphasis upon cost or supply conditions and the neoclassical emphasis on utility or demand conditions into the partial equilibrium analysis of demand and supply, which is such a major concept in the development of Western economic thought.

The neoclassical revolutionaries argued, in essence, that the value of a good depended upon the utility received by the consumer when he consumed the good. *Utility* may refer to *usefulness* in the common-sense meaning of that term as, for example, when it is said that water is useful; but utility also refers to that subjective valuation that an individual places upon an item for whatever reason. If a good has the capacity to satisfy a want, then it is said to have utility. Different individuals have different tastes, and therefore the same goods may have a different utility to different individuals. Thus individual preferences give rise to value in exchange. Cost curves, or supply curves, may be thought of as negative demand curves, so that supply conditions as well as demand conditions are formed by individual tastes.

Not long after neoclassical economists proposed these revolutionary ideas, philosophers objected that utility, as defined, was not a *measurable* concept; it was, rather, a subjective concept which defied measurement. They questioned the efficacy of building an analytical construct to explain economic behavior on a nonobservable concept. Their concern was well received. Francis Ysidro Edgeworth responded to the challenge presented by the critics of the neoclassical approach by creating the indifference curve which plays such a monumental role in the modern theory of consumers' choice.[2]

By using indifference curves economists side-step the necessity

[1] Leon Walras also created the general equilibrium, to the exposition of which this intermediate level text is devoted. His Italian follower was Vilfredo Pareto, after whom the paretian optimality conditions that play such a large role in welfare analysis are named. A. J. E. J. Dupui, a French engineer, also arrived at the concept of marginal utility in 1844; but his work did not gain widespread recognition among economists.

[2] F. Y. Edgeworth, "Mathematical Psychics," Kelley, 1881. See the selection reprinted along with other classical articles in A. N. Page (ed.), "Utility Theory: A Book of Readings," John Wiley & Sons, Inc. New York, 1968.

of *cardinal* measurement of utility. As long as indifference curves can be ranked in ascending order of importance, then an *ordinal* measure of utility is all that is required. In the eight-equation model of the consumers' market in Chap. 2, it was assumed that Mr. A and Mr. B could measure utility in terms of utils, a cardinal measure. However, marginal rates of substitution can be derived from the ordinal measure described by indifference curves. With marginal rates of substitution it is possible to solve the set of six equations that determine prices and quantities. The remaining two equations merely allow one to find the number of utils of satisfaction received by each consumer. Thus, a cardinal measure of utility is not required in order to explain price and quantity, which is, of course, the objective of price theory.

Cardinal measurement of utility *is* required if one wishes to set a numerical value upon the amount of satisfaction that he receives from consuming a particular package of commodities. In theory two ways of measuring utility exist. The first we might call the *method of ordered differences;* the second departs somewhat from the neoclassical frame of reference in that it measures the utility received in the purchase of assets (rather than flows of consumer goods) when choice among assets involves *risk.*

Ordered Differences[1]

Assume there exists a set of consumption packages representing points in a multidimensional commodity space a, b, c, d, ... Let U_a, U_b, and so on, represent an individual consumer's utility level corresponding to consumption packages a, b, and so on. Assume that the individual can arrange the packages in a unique and consistent order of ascending preference such that, for example,

$$U_a < U_b < U_c = U_d < U_e$$

and so on. By presenting the individual with a large set of alternative packages and allowing him to "reveal" his preferences in the manner described, an ordinal preference function can be specified. In the example, b is preferred to a and c

[1] R. G. D. Allen provides a complete analysis in his "Mathematical Economics," pp. 669ff., The Macmillan Company, London, 1960.

is preferred to b, while c and d are points on the same indifference curve, and so forth.[1] Some technical mathematical difficulties remain, but the idea that utility is ordinally measurable in this fashion is generally accepted.

To arrive at a cardinal measure of utility Sir Dennis Robertson suggested this procedure be extended another dimension. He suggested that the consumer be asked not only to order his preferences but to order them in an "orderly" manner; that is, ask the consumer to order the *increments* in utility derived from different packages of goods. Thus, observe increments of $(U_b - U_a)$, $(U_c - U_b)$, ... Then arrange these in a unique and consistent order of ascending preference:

$$(U_b - U_a) < (U_c - U_b) = (U_d - U_e) < (U_c - U_d)$$

and so on. If the consumer can provide such an ordering, then one may construct *for this consumer* a cardinal measure of utility with an arbitrary base.[2] The base can be chosen from among the set a, b, c, ... If a represents a certain consumption package and it is assigned to be the base package providing 1 util of satisfaction, then other packages can be said to contain, say, 3 utils, 10 utils, and so forth. Thus, this consumer can answer a question about "how many" utils of satisfaction he receives from consuming a certain package of goods. All cardinal measurements, of course, require the establishment of an arbitrary standard or base in terms of which numerical statements are made.

If Mr. A were to establish a preference function with package a as the standard unit providing 1 util of satisfaction, and if Mr. B were to do likewise, we still would *not* be able to compare the satisfactions received by the two individuals by reference to the utils received by each. Measuring utils in the manner described does *not* allow interpersonal comparison of utility. Mr. A might receive 20 of his utils from package c whereas Mr. B might receive 30 of his utils from package c. Does this mean that a net increase of 10 utils of satisfaction would occur in this two-person economy if package c were taken away from Mr. A and given to Mr. B? The answer is no. While each individual might have a cardinal measurement

---

[1] This analysis was developed by Samuelson, Houthakker, and others. For references, see Allen, *op. cit.*

[2] For a numerical example of the procedure see Allen, *op. cit.*

for utility, so indifference curves (and box diagrams) used in the theory of consumers' choice can have cardinal units of utility attached to them, the utils received by Mr. A and the utils received by Mr. B cannot be compared directly with each other.

Choice Involving Risk[1]

Another cardinal measure of utility can be constructed for an individual faced with choices involving risks. Many consumption decisions of individuals do involve purchase of assets. We rent houses for a month at a time, or we sign a contract for a year's lease, or perhaps we sign a purchase contract that intermixes a savings decision (building of equity in ownership) with a consumption decision (paying interest, depreciation, and taxes for the privilege of living in the house and discretionary privileges related to resale, remodeling, etc.).

Signing a lease or purchasing a house involves a contract—a purchase of a stream of utilities expected to accrue over time. There is a risk that the purchase will be unsatisfactory, resulting in a loss in real income. There is also risk of gain from the purchase. By *risk* we mean the attachment of a probability to the outcome of loss or gain.

Let E be the expected value of a purchase involving risk, let G be the monetary value of the gain to be realized if the outcome is favorable, and let L be the monetary value of the loss if the outcome is unfavorable. If p is the probability of gain, then

$$E = Gp - L(1 - p)$$

For simplicity assume both G and L equal \$100. If $p = .5$, then $E = 0$. If $p = .6$, then $(1 - p) = .4$ and $E = \$60 - \$40 = \$20$, which is the expected monetary value of the outcome.

For a given individual, if $p = .6$ is just sufficiently large enough to induce him to make the bet (purchase), then *for him E* $= 0$, the expected utility of the outcome. Thus

$$0 = Gp - L(1 - p)$$

or $\qquad Gp = L(1 - p)$

---

[1] The method of utility measurement was devised by John von Neumann and Oskar Morgenstern, "Theory of Games and Economic Behavior," Princeton University Press, Princeton, N.J., 1943.

If we choose an arbitrary value of, say, 10 utils of satisfaction for the expected utility loss from the bet, we can write

$$G(.6) = 10(.4)$$
$$G = 10(\tfrac{2}{3}) = 6\tfrac{2}{3}$$

which is the expected gain in utility from the outcome. By facing the individual with many different choices, the utility of gain in any given case can be calculated. This would be a cardinal measure of utility for any choice among risky assets.[1]

The subject of measurability is much more complicated than this brief introduction might suggest. Practical attempts at actual measurement of utility, either ordinal or cardinal, have been rare and have not been noted for their success. But, in theory at least, measurement is possible.

[1] For a different summarization of this method of measuring utility see Donald F. Watson, "Price Theory and Its Uses," 2d ed., chap. 7, Houghton Mifflin Company, Boston, Mass., 1968. Also see A. A. Alchian, The Meaning of Utility Measurement, *Am. Econ. Rev.*, vol. XLIII, pp. 26–50, March 1953; reprinted in Edwin Mansfield (ed.), "Microeconomics: Selected Readings," W. W. Norton & Company, New York, 1971.

Index